Two Immigrants

from

Italy

Luigi & Nicla Chiarappa

Printed in the United States of America

First Edition

Library of Congress Catalog Card Number: 98-93351

Chiarappa, Luigi and Nicla
    Two Immigrants From Italy: A lively tale of a wonderful
life / Luigi and Nicla Chiarappa - 1st ed.

          p.   cm.

Includes bibliographical references and index

ISBN 0-9665594-0-1

        1. Italy--World War II--Emigration--California--
Biography. 2. Plant Disease. 3. FAO--United Nations--Plant
Protection. Title

COVER DESIGN BY DAN WILLIAM MILLS

Published by: (G)
                    P r e s s
              Post Office Box 2455
              El Macero, CA 95618

❖

To our three wonderful daughters

Victoria, Marina and Cynthia -

the source of our greatest

satisfaction and joy in life.

❖

To our good friend June
we dedicate this book
sharing together many good
memories.

  Luigi and Nicky

November, 1999

Contents

Acknowledgments

Authors usually owe more thanks than they can possibly enumerate. From inception to completion of this book it took a period of five years. During this time, many people helped in one way or another to the improvement of the manuscript. First was our daughter Cynthia, who in the early period assisted in correcting "our bad English." Then came Marion Lopes who provided advice on some parts of the text. Special thanks are given to Karen Van Epen for her endless patience in editing the final draft. The help of Frank Duba is acknowledged for his rewarding commentaries. Our warmest gratitude goes to Marguerite Di Giorgio and Bob Thomason for providing some of the photos used in the illustrations, and to Dan Mills, Bill Wallace and Lisa de Lalla for their photographic work. The good work by Honda Ngo for electronic design and text composition is also acknowledged.

Introduction

Human life is an extraordinary phenomenon—a mystery of faith, biology, genetics, and psychology. It is difficult to explain what attracts and binds two individuals when they first meet, become engaged and then marry to begin a family with a pattern of their own. When the pattern is like ours, life becomes a rich sequence of unexpected events, of deep and continuous love, and of unusual experiences. Towards the end it becomes a story that deserves to be written.

As the writing of our story progressed, it became apparent that this was also part of the many unwritten accounts of people who emigrated to the United States or Canada. Many families in America have their roots in faraway places and have lost contact with their country of origin, its traditions and culture. Our book may stimulate these people to learn more about their homeland as they read about our family's saga. After all, America is a continent of immigrants. Readers may see themselves, their parents, or their grandparents at the time when they decided to leave the "old country" to face new realities in America. They may relive the great anxiety of the days when they departed from the comfort and intimacy of a familiar environment to face the mysteries and the challenges of a "New World."

People write autobiographic books for many reasons. Some authors are driven by the money they can make if the book becomes popular. Others are after recognition, fame, and social status that come with well written books. A few autobiographic writers want to make sure that history is recorded from their own viewpoint and not someone else's. Often these authors are political figures who use their name and fame to write about events that satisfy popular curiosity.

Then there are the very good writers who are destined to be the chroniclers of special events, and who vividly portray people's characters and life situations. Their books are classics in world literature. Their thoughts, words, and way of describing events and interpreting the mysteries of the human mind are truly unique.

As for ourselves, Nicla and I are not professional writers. We have never thought of or attempted to write a book before. We are not after money or glory. Furthermore, we did not want to impress anybody, nor did we have any desire to become part of history. Instead, we strongly believe in something more concrete and tangible than reported historical events: we believe in our family. And it is to our family, and to those who will follow, that we wish to leave a tangible record of our life, to serve as a link to their past and as a stimulus to their future.

This book, written mainly for our daughters and their children, has three major objectives. The first is to let them know where their family "roots" are—where we and our parents originated, and which traditions we tried to maintain. We also wanted to tell them something about the old country, its recent history, and about the Italians in general. This could be useful in their search for a new perspective about their lives.

A second objective is to let our daughters, grandchildren and others appreciate what we have done to overcome the many obstacles we encountered during our existence. This may provide some inspiration and encouragement in times of hardship.

The third purpose is to leave a message about appreciating the true values of life. Although "experience" can hardly be transmitted to others, a word of wisdom could always be useful to counteract the prevailing materialism and superficiality of modern times.

When it comes to writing a book, a nonprofessional writer first wonders who the reader is going to be. This can be a frightening thought. The second concern is how the book is going to be received. The third deliberation is how much material is to be included and in which order it should be presented. Of the two of us, I had to address all these issues. Clearly, I was on the front line of the writing exercise. Nicla, instead, remained in the background. But she provided valuable and accurate information for the completion of Part II. She made available the entire collection of letters she had written to her family from 1951 to 1962. These letters had been guarded by her parents and returned to her only a few years ago. They contained a wealth of information on people, places, dates, and special events. They served to enrich and to safeguard the accuracy of our text.

I have had some previous writing experience, but it was limited to scientific or technical papers, which use an entirely different vocabulary . This means that all my expertise was of no value for this book. It would seem that this would be easier to write because we were free to select subjects and words. But in the end, the freedom was not there. The book was to factually describe what happened, and to narrate stories and portray characters that really existed. In doing this, there was no place for fiction. So, the best way for us to proceed was to use the same technique employed in producing an oil painting: first lay out the background colors, and then apply all the coats and details to complete the picture.

The background of this work is essentially given in Part One. Following this, all the remaining chapters proceed in chronological order. Wherever possible, we stayed away from technicalities or tiring descriptions of matters that are of interest only to ourselves. This was done out of respect for the intelligence and busy schedule of the reader, who should not be expected to "suffer" through long descriptions of trivial events.

The reader will also find that a bit of humor is used sparingly throughout the text. This is to make reading more palatable and to underline that wit is a priceless component of human life.

Finally, the reader is advised to "digest" this book in small installments: this should help everyone appreciate the many details we tried to faithfully portray on the large canvas of our colorful story.

PART ONE

Early Life in Italy

1

Something Special about the Italians

A man who has not been in Italy is always conscious of an inferiority.

—Samuel Johnson, 1776

Italy is smaller than California, but it has more than twice its population. The country is composed of people with very different traditions, dialects and behaviors. For example, a man from Bolzano, in the North, has less in common with one from Palermo, in the South, than a Frenchman has with a Russian. The person from Bolzano lives close to Austria and is likely to be tall, blond, and blue eyed. He speaks German, eats sausages and drinks beer. The person from Palermo is likely to be short and dark. He speaks Sicilian, eats pasta and drinks wine. The two have entirely different backgrounds. Bolzano, once part of Austria-Hungary, is ethnically part of the Tirol (which also includes

Bavaria, Switzerland and Austria). Sicily, in contrast, is an island that was occupied in turn by the Greeks, the Romans, the Arabs, the Spaniards, the Normans, and, finally, by General Garibaldi for the King of Italy. The social and economic differences between Sicily and other Italian regions are so great that after World War II there was a strong movement in the island to become an independent state. Likewise, a special status was granted to Bolzano to become administratively autonomous. All this is to explain the remarkable diversity of Italy and the Italians.

Italian society is extremely complex and difficult to understand. For many centuries the country was kept divided into small and independent states, and each of these states was run by some type of tyrant with a title varying from king to prince, duke, baron, or pope. Each of these despots was surrounded by an aristocracy composed of rich families who owned land, money and soldiers. With their riches these "noble" families could buy all sorts of favors, including honors, titles and even education. The greatest majority of the population was composed of the poor, the ignorant, the illiterate, and the derelict. They were the hopeless part of society and the ones most vulnerable to wars, depredations and epidemics. Between these two social groups stood the middle class. This included storekeepers, artisans, artists, and the like. It was inconceivable for most people to move up the social ladder, and it was impossible to change the course of events once these were started by the tyrants at the top.

It is no surprise that an Italian was the first to write about the "art" of surviving in treacherous political times. He was Francesco Guicciardini from Florence, who published his book entitled "I Ricordi" (The Memoirs). For understandable reasons, this book became only publicly available two hundred years after Guicciardini's death in 1540. The French Revolution of 1789 had a substantial effect on Italian social conditions, and the Industrial Revolution which followed greatly contributed to the shuffling of social classes. The latter also created conditions for better distribution of economic wealth and more generalized education. However, all this did not prevent other tyrants and privileged classes from reestablishing themselves in recent times. The Fascist Revolution—which included Mussolini's reign from 1922 to 1943—followed by the period of "tangentopoli" (pluralism of bribery) during the last twenty years, are good examples. These and other historical events have greatly influenced Italians and Italian society.

As a group, Italians (either from Bolzano or from Palermo) are different from other Europeans. They are individualistic and shrewd, loud and temperamental, kind and stylish. They are something else! One point is almost sure: they are no fools. No one is able to explain the discrepancy between the excellent character of the majority of individuals and the poor destiny of the country as a whole. In Italy there have always been a great number of eminent people, way above the need of the country itself. Stendhal once wrote, "In Italy the plant man grows more vigorous than elsewhere." But the country, as a whole, has always been weak and irremediably fragmented like a fragile wall that even gentle winds can easily knock down. The individual stones are all excellent and exceptionally solid, but without a good mortar to keep them together, they are nothing more than a "muro a secco" (loose rock wall).

During the last war, after a number of defeats, Mussolini himself had to admit that there was something wrong with the Italian people, or, as he put it, with the "raw material" that made up the Italian soldiers. "Even Michelangelo needed good marble to carve solid statues," the duce mused. "If he had had only clay, he could have created only friable ceramics." Never did Mussolini consider that the world as a whole has greatly gained by the overflow of Italian genius and creative capabilities.

But it is not only Italian geniuses who have contributed to world progress. Many less famous Italian men and women, from different places and backgrounds, with no resources other than their intelligence and their strong desire to work and succeed, have contributed in a significant way to the improvement of life in Europe, the Americas and Australia. It was an Italian who discovered America for the Americans. Italians invented pizza, cappuccino, Chianti wine, and Bologna sausages. They established some of California's finest orchards, vineyards and cellars, decorated Sacramento's Capitol building, and designed St. Mary's cathedral in San Francisco. Italians were the first daring commercial fishermen to sail the cold Pacific waters of California. The man who founded the Bank of America and Italy in San Francisco, and built it into one of the world's largest banking systems, was also an Italian.

Italy, as a country, is not always good to the outstanding people she is capable of generating. The examples of great Italian scholars or artists who were mistreated, persecuted and forced to leave their country are many and frequent. Enrico Fermi and Arturo Toscanini come to mind. But one need not be prominent to receive harsh treatment. For example, it is common in Italy to be distrustful towards young people. While in other countries there is an open process of selection which allows the best and most qualified young professionals, artists, artisans, or politicians to access top positions early in their life, this is most unlikely to happen in Italy. Instead, here the prevailing custom is to let young people "stand in line waiting for their turn." As a result, young people have greater difficulty in getting started in their careers than in other countries.

To overcome this situation, Italians make frequent use of the "recommendation." This is simply a letter or a timely phone call by someone high enough in society to influence or overturn the results of an exam, a job interview or any other selection process. This applies to jobs in private business, in public offices and even in the military service (to exempt young people from the draft or to assign them to serve comfortably in their home towns). In fact, there is no greater aspiration in any Italian family than that to have their young son or daughter placed in a job through a well prepared and well timed "recommendation." To secure this type of intervention, there are commonly two routes to follow: an expensive and showy gift at Christmas or Easter to the "important" recommending person, or the use of a "bustarella." This is nothing more than a sealed envelope containing plain cash and no written explanations.

The use of the "bustarella" (also called "mazzetta" or "tangente") has grown out of proportion in the Italian business world in recent years. It now involves most politicians and their political parties, financial institutions, and even the judiciary system. Corruption has become so common it is considered the normal way of conducting business. This could be compared to papal Rome in the 1500s when it was perfectly normal to sell indulgences in the form of bribes to the Pope or his close collaborators. A "donation" properly placed would then secure a shorter stay in purgatory. Machiavelli, after all, was an Italian. He was the first to write in his book "The Prince" that political expediency is above morality. Modern Italians have pushed this concept a step further, to that of double-track morality: one for the government and one for the citizens; one for the political party and one for the people. Many even conclude that they could do better without any morality: it would be easier to fatten their illegal account in some respectful Swiss bank.

There are many more customs that have become common heritage in modern Italy. For example, Italians are (or, at least, they believe to be) all smart. "Ca' nisciuno e' fesso!" is an old Neapolitan saying which literally translates, "Here no one is a fool." This means that in a country of more than fifty million "non-fools," each individual must always try his best to outsmart the others. This phenomenon can actually be seen out in the open. For instance, look at the way Italians drive on their highways or in city traffic. They all want to pass each other, trying to squeeze in from all sides at intersections, daring to push their way through red lights without hesitation. For the same reason, Italians do not like to stand in line; so they are always trying alternate ways to be first at the counter or service window. There are many other situations which the average Italian plainly dislikes. For example, they consider fools those who pay taxes, who comply with laws and regulations, or who declare the true value of real estate. Italians are also fatalists: the laws of the unavoidable persistently underlie their psyche and behavior. Italians are extremely individualistic: they rarely agree on anything. As Guy Talese puts it, they are fine as soloists, but not in the choir; fine as heroes, but not so good in a parade.

Italian laws are many, complex, and, most of the time, outdated. In the country where Western jurisprudence was born, it is difficult to apply justice through proper legal process. The entire country's economy and its many business relations are based on a very fine, almost invisible division between legal and illegal. Again, where there are too many "smart" customers and an excess of capable attorneys, the law becomes flexible, slow and frequently unreliable. The consequence is that there is no confidence in the judicial system, nor in the police, nor in any established authority. In fact, there is no trust in other people. This is clearly embodied in an old Italian proverb that says, "Fidarsi e' bene, ma non fidarsi e' meglio" (to trust is good, but not to trust is better). This lack of trust greatly complicates everyday life. To get a loan from a bank, or a simple checkbook, or to cash a traveler's check, numerous forms must be filled out, and many signatures are always required. This also applies to the abundant documentation demanded of any person applying for a job, a driver's license or any kind of permit.

Italy is a country that appears created for the delight of tourists. Year after year, millions of foreigners invade Italian hotels, beaches, mountains and lake resorts. Just like California, Italy possesses a natural beauty, with its magnificent and varied landscapes, long and winding coastline, scenic interior valleys, mountains, lakes, islands, and volcanoes. Just like California, the climate is mild and caressed by the breeze of the nearby sea.

The Etruscans, the Romans, and then the Italians built their beautiful cities, arenas, castles, churches, and highways in harmony with these very special natural conditions. They terraced their hills and planted orchards and vineyards. They captured the waters and leveled the soil to grow very fine crops. Nowhere in the world are the results of so much dedicated human work so apparent as in Italy. And nowhere in the world is the quality, and expression of what is beautiful so well documented as by the Italian painters, sculptors, architects, and musicians.

For example, according to Indro Montanelli, the famous writer from Tuscany, his countryside is a masterpiece of harmony. At its foundation is a miracle of intelligence and good taste, both following rigorous schemes of sober lines and balanced proportions. This reflects the mentality arising from Tuscan art. If one compares today's countryside with the ancient landscapes depicted in 1,300 or 1,500 paintings, one wonders if these painters copied the farmers, or if the

The hills in the Chianti area between Florence and Siena (1997).

"The clays near Siena" (Fresco by A. Lorenzetti, early 1300).

farmers were inspired by the painters. In either case, one can see the same rejection of embellishment for the sake of ornamentation, the same allergy against whatever was Baroque, rhetorical or superfluous. Instead, in both cases one finds the same brightness of light, and the same search for ascetic simplicity. All this reveals the "Tuscan style," which can equally be found in a painting by Benozzo, a page by Guicciardini or Machiavelli, or on a farm in Chianti or Valdarno.

There is also the Italian character, which appears always kind and friendly, in harmony with the beauty of the landscape. This could be part simulation and part fun: but it is always nicer to receive an amicable smile from an Italian police officer than a stiff ticket for a well deserved parking violation!

Through the centuries, Italians have developed the fine art of masking their problems or aspirations. Their main concern is always that of "fare bella figura." These words can hardly be translated into English because there is no equivalent vocabulary. Probably this is because there is no need in the Anglo-Saxon world to use this art as commonly and effectively as do Italians. Essentially, what Italians are much concerned about is to not appear to others either cheap or sloppy. So, everything must respond to an unwritten code of class, elegance and distinction. Appearance is extremely important to Italians, often more so than substance. This is quite different from "showing off," which is so common in America and elsewhere. "Bella figura" is a much finer and more subtle matter. It probably derives from another important value the Italians have in great abundance: their appreciation for good "design." A car by Pinin Farina, a pair of shoes by Ferragamo, or a belt and purse by Gucci are generally recognized for their unique class and high quality of design. The same could be said for the choreography of operatic settings or movies for which Italian directors like Franco Zeffirelli or Luchino Visconti are internationally acclaimed.

But design can be also exploited for political use. The best example was Mussolini himself, who believed he was the designer of Italy's destiny. He wanted to be called "duce" (from the Latin "dux," meaning leader), and he wanted to lead others, even in their way of dressing. He always wore well designed, showy uniforms. Furthermore he wanted Italians—rich or poor, men or women, children or adults— to hide their individual taste and preferences by wearing uniforms that he (or someone close to him) designed for the entire country. In this way, the "bella figura" was firmly assured. A good front was displayed to friends or enemies, in Italy or abroad. All these uniforms, when brought together at ocean-like rallies in Piazza Venezia or elsewhere, created a most spectacular show. The choreography was splendid: thousands and thousands of people crowded together in a historic plaza, the men dressed in black shirts contrasting with the white blouses of the women and the deep blue scarfs of the young "balillas." Strategically located floodlights illuminated the nearby Roman ruins, while music was playing in the background and flags, many large flags, waved freely in the evening breeze. And finally, after a long, purposely-planned wait, the windows of the balcony slowly opened and the "duce" appeared to the crowd in the plaza. All floodlights were directed on him and he smiled to the crowd in his elegant uniform. The people responded with a roar of applause and with the seethed chanting of "duce, duce, duce, duce." There appeared to be no end to this chanting.

Recalling these rallies after so many years, one wonders what really happened to these intelligent, sophisticated, individualistic, incredulous, treacherous, but yet resourceful Italians? How could they accept twenty or more years of these kinds of shows, promises and downright lies? Luigi Barzini, Jr., author of "The Italians," compared Mussolini to men like P.T. Barnum or Cecil B. De Mille, who tried to create in America the greatest show on earth. Mussolini, no doubt, succeeded in Italy. From the moment he took power, he dedicated his life to running an impressive, but very dangerous, show. Unconsciously, however, he became the victim of his own dreams. In the end, he no longer was able to separate reality from appearance, spectacle from verity.

In this unique and artificial situation, half circus and half truth, Nicla and I were born and raised. No one wished to explain to us what was going on in our country, and we asked no questions. Life was accepted at face value. The subtle fascist propaganda had completely infiltrated radio, newspapers, movies, and schools. It was so powerful that no one, least of all a growing youngster, could object to it. Because of some natural defense mechanism, both Nicla and I gradually but steadily developed a personal resentment against this situation. For instance, I was fed up with having to wear a uniform on Saturdays and march all afternoon in preparation for some future parade or rally. To me this was a waste of time. I soon discovered that by wearing an incomplete uniform, I could be easily dismissed from parades or other similar events. I then started wearing brown shoes when black ones were required. When apprehended for the brown shoes, I candidly explained that my black shoes were being repaired. My only alternative would have been to go to school barefoot. When this excuse could no longer be used, I made sure that I did not have a dagger to go with my uniform. In this way, I succeeded again in being set aside.

In Nicla's case, she was dismissed because the little numbers she had to wear on her uniform never matched those of her unit. We were very young then, but we were already typical, resourceful Italians: we enjoyed a subtle form of rebellion against established authority and authoritarians, if only by using the wrong shoe color or group numbers. After all, people young or old must fight only those revolutions which they can manage best!

In a country with more than fifty million "non-fools," life could be extremely difficult for someone who was young, just starting a career, not belonging to a political party, and not willing to compromise or depend on any form of "recommendation" or "bustarella." These were a few of the reasons we did not want to stay in Italy. We preferred, instead, to risk our lives abroad, in a world that promised to be free, more open, and with greater opportunities for young people willing to work hard and to succeed only on their own merits rather than by political affiliation.

2

Roots

*Next to the family, it is work and
the relationships established by
work that are the foundation of
society. If the foundations are
unsound, how could society be
sound?*

—E. F. SCHUMACHER

Nicla's mother, Ambrogina Franz (called Gina), was
born in Udine on October 2, 1894. She was the
daughter of Ferdinando Franz and Elisabetta
Rizzi. Gina's parents came from two families with entirely
different social status and background. The Rizzi family,
which was in the upper middle class of the Udine society,
had generated medical doctors, poets and humanists.
Ferdinando Franz and his family were   builders and

contractors in the small town of Moggio Udinese. They had more humble origins but they were well known for having built the Grand Hotel of Abbazia, a famous resort in Northern Italy. Gina was the oldest in a family of five. She had two sisters (Rita and Anita) and two brothers (Aurelio and Attilio).

After graduating from the Academy of Fine Arts in Florence, Gina taught in Udine for a short period. However, she did not like teaching. She much preferred to perform in the arts. Gina enjoyed producing fine ceramics, tapestries, and exquisite miniatures. Later in life she took up embroidery and became outstanding in this field as well. Gina loved flowers. She could take their colors and shapes and translate them into some of the most beautiful needlework. Gina was remarkable for her beauty, quick intelligence, wisdom, and a unique ability to be decisive. She was also a very sensitive woman, who could exercise perfect control over her feelings so as to appear somewhat cold and reserved. She was tall, had a nice figure and always dressed in elegant clothes. Gina had a strong personality of her own. She proved to be an outstanding wife, and an unforgettable mother and grandmother.

Nicla's father, Ronchi, Vittorio, was born in San Dona' di Piave (near Venice) on September 22, 1892. He was the son of Maria Vianello and Taddeo Ronchi. The latter was a grammar school teacher who gave up teaching for a diploma in Agriculture. He then became manager of a large farm estate, called "Palazzetto" (small palace) bordering the Piave River. This is one of the many streams flowing south from the Eastern Alps into the Adriatic Sea. Since Roman times, attempts have been made to regulate this river known for its severe floods and sudden changes of direction. After the defeat of Caporetto in October, 1917, the retreating Italian troops chose the right bank of the Piave to stop the advancing enemy armies who attacked fiercely in November and again in December, but only with modest results. The Italians were able to contain and, later on, to eliminate the two beachheads established in their territory. This success was mainly due to three factors. The first was that the Austrians had overextended their lines, scattering their troops on a wide front in hostile territory. They arrived at the Piave River without bridging materials and with insufficient supplies. The second factor was the withdrawal of seven German divisions, needed on the French front. And the third was the severe weather and torrential rains that made the Piave impossible to cross. The city of San Doná and the Palazzetto farm, caught in between the fighting armies, were totally destroyed. It was on this farm that Vittorio had spent his entire childhood. Vittorio had one brother, Giovanni, and three sisters, Angelica, Ida and Ester. In 1907, he started his technical training at the School of Viticulture and Enology at Conegliano. By 1911 he was able to enroll at the School of Agriculture in Pisa. The war interrupted his studies, and from 1915 to 1919 Vittorio served as an officer in an infantry regiment. He spent most of this time in the line of battle, surrounded by his faithful soldiers, most of whom were from the South. He endured with them the tormented life in muddy trenches, where he was always able to keep up their morale and fighting spirit. These were the soldiers called "pieces of walking mud," poor and ignorant peasants sent to fight a war they could not understand. Vittorio distinguished himself for his courage and military performance. He was promoted captain in November, 1916, and awarded bronze and silver medals.

After the war, Vittorio returned to Pisa and obtained a "laurea" degree in Agricultural Sciences. He then went back to San Doná and to the "Palazzetto" farm to engage in reconstruction work for nearly two years. After a short

Ambrogina Franz, called Gina.
Nicla's Mother.

Vittorio Ronchi, Nicla's Father.

period of teaching at the School of Viticulture and Enology at Conegliano, Vittorio began a career that rapidly elevated him to top positions in government and private business.

Vittorio was a nice-looking man with a short butch haircut, blue eyes, and an open, honest smile. He would claim at the age of 90 that he never had dental cavities because he drank plenty of water from the Piave River during his childhood. Vittorio had an exceptional memory, allowing him to remember events and situations to the smallest detail. He inspired people and was always respected as a leader. During the later years of his life he became religious. This late encounter with the Christian faith gave him added moral strength. Vittorio's friendly personality was also exceptional. He was an optimist and always felt good toward others. Vittorio, however, disliked politics and politicians, who seemed attracted to him for his great honesty, deep technical knowledge and exceptional managerial skills. These were things they did not possess, but desperately needed.

Vittorio and Gina met in Udine in February, 1922, during the carnival festivities. Vittorio, who was then teaching at the School of Viticulture and Enology at Conegliano, happened to be in Udine to pay a visit to his sister Ester. Gina, who was very popular in the local high society, did not feel like going to the carnival dance. She felt she did not have the proper dress for the occasion and preferred to stay home for the evening. At the last minute, a friend was able to convince her to attend the dance. This was a very special event, taking place in the local opera house. Gina and Vittorio were introduced to each other by this same friend. It was love at first sight for both. They danced together all night and made plans to see each other soon. In a matter of months they were engaged, and by August they were happily married.

The suffering of the war appeared almost forgotten by both except for Caporetto. This is the Italian name for Kobarid, a village in Croatia where Italy suffered one of the greatest defeats of its history. Toward the end of October, 1917, the German High Command decided to concentrate its war effort on the Italian front. It was hoped in this way to overcome the deadlock on the French front. A breakthrough in Italy would allow German penetration into France from the south and a consequent attack from behind the French lines.

To implement this plan, seven German divisions were sent to the Italian front with special battalions dressed in Austrian uniforms. One of these was under the command of a young captain who was to make a name for himself in World War II: Erwin Rommel. He was the promoter of a new tactic developed on the Russian front. This was to concentrate surprise attacks on a very narrow sector of the enemy front line, and to rapidly infiltrate through it with specially trained troops. These would then advance deep into the enemy's territory to assault from the back.

During the lightless and foggy autumnal nights, Rommel's troops moved quickly through the valley floors, escaping Italian attention. In only four days they were 60 miles deep into the Italian territory. With the use of newly developed suffocating gases, modern weapons and explosives, they attacked from behind, annihilating most of the Italian soldiers and capturing 10,000 prisoners. The rest of the Austrian and German divisions then rushed like flood water into the opening at Caporetto, advancing rapidly in the direction of Udine and the plains toward the sea. It was total chaos. The entire Italian Second Army collapsed and 300,000 men surrendered at once. An estimated one million troops and a half million civilians were desperately on the run.

Gina was among these refugees. She left her home in a great hurry and fled to Florence. She took with her all of her young sisters and brothers and only a few personal effects. Gina's mother Elisabetta was left behind in a local hospital which was occupied by the Austrian troops on October 29. She died in this hospital in complete solitude and was buried with many other patients in a large common grave. Also incapacitated and hospitalized in Udine during this period was Vittorio. Fortunately, he was able to leave the hospital before the enemy's arrival, and safely reached the town of Conegliano, where he had been a student years before.

A much happier period started in Gina's life after she met Vittorio. They settled in Treviso where they had four daughters: Lisa, born in 1923, Francesca in 1924, Vittoria in 1928, and Nicla in 1930. Vittorio was then director of a special Agency for the Reconstruction of the Venetian Regions. This agency aimed at rebuilding what the war had destroyed, and at spurring economic development of local agriculture. Many important projects were carried out during the nine years of Vittorio's leadership. This period of apparent happiness was cut short, however, when, in 1932, Vittorio was arrested by Mussolini's secret police. The accusation was of "maintaining contacts with antifascist groups trying to overthrow Italy's legal government." Vittorio had just returned to Venice from Paris, where he had secretly met his old friend Silvio Trentin, a socialist who had fled Italy several years before. Vittorio felt totally sure that no one had seen him with Trentin. Yet Mussolini's secret service must have been tipped off about his encounter.

During the following three months, while Vittorio remained in prison without any form of legal assistance, his family was continually harassed by the police looking for incriminating documents. During one of these searches in the

Ronchi apartment, one of the policemen took a book from a shelf to see if compromising letters were hidden inside. Gina stood in the room facing the prying policeman. Suddenly, a letter dropped out of the book and fell to the floor. Gina was quick to recognize it as one of the letters she had written to Vittorio during their engagement. She waited until the agent snooped through a few lines of the text, and then with a cold smile she said, "I hope you do not wish to go through all my love letters, sir. But if you so wish, I have many more letters in my desk." The agent, evidently embarrassed, promptly returned the book to the shelf and quickly cleared the apartment. The secret police never discovered that inside that book there were some very compromising letters from Silvio Trentin and other Italian exiles. Shortly after, Vittorio was allowed to return home. His release was mainly the result of a plea by growers and politicians from the Veneto region. They requested of Mussolini that Vittorio be set free and reinstated in his position. Lacking any incriminating documentation, the duce obliged this petition.

In 1930 there was a nationwide contest to select top level agriculturists as Regional Directors of the Ministry of Agriculture. Vittorio was invited to participate and he qualified at the top of the list. For the next seven years he worked in this position in the Venetian Region, where his popularity grew very rapidly.

In 1937, the Ronchi family moved to Rome. Vittorio was offered the position of Director General with the "Maccarese." This was a very large agro-industry complex, operating on nearly 12,000 acres of land a few miles from Rome. Most of the land had been reclaimed from old marshes that were once used only for fishing and hunting. On this property there was also a beautiful castle built in the 1500s by Prince Rospigliosi's family. The castle was frequently used to host dignitaries visiting the estate or foreign guests of the

Ministry of Agriculture. Part of the castle became a summer home for the Ronchi family. In Rome, Vittorio and Gina moved into a rental apartment in Via Crescenzio, not far from Saint Peter's Square, while they were looking for something to buy. This purchase happened very suddenly once they saw an apartment in Via Ovidio which had just been placed on the market. It had been beautifully decorated for a young couple who were going to be married but changed their plans. The apartment was large enough for a family of six. Gina liked it and in no time the decision was made to purchase it. This was in 1939, one year before Italy declared war, siding with Germany—a time when there was a total freeze on the sale of apartments, and incredible real estate increases were to take place.

My mother, Maria Rass, was born in Essen, Germany, on February 6, 1887, into a family of wealthy business people. Her mother, Maria Smalenberg, came from a family of affluent building contractors. Her father, Theodor Rass, was the owner of a large, fancy restaurant. She had three younger sisters, Elizabeth, Iolanda and Alexandra. Maria spent most of her youth in the city of Essen where she developed into a beautiful teenager. In Essen was the headquarters of the Krupp works, the strongest armament industry in Europe. In a complex of sixty different factory buildings, 41,000 workers were employed in manufacturing the heavy weapons Germany used during World War I. This huge industrial complex was a city within the city, with its own security, hospitals and traffic laws. Maria was actually born inside the complex. When she was only 16 years old she married an older man by the name of Gödde, who gave her a son, Theo. Life was no longer happy for Maria after she discovered that her husband was a gambler and an adulterer. They divorced shortly after Theo's birth and Maria decided to start a new life of her own. She began working as a cashier in her father's fashionable restaurant. Maria was a very attractive young lady with deep blue eyes, dark hair and a very nice figure. Her character was extremely sweet but she was also a strong-willed woman. She had a great sense of humor and was exceedingly responsive to music and art in general. Maria graciously displayed great generosity towards others, while paying little or no attention to herself. She loved good food and knew how to cook well. Raising a large, healthy family was her first priority in life.

My father, Luigi, was born in Bari, in southern Italy, on March 6, 1890. His father Saverio was a musician by trade who played double-bass in small orchestras. Luigi's mother, Lucia, came, instead, from a noble family (Sagarica-Visconti) from Giovinazzo, a small coastal town north of Bari. Luigi was the oldest in a family of four. He had two sisters, Olga and Suzel, and a much younger brother by the name of Antonio.

Luigi showed great musical talent at a very young age. He first played the violin and later switched to cello. He was an attractive man with abundant, thick, blond hair, brown eyes, and a tall frame. In many ways, Luigi had the features one might expect from an artist. His personality was very complex and difficult to understand. During the time he lived with his family he appeared to be very sensitive, somewhat weak, and with little sense of humor. He was a good father and a hard worker. He loved his wife and six children, and enjoyed being at the center of the universe. He was not an authoritarian, but he always demanded great respect from others. He seemed, at times, somewhat distant and self-contained. One problem he had was that he was very tight with his money. When later in life, Luigi left the family, he appeared very weak, fearful of the outside world and completely blind to the real values his long life had generously given to him.

Maria Rass, a German
lady who loved Italy and
the Italians.

Luigi Chiarappa, a first class
cello player.

Luigi met Maria in Essen just before the beginning of World War I. He was part of a small musical band playing in Maria's father's restaurant. The two fell in love almost immediately and decided to get married. Maria's father, Theodor Rass, was very much against this wedding. He did not want to see his beautiful daughter marry "an Italian gypsy." On this occasion, Maria's personality came out strong and clear: she was fully determined to leave her family and her secure job for the young Italian musician she loved. And so it came to be. The marriage took place at a time when there were great problems in Luigi's own family. His father, Saverio, in a moment of depression, committed suicide, leaving his family in Germany with no financial support. Maria and Luigi went ahead with their wedding plans just the same. With their limited savings they decided to repatriate Luigi's mother and two sisters, but to keep with them little Antonio, who happened to be the same age as Theo. With these two young boys already in their family, the freshly married couple moved from Essen to Berlin.

The war had already begun and Italy, which had been part of the Triple Alliance since 1882, was brought out from the old treaty to fight with England and France against the Austrians and the Germans. Luigi, now a full-fledged enemy, had to hide his true nationality and suddenly "became" Dutch. In this way, he could continue to play cello with small orchestras in smoky restaurants crowded with drunk German soldiers on leave from the front line. Maria, instead, having married an Italian, was under constant surveillance by the Berlin police. Twice a day she had to report to the police station to have an identification document stamped.

Berlin was close to starvation in those years and there was no food to be found anywhere. Belt tightening had already began in 1915, but toward the end of the war it was severe starvation. Foodstuffs were not available mainly due to the lack of nitrogen fertilizers and copper fungicides. Both chemicals were used almost exclusively by the armament industry for the manufacture of explosives and brass shell cases. Many potato crops, lacking protection against blight disease, were ruined, causing severe shortages. German authors claimed later that 750,000 of their countrymen were killed by lack of food. Under these difficult conditions, Maria gave birth to Umberto in February of 1915, Italo in March of 1917, and Bianca in June of 1918.

The war finally came to an end. Almost ten million men and women had been killed and nearly six million had been crippled. This was the human price that had to be paid to reach a peace treaty in Versailles which strangulated Germany's economy and planted the seed for another world conflict twenty years later.

Right after Germany surrendered in 1918, the family decided to move to Belgium, where living conditions were reported to be better. Another daughter, Irma, was born in October of 1923 in Brussels. Not long afterwards, Luigi wished to return to his native Italy and decided to move his family of six children and two adults to Bari. He did not realize the cultural shock he was going to give to his German wife. As already mentioned, Maria had been raised in a very wealthy environment in northern Germany and had never traveled south before. She was totally unprepared to face the primitive social and sanitary conditions of southern Italy. For the first time she realized that she really was sharing her life with a "gypsy." She refused to stay in Bari, and shortly afterwards the family moved north to Rome.

These were difficult times for Italy's capital. Mussolini had taken over the government a few years earlier, and there was still much social unrest throughout the country. This was especially true in the outskirts of Rome, where poverty was most evident and conflicts between fascist strong-arm squads and communist workers were still frequent. The only lodging Maria and Luigi could find was in the Ponte Milvio area, on the northern outskirts of the city. This was far away from downtown, where Luigi found a job in a small musical band playing in "Galleria Colonna." The home they purchased was small, but had the advantage of a good-sized backyard for the children to play outdoors and for my mother to grow vegetables and fruit trees. It was in this small house in Via Ferdinando Galliani that I was born on a very cold December day of 1925. As stated, life for the family was not easy. At the age of fourteen, Antonio and Theo were sent out to work in hotels or wash dishes in restaurants. The only income supporting the rest of the family was that of my father, who returned home late at night, riding a bicycle accompanied by a stray dog. He always carried a loaded gun in his pocket, a needed precaution in difficult times.

Umberto and Italo made several good friends in our neighborhood of low-income people. One of these was Rosa Ciavatti, who married Umberto when they reached their early twenties.

One day my father found out that there was an opening for a first cello soloist at the "Augusteo" symphonic orchestra. He had no confidence in himself, however, and did not want to consider this opportunity. It took Maria's German determination to convince him to apply. She also decided to accompany him to the audition, afraid that he might stop halfway and return home. The audition, however, was a great success and Luigi qualified for a job that he maintained until his retirement.

A steady income allowed the family to make important changes, including the move to the city's center, where my father was working and where better schools were available for the children. The house in Ferdinando Galliani was rented out and the family moved into an apartment in Via G. Ferrari first, and then in Via degli Scipioni. Both were rentals, but they represented a substantial improvement in living conditions and neighborhood. After a few years, the apartment in Piazza dei Quiriti was purchased. It is here that Gilda was born in October of 1933. The family was large, the expenses were many, but Maria managed her finances incredibly well. Soon there were sufficient savings to invest in the purchase of a store in nearby Via Fabio Massimo. This music shop was opened in partnership with a man by the name of Bertucci, who owned a similar store in Via del Corso.

Luigi continued to spend all his time playing cello in the orchestra or giving solo concerts all over Italy and throughout Europe. Maria took care of the shop and her family. Her patience and sweet personality attracted numerous clients, including those from several music bands in nearby military barracks. Maria always maintained a strong German accent, which was much appreciated by all costumers. She deeply loved Italy and Italians, and never looked back to Germany or her relatives. In fact, her father ostracized her from the family and Maria was never given any part of her wealthy inheritance. But she never cared, being perfectly at ease in her new environment, enjoying a loving husband and many healthy children.

By the mid-1930s, Theo was working alternate seasons as a concierge in first class hotels in Sicily and Fiuggi, near Rome. While in Palermo he met Bice, a Sicilian girl whom he married. Walter was born from this marriage.

Umberto studied first at the "Marcantonio Colonna" gymnasium, a Catholic school run by Irish priests. Then he transferred to the "Mamiani" lyceum, where he never completed his studies. He was in love with Rosa and wanted to marry her without delay. He joined Theo in the hotel business and by October, 1935, he was financially independent and able to wed Rosa.

Italo, though was a bit of a problem. He did not like any form of discipline nor of schooling. He left a trade school to work as apprentice car mechanic and, later, as an actor in cheap variety shows. He wanted to play the cello, but it was evident that he was not going to make it in this field, either. He was liked by his brothers and many friends because he was a saint and a rebel. He was also a constant problem for my father who only saw the rebel in him. The saint came out much later, when Italo met Anna and he had to marry her on a very short notice!

Bianca, and subsequently Irma, helped my mother in managing the apartment and supervising Gilda and me. Bianca met Romolo Branchi, a cousin of Irma's best friend, who was a salesman for well drilling equipment. Romolo, who had just returned from Asmara in Erithrea with an outstanding suntan, was immediately nicknamed "the African" (after the name given to Scipio the Younger, the Roman general who destroyed Carthage). As a salesman, Romolo knew how to sell himself to people, and as "African" he carried sufficient charm to win Bianca's hand in marriage.

With Irma, things went in a different way. Ottavio Basile, a top clarinet player in the Air Force music band, was attracted to our shop in Via Fabio Massimo. Ottavio was born and raised in Grottaminarda, a small mountain town between Naples and Bari. Like many other men from the South, he was strongly attracted by blond women of the North. And Irma was a splendid, light colored blonde in a music shop, only a few steps away from Ottavio's barrack and from his never ending desires.

I was a quiet little boy who attended the "Umberto I" elementary school (the same one Nicla attended), and then the "Mamiani" gymnasium (also a school where Nicla went for a few years). I spent most of my time with friends of my age living near the music store, or with those of the nearby "San Gioacchino" parish. I enjoyed playing soccer and always loved swimming. All boys of my age had to belong to the "Balillas," a youth organization created and made compulsory by the Fascist government. I deeply resented going to their rallies every Saturday afternoon, when time was better suited for soccer games or swim races.

Occasionally, I had to help in the music shop. When I was old enough to go by myself to Piazza Venezia (where Mussolini's famous balcony was located), I was often requested to collect music for the store from Ricordi & C., the publisher and wholesaler of concert scores. It was a long distance from Via Fabio Massimo to Piazza Venezia, but I gladly walked all the way there and back, saving the bus money to spend on something else.

Gilda was born when my mother was 46 years old. She was a most beautiful baby girl, with blond hair and dark blue eyes, a real surprise to her family, to our friends, and to the many shop customers. Gilda' s mission in life was to take good care of my mother in later years, when everyone else in the Chiarappa family was either married or living in faraway places. She married Gianfranco Aragozzini, a businessman and interior decorator.

Towards the end of the 1930s, life appeared fine and normal for the entire family. By this time, my father was a well known artist, giving concerts all over Italy and in many European cities. The piano player who accompanied him in these concerts, was Enrichetta Petacci. She was the aunt of Claretta, Mussolini's lady lover who died dramatically with him during the 1945 uprising in northern Italy. On one occasion Enrichetta warned my father, saying that he should be careful with her: she had "powerful connections in very high places."

No one in the Chiarappa family expected the dramatic events that were on the horizon and that would change life for everybody. The first event occurred in 1939, when Marichen came to Rome. She was my mother's niece, visiting Italy for the first time. She was an attractive young woman who immediately liked Italy and the Italians. My father took special care of her and probably spent too much time touring her around in his second-hand coupe car. This stirred a flare of jealousy on my mother's part. One day, this exploded in violence at our apartment, when Umberto was called in to throw Marichen into the street. This was enough for my father to pack a suitcase and walk out on his family. He felt that his wife and all his children were against him, and that he had to find other arrangements for himself. He never filed for a divorce or legal separation. Instead, he created an ambiguous and sad situation for everyone concerned. He stubbornly maintained this situation for the rest of his long and pathetic life.

One year after this incident, King Victor Emmanuel III and Mussolini declared war on France and England. Many important events took place which affected our family, our country and the entire world.

3
The War Period (1940-1945)

The quickest way of ending a war is to lose it.

—George Orwell, 1950

No one wanted the war against France and England except for Mussolini, a few over-enthusiastic fas cists and a handful of irresponsible generals. Italy was totally unprepared, not only materially but also psychologically exhausted, tired of the pre-war government rhetoric and convinced that any future victory would be the victory of Germany, something more dangerous than a defeat. The standard army rifles were still 1891 models. Most of the artillery consisted of cannon pieces taken from the Austrians at the end of World War I. The Navy and Air Force ignored the existence of radar equipment. The Italian troops, poorly equipped and inadequately trained, were thinly scattered over a huge front including the French and Yugoslavian borders, Albania, Libya, and East Africa (Eritrea, Somalia and Ethiopia).

Civilian infrastructures to support and maintain the war effort were deficient or non-existent. The critical area of food procurement and distribution had been totally overlooked. A few days after the war's declaration on June 10, 1940, Nicla's father Vittorio, who was then managing the "Maccarese", was asked by the Minister of Agriculture to become the Director General of the Department of Food and Nutrition. This department, just conceived by the Council of Ministers, had to be organized immediately. This meant that manpower had to be recruited, office space had to be found, and sources of essential foods (wheat, rice, flour, sugar, fats, and meats) had to be identified and safely stored in strategic locations throughout the country. To further this plan, an army general assigned to the Ministry of Agriculture turned over to Vittorio numerous documents classified top secret. They consisted of incomplete and outdated statistical information, and typical military plans directed at feeding the troops only. No plans existed, however, for feeding the civilian population. This was to be Vittorio's responsibility for the next five uncertain years.

The war against France only lasted 100 hours, long enough to cost the life of 600 Italian soldiers sent to die with the same indifference as thirty years before against Austria. This ephemeral success gave hope that the conflict would not last very long. But after a few months, it became evident that no progress was being made in North Africa, where unexpected defeats were being experienced. Marshall Rodolfo Graziani penetrated Egypt at Sidi el Barrani in September, 1940, but he was forced back three months later by the so-called Army of the Nile, under the command of Sir Arcibald Wavel. In this British counterattack the Italians were driven back deep into Cyrenaica and lost large quantities of arms, supplies and over 100,000 men. Graziani himself seemed as if he had lost his head. In a pathetic letter to Mussolini he asked to be relieved from his responsibilities. It became evident that the destiny of North Africa could not be left in the hands of Mussolini and his incapable generals, and Hitler assigned Field Marshall Erwin Rommel to lead the armored Afrika Korps.

Rommel had already visited North Africa and had seen the type of strategy used by Graziani. In his judgment, this was a mixture of short-sightedness, megalomania and plain fear. The war in the desert could not be won by static troop concentrations in faraway strongholds scattered over acres and acres of flat, hot sand. When he landed in Tripoli, Rommel was nearly 50 years old. His reputation of fearless commander and quick strategist had preceded him. He was a handsome man of below-average height. His profile resembled that of a bird of prey, while his mobile blue eyes revealed quick intelligence and unshakeable resoluteness. He had the cold, cruel smile of a fearless poker player.

Rommel opened his first offensive on March 24, 1941, with two objectives: to beat the British in Cyrenaica and to rapidly proceed to Cairo. In a matter of weeks, his Panzer troops arrived in Sollum, on the border with Egypt. The problem he now confronted was the great distance from the port of Tripoli. He faced a severe shortage of supplies. He was low on fuel, ammunitions, spare parts, and even water for his thirsty vehicles and men. Overextension became the principle factor of Rommel's forthcoming defeat in Libya, a country where rich oil deposits were yet to be discovered.

In spite of the dubious situation in North Africa, Mussolini decided to attack Greece from Albania on October 28, 1940, just before the onset of the winter. This offensive was not part of any well developed strategic plan, but only

Mussolini's strong desire for a quick and glamorous success, in response to Hitler's decision to occupy Romania. Mussolini complained to his Secretary of State that the Führer never informed him about his plans. "This time I will pay him back in the same manner. He will learn from the newspaper that I have occupied Greece." The Greek army, however, reacted with a fierce counterattack, beat the Italians and invaded Albania. A very cold winter followed. This contributed to the death of many thousands of Italian soldiers.

By early March, 1941, British troops from North Africa landed in Greece, expecting to open a second front in southern Europe. At this point, Hitler decided to help Mussolini in his poorly conceived and badly conducted Greek campaign. Before doing so, he signed an agreement with Prince Paul of Yugoslavia to let him join the Axis. Word of this agreement touched off a rebellion in Belgrade where a coup was promptly arranged and neutrality re-instated. On April 6, Hitler, infuriated by this insult, ordered the invasion of Yugoslavia and Greece. Yugoslavia capitulated eleven days later, and Greece shortly afterwards. The Air Force general who had arranged the coup in Belgrade fled to Cairo with most of his planes and pilots. Among these was a tall, good looking Serb by the name of Jovanovich. He was to come to America at the end of the war and become the father of Stevan, our future son-in-law.

The war at sea was not developing any better for Italy. The speedy Italian fleet suffered numerous blows from the British Navy, which literally dominated the Mediterranean Sea from its strongholds in Gibraltar, Malta and Alexandria. One of the most important defeats was the surprise air raid of Taranto. This naval base on Italy's heel, was attacked on November 11, 1940. Two waves of slow and obsolete Swordfish aircraft, launched by the carrier Illustrious were able to destroy or take out of action half of Italy's battle force. It was a sort of Pearl Harbor, the only difference being in the number of attacking planes: three-hundred-fifty in the case of Pearl Harbor and only twenty over Taranto!

On March 28, 1941, the Italian Navy was again shattered by British naval and air forces in the battle of Cape Matapan. On this and future occasions the Italian naval forces showed that they could not compete with the more modern and better equipped British fleet.

In spite of the adverse military situation in North Africa, Greece and at sea, Vittorio was doing his best to organize his department, to ration bread and other basic food commodities, and to ensure their distribution in cities and villages throughout Italy. There were serious difficulties in reaching populations in Sardinia and in the south, due to heavy bombing of ships, railroads, and highways by enemy Air Forces. Furthermore, Italy could no longer count on food imports from overseas. The British Navy and Air Force sank most of the cargo ships daring to cross the Mediterranean Sea.

At the same time, national crop productivity declined rapidly all over Italy. There were no tractors or trucks left on the farms, no gasoline, no seed, and no fertilizers. Even horses had been taken away by the army. The labor force consisted essentially of women, children and old men.

Vittorio and his newly established organization faced increasingly difficult problems in procuring food supplies for hungry Italy. In the spring of 1941 his attention was called to the urgent need of making food available to the Axis-occupied territories of Yugoslavia and Greece. An Air Force plane was placed at his disposal for an immediate assessment of the food situation in both countries. By mid-May, upon completion of his survey, Vittorio reported to the Minister of Agriculture the impossibility of providing food from Italy to these territories. Supplies had to be found in the Balkans, where German occupation authorities were to be made responsible for the matter.

Shortly afterward Vittorio received a visit from Pellegrino Ghigi, the Italian ambassador in Athens. As he entered his office, Vittorio promptly told him, "Please, your excellency, do not ask me for food for Greece. We do not have reserves in store to feed our own army and population." The ambassador expected this reaction. He patiently sat at the other side of Vittorio's desk, and started describing the situation in Athens, where people were dying of starvation in the streets. Most affected were the children. Vittorio realized at once that he had the lives of these children in his hands. He had to help them. Without further hesitation, he issued an order for the immediate delivery of nearly 3,000 tons of rice to Italy's former enemy. Greece never forgot this unexpected gift.

Vittorio was able to swap some food supplies with the Germans, who wanted rice from northern Italy in exchange for potatoes and modern weapons. During the spring of 1943, on one of these exchanges with Germany, something went wrong in one of the imported freight cars. A consignment of potatoes was spoiled on arrival in Bergamo, in northern Italy. The spoiled potatoes were promptly dumped into a local creek, but this did not escape the attention of some local fascists who reported the matter directly to Mussolini. Vittorio at first ignored the spoiled potatoes but in the following months he became increasingly aware that someone in the high ranks of the Fascist Party had organized a press campaign against him and his department. He was publicly reprehended in the newspapers for being responsible for a waste "that seriously undermined Italy's war effort."

By this time, the internal situation in Italy was rapidly deteriorating. People were waking up from the illusion that the war was to be short, easy, and possibly conducted by proxy in far away lands. The Fascists were becoming increasingly aware that the war was also being lost, and, accordingly, they started directing their blame toward the existing bureaucracy. This was considered slow, inefficient and willing to sabotage the country.

As a result of a few spoiled potatoes, Vittorio had to resign from his office. He returned to manage the "Maccarese," but even there he was continually harassed by Fascist groups. Almost daily they organized audits and inspections to ensure that all commodities produced on the farm were duly delivered to government storehouses. This harassment became so bad that Prince Boncompagni, "Maccarese's" chairman of the board, called for a meeting with Mussolini. He wanted to bring this matter directly to his attention. With great surprise he discovered that Mussolini was not aware of what was going on. Instead, Mussolini openly recognized that "Professor Ronchi, being a faithful Republican, was a gentleman who deserved full respect." This signaled the end of any further persecution.

In the meantime the war in North Africa, which had been fought with alternate attacks and retreats by Italian troops and the German Afrika Korps, was coming rapidly to an end. On November 8, 1942, the British and Americans invaded Morocco and Algeria, thus opening a second front in this war zone. The British Eighth Army in Egypt, now commanded by General Bernard Montgomery, and reinforced with powerful American tanks, struck at El Alamein on October 23, forcing the Axis armies into one of the longest retreats in history. In eighty days these troops traveled seventeen hundred fifty miles, leaving behind a desert filled with burnt-out artillery, tanks, trucks, and thousands of dead or wounded soldiers. Occasionally, the Germans borrowed Italian transport at gunpoint and left their allies to make their way back on foot in the desert, without food or water. At the end of this retreat, Rommel ran into the fresh British Army and the Americans closing in from the west. He recognized that the war he had fought with such astuteness, earning the nickname Desert Fox, had come to an end. On May 12, Rommel flew back to Germany leaving some 250,000 men, part Germans and part Italians, to surrender to the Allied forces. No one realized that this was the turning point of the war. Later Churchill admitted, "Up to El Alamein we survived. After El Alamein we conquered."

In the early morning of July 10, 1943, American troops, under the command of General George S. Patton, landed in Gela and Licata on Sicily's southern coast. At the same time, Montgomery's Eighth British Army invaded the island's east coast and swiftly moved north to Syracuse and the Catania plains.

Although German Panzers struck back with great fury, most of the Italian defenders put up a very weak fight. A good number of these soldiers were ready to surrender or vanish into the island's interiors. The local population exulted at the arrival of the invading armies and welcomed them with flags, flowers and plenty of robust Marsala wine.

The effect of the successful Allied landing in Sicily was immediately felt throughout Italy and especially in Rome. There was a general feeling that the war was soon coming to an end. Shortly afterward, the city was heavily bombed from the air. Seven hundred American aircraft flying in formation in full daylight bombed Rome, on July 19, without interference by Italian anti-aircraft or fighter planes. Wave after wave of B-24 Liberators were seen discharging thousands of bombs from high altitude. Nicla and her sister Francesca, who had hurriedly returned to Rome from northern Italy, arrived just in time to observe the outcome of these powerful air strikes. From the open countryside where their train was forced to stop, they could see flames and heavy smoke rising from the devastated city outskirts.

On July 25, Mussolini was forced to resign as prime minister, following a majority vote against him by the Fascist "Grand Council." This meant that he was recognized by his own party members as no longer capable of ruling over the nation's Army and economy. Among those voting against him was his own son-in-law, Count Galeazzo Ciano. The following day, after a brief meeting with the King, Mussolini was arrested by the carabinieri (the equivalent of military police), placed in an ambulance, and taken prisoner to an undisclosed location in central Italy. Field Marshall Pietro Badoglio, the former conqueror of Ethiopia, was requested by King Victor Emmanuel III to take over the government and to announce to the Italian people that "the war was to continue." Instead, secret plans for Italy's capitulation were already underway with the Allied command. Royalist General Giuseppe Castellano met Americans and British representatives in Lisbon to sign an unconditional surrender and to propose a switch in sides. This would allow Italy to join the Allies against Germany, and signal the beginning of a civil war in the country.

In the days of confusion and apprehension that followed, Vittorio was called back by the newly established government to again direct the Food Department. This took place shortly before another severe air raid on Rome caused the destruction of many freight cars and rail tracks, adding to the difficulties of distributing food to the civilian population.

Badoglio's government, which lasted only 45 days, was called "the government of fear." Fear of the Americans and the British who continued the bombing of Italian cities and coastline, fear of the Germans who were moving fresh troops to Italy to occupy the country in case of Italy's capitulation, fear of the return to power of the Fascists, and fear of an uprising by the anti-fascists. Even Badoglio's procedure for the secret armistice was a comedy of deception that did not deceive anybody.

There were, in fact, two Italian generals in Lisbon, negotiating separately for the suspension of hostilities: the above mentioned Castellano and Giacomo Zanussi. The latter had been secretly sent to Lisbon on August 24 by a different faction of the Italian High Command. To the Allied, this second visit came as a surprise. They even suspected that Zanussi might be spying for the Germans to find out the terms of the armistice. Then they thought that this might only be Italian Machiavellianism. Instead it was only Italian distrust, inefficiency and plain clumsiness.

The result of all this was that Castellano, who had already left Lisbon when Zanussi arrived, was given copy of a short document on surrender conditions. Zanussi, instead, received the full length text containing expanded and much harsher conditions. Its title read in bold letters, "Unconditional Surrender," words that had been carefully left out of the short document, to avoid delays in terminating the war.

On September 3, Castellano received authorization by the King and Badoglio to sign the acceptance of the Allied conditions. The signing ceremony took place in the mess hall of Fairfield Camp near Cassibile in Sicily. Eisenhower stood behind a long table. surrounded by English and American high ranking officers. Castellano, dressed in civilian clothes, appeared confused and disoriented by so many uniforms and the sound of a totally unfamiliar language. He signed the short text and only afterwards was given the full length document. Then it was the turn of General Bedell Smith to sign on behalf of Eisenhower. Apparently Ike did not want to sanction with his signature what he considered "a dirty affair." Then came the photographers, and some whiskey, but no toasts. Many photos were taken to immortalize an event which remains one of the most humiliating in Italy's history.

The same distrust, inefficiency and clumsiness characterized the negotiations for the date of the official announcement of the armistice. While Eisenhower wanted this to be on the 8th of September, to coincide with the American landing in Salerno, no one informed Castellano about these "secret" plans. He therefore guessed that the announcement would be given "between the 10th and the 15th, possibly the 12th." This guess became "certainty" once it reached Badoglio's High Command in Rome, which was to organize the defense of the city and the trapping of German troops south of the Alps.

For capturing Rome, the Americans had agreed to provide the 82nd Airborne Division under the command of General Maxwell Taylor. The objective of Operation Giant 2 was to parachute troops or land them on gliders at several airports in the city while the Italians were to maintain a corridor five miles wide and twenty miles long on both sides of the Tiber river.

On the evening of September 7, an ambulance from the port of Gaeta drove through Rome heading for the high command of the Italian armored division. In the ambulance were General Maxwell Taylor and one of his aides. They were both in their uniforms and ready to finalize Operation Giant 2 set for the following night. But there were no Italian generals at the command nor in the city to discuss these plans. Finally, they decided to talk directly with Badoglio, who was sound asleep in his family villa. The old Marshall was very surprised to see the Americans in his house and to learn from them that the official announcement he had to give was for the following day. "But the Italian troops are not yet prepared," protested Badoglio. "We have fuel and ammunitions to resist the Germans for only six hours." General Taylor lost his temper and told Badoglio that the armistice had to be announced on the 8th or the Americans would bomb and destroy Rome. Badoglio, feeling the pressure of the situation, immediately drafted a cable to Eisenhower asking to postpone the announcement and to cancel Operation Giant 2.

Ike's reply was quick and unequivocal: "Either you announce the armistice today or I will reveal the details of this dirty affair. You must do your part NOW." And Badoglio could no longer avoid the destiny he had helped to create.

As requested, on September 8, 1943, at eight o'clock in the evening, Marshall Badoglio announced on the radio that Italy had given up the fighting. The following day, very early in the morning, he, the King and his family, two of their servants, and a selected number of generals and admirals secretly fled Rome for Brindisi, a city in southern Italy occupied by American and British troops. They left behind no orders or instructions: only chaos. It was the signal for a dramatic, immediate and total collapse of the Italian armed forces. Most units, left without directives, food or supplies, melted away like ice in the sun. Each man was left entirely on his own to make whatever decision he felt necessary. Soldiers and officers alike quickly dropped their uniforms for civilian clothes and ran away. Buses, trains, horses, bikes, anything that could be used for transportation, were taken by thousands of men anxious only to reach their families and safety. It was the terrible finale of an unbelievable human tragedy.

The German troops watched incredulously what was happening to their former partners. Within hours of Badoglio's announcement, German patrols reacted to the new situation by promptly occupying all strategic points in Rome. The same happened throughout northern and central Italy. Rommel seized Trieste and the routes to Yugoslavia. As many as six-hundred-forty thousand Italian troops were taken prisoner in Italy and the Balkans. Officers and soldiers were tightly packed in sealed freight cars and shipped to internment camps in Germany. On September 11, Field Marshall Kesserling proclaimed Italy a war theater under German control. He also declared Rome an open city under his authority. A puppet civilian government was established and Vittorio was called back to work as Food Commissioner.

On September 22, Mussolini was freed from his confinement on the "Gran Sasso", a range of high mountains northeast of Rome. A German airborne commando landed gliders and light planes near the ski resort where Mussolini was being kept under surveillance. Without firing a single shot, the German soldiers liberated Mussolini, and flew him to Rome, then to Vienna and, finally, to Rastenburg, in eastern Prussia. Here, he was met by Hitler who reassured him that he was to be re-established as the Fascist leader of his homeland. A new Fascist Republican government was formed and moved from Rome to Salo', in northern Italy. Vittorio was asked to leave Rome for Treviso, near Venice, where the Ministry of Agriculture was to be relocated. This decision greatly upset Nicla's mother. Gina immediately arranged to meet the Minister of Agriculture to request him to allow Vittorio to remain in Rome. Her request was not granted, and Vittorio was forced to leave for Treviso. A letter of resignation, which he submitted to the Ministry, was also rejected.

By October 13, 1943, Victor Emmanuel III formally declared war on Germany. By doing so, he was probably one of the few head of states in history who was able to declare war twice during the same conflict. It was a miserable expediency to save his throne and, probably, lessen the punishment Italy was to receive for having lost the war.

Vittorio returned to Rome in January, 1944, when amphibious Allied forces landed in Anzio. Shortly afterwards, he was hospitalized with a stomach ulcer. The German SS and Fascist militia established a 24-hour hospital watch to discourage him from escaping. He had hoped, like many others in Rome, that the Allied troops could quickly reach the city, only one hour's drive from Anzio. Instead, this never happened.

For more than a year the Allied troops remained pinned down to a semi-circular strip of the Italian seashore, fifteen miles long and seven miles deep. The troops, constantly engaged by heavy German bombing, suffered days reminiscent of World War I. Their agony came close to being a military disaster. Churchill, who was responsible for Anzio's beachhead, summarized this situation by stating: "Such is the story of the struggle of Anzio; a story of high opportunity and shattered hopes, of skillful inception on our part and swift recovery by the enemy, of valour shared by both." Beautiful words pronounced by a most eloquent British politician, who never saw the thousands of white markers left behind in the American cemetery in nearby Nettuno, the tragic reminder of a military operation of very questionable value.

On April 14, the police stepped into Vittorio's hospital room and, without consideration for his medical condition, placed him under arrest. He was loaded on a bus and taken with other prisoners to the penitentiary of Castelfranco Emiliano, not far from Modena. Vittorio was kept alone in a security cell but, through the prison grapevine, he soon learned of the execution of many political prisoners. He suspected that his turn had arrived. During the ensuing sleepless night, Vittorio engaged in long prayers. The following day, he was surprised to see that he was loaded on the same bus and taken to his final destination in Treviso, where he was "delivered" to the Minister of Agriculture. Only then did Vittorio learn that his letter of resignation had been interpreted by fascist authorities as "an act of treason for not reporting for duty at time of war." This meant that he had to be referred to a special military tribunal and that the death penalty was almost certain. Then came the great surprise. For unknown reasons, the same Minister of Agriculture who had refused Gina's early plea, agreed to let Vittorio go, but not back to Rome. He and his family were to remain impounded in northern Italy so that Vittorio's technical skills "could not be used by the invading enemy."

Cortine di Nave, a small village near Brescia, was selected for the Ronchi family's confinement. Vittorio's sister, Ida, and her husband Benedetto Mombelloni, lived in Brescia with their five boys: Paolo, Gianni, Simone, Piero, and Vittorio. Benedetto was very popular in the area, having the reputation of being a first class physician. Gina and her four daughters, Lisa, Francesca, Vittoria, and Nicla, arrived from Rome with only a few belongings to settle down in a small farmhouse requisitioned for this purpose. The house was a few miles away from the village, where it stood lonely on a small, bare hill. The owners of the house kept half of the building and the Ronchi family camped in three bedrooms and a country-style kitchen.

There was no running water in the old house, only an outdoor well from which water had to be transported to the house in metal buckets. A sturdy iron rod, running parallel to one of the kitchen walls, was the support on which these buckets were kept aligned like soldiers in a parade. During the winter nights it was so cold in the house that the water froze in the buckets and ice had to be broken the next morning before water could be used. The only source of heat in the house was a large cookstove in the kitchen which operated on firewood. The Ronchi family spent most of their time around this stove when at home. Gina was occupied knitting sweaters or making heavy clothes for the girls. Vittorio spent his time reading and writing. One of the documents he produced was a new Agrarian Reform for Italy. He also had a bicycle at his disposal with which he was able to ride around in the countryside, visiting nearby farmhouses and, occasionally, procuring food supplies. On one of these bicycle excursions Vittorio happened to meet a long military convoy of Fascist troops moving on a country road. He quickly descended from the bicycle and took cover behind some bushes. Suddenly he recognized Mussolini, sitting alone in one of the convoy's cars. The "duce" appeared pale, thin and incredibly aged. He was staring around without interest, almost as if he already knew that his dramatic end was irrevocably close. Vittorio felt only compassion for a man whose dreams and ambitions had ruined Italy.

During the long stay at Cortine di Nave, Nicla and her sisters were able to find local instructors to tutor them, in the absence of public schools and transportation. The hardship of being confined to a small village and an uncomfortable house weighed much less heavily on the girls than on their parents.

More than a year was spent under these conditions. Finally, in the spring of 1945, partisan forces rebelled against the Germans and Mussolini's Fascist troops. Milan and the rest of the Po Valley remained in their hands for some time, due to delays in the Allied Force's arrival. This led to much bloodshed throughout northern Italy.

Mussolini and his mistress, Claretta Petacci, were recognized by a group of partisans while trying to cross into Switzerland as part of a German military convoy. The "duce" was no longer wearing one of his showy uniforms. Instead, he was hiding in an old, shabby army coat and his head was covered by a German helmet. His once robust jaw and his conceited appearance had both clearly shrunk. He was no longer smiling as he used to from Piazza Venezia's balcony. Mussolini appeared as he really was: a scared old man who realized, at last, that the great show he had started was coming to an end. He was now facing a reality he could no longer escape. Without any trial, he and Claretta were brutally killed by the partisans, who then took their corpses to Milan to hang them head down in a gas station of Piazza Loreto. A barbaric finale in one of the most civilized countries in the world.

By April, 25, 1945, the war in Italy was practically over. Vittorio, accompanied by Lisa, was called to Milan to work with the newly established Economic Commission of the Liberation Committee for Northern Italy. He then returned to Rome to a newly formed Ministry of Food. By June the rest of the family followed him to the city, after having suffered in confinement one of the coldest winters on record. On arrival in Rome, Nicla and her sister Vittoria were dropped off at Piazza Mazzini because the car in which they were traveling was headed elsewhere. For the two young girls the distance from this piazza to the apartment in Via Ovidio was not a problem. They were so happy and excited to be back in their city and their environment that they ran all the way home without stopping. The war was over and a great feeling of hope was now filling their young hearts.

There were many events during the war which had important effects on my family. This was mainly because my mother had four "boys" in two of the fighting armies, and all of them were of "fighting age."

Theo was drafted by the German army at the onset of the war. He participated in the invasion of France in 1939, but only as part of the occupation forces. Of this campaign, Theo could only recall how much good wine he was able to drink. The cellars in the French countryside were well stocked with superb wines, and no one was there to guard them. Everyone had left in a hurry to escape the "blitz" war and the rapidly advancing German troops. For Theo, his military service in France's Champagne district remained a memorable affair. Many years later, he would remember that visiting so many French cellars without being formally invited was, for him, a "civilized way to be part of an otherwise cruel war."

Umberto was called to serve in the army on June 10, 1940, the same day Italy declared war on England and France. He was assigned to a trucking regiment stationed in Rome, where he discovered that his head was too big to fit the largest Italian helmet, and that his calves were too fat to squeeze into the largest army boots. So Umberto was not given the opportunity to wear a helmet for the entire war, while he had to buy his boots with his own money from a private store. Definitely, Italy was not prepared to dress its soldiers nor to fight a war.

After a few days of service, Umberto learned that most of his comrades were being shipped to Albania, in preparation for the invasion of Greece. He also learned that his regiment needed a cook for the troops remaining in Rome. Umberto immediately volunteered for this position. His face was round, his body was large around the waist, and he had the look of a good cook. But he had no cooking experience.

My mother then became Umberto's adviser. Every morning she would tell him over the phone what to cook and how to cook. I was a 15-year-old boy, growing rapidly, and always in search of food. I soon discovered that by spending certain "critical" hours of my day in Umberto's kitchen, I could secure free and abundant lunches. More important, I could still taste genuine "mamma's dishes." All the service men shared my appreciation for Umberto's excellent food. It was probably the first time in history that a mother was willing to spend so much time on the phone, and that a soldier son was honestly using all the ingredients received from the Army. When Umberto was transferred to a local transport command as a German-Italian interpreter, it was for me and his fellow soldiers a most serious loss of abundant and tasty food. It was, in fact, the actual beginning of the real war.

Italo was also in the Italian army. He was serving in an infantry regiment located a few hundred yards away from his family apartment in Rome. At first, he had a very comfortable life as a drafted soldier in wartime. He transcribed music for the military band during the day, and slept comfortably at home at night. No one imagined that his regiment was soon to be sent to Dalmatia during the German invasion of Yugoslavia, and later to the Don River in Russia. The latter campaign was a total disaster for the Italian Army. Only a handful of survivors came back from this tragic ordeal, and Italo was one of them. This was due to Umberto, who, in the meantime, had been transferred to Warsaw in Poland, as interpreter of the Transport Command serving the Italian troops on the Soviet front. When he found out that Italo was in Russia, dangerously exposed to a harsh winter and a failing military operation, he asked his superiors to have him assigned to Warsaw, where there was need for more German-Italian interpreters. Both Umberto and Italo remained safely in Poland until the retreat of the German Army from Russia was completed. They were then relocated to Munich.

At the same time, Theo was assigned to a German Transport Command in the Hotel de la Ville in Rome. His fluent knowledge of Italian also qualified him to procure food for the cafeteria he was running in the nearby Hotel Internazionale in Via Sistina. This was very helpful to my mother and the rest of our family, now suffering for lack of food. In fact, the strict rationing enforced by Nicla's father's department allowed each person only 100 grams of black bread per day, half a pound of potatoes per month, and no coffee nor sugar. Olive oil could only be procured if one could trade it for gold, shoes or clothing with farmers in the countryside. Occasionally, Theo was able to drop off at our apartment a bag of potatoes or a sack of rice from his cafeteria. This helped to fight the everyday battle of food procurement for the family.

In 1941, I joined the Military School in Naples. There were three such schools in Italy: in Rome, Milan and Naples. I had always admired the young cadets walking in the streets of Rome in their elegant uniforms, and I felt that I could also pursue a career in the Army, or maybe in the Air Force. An added advantage for me was to defer the draft in wartime.

My father accompanied me when I reported to the School. I had never seen Naples before. The streets were crowded with people and not as clean as in Rome. There was also much noise in the air.

The Military School was located on one of the hills overlooking the bay, and I was immediately captivated by the view and the beauty of the large baroque building and the nearby "Nunziatella" church dating back to 1588. It was during the Kingdom of Ferdinand the Fourth in 1787, that the Royal Academy of the Bourbon Army was first established in this building. During the following years, the Academy changed to Military College and then, in 1860, to

Maria's four "fighting boys": Luigi, Italo, Umberto, and Theo.

Military School. King Victor Emmanuel III was a cadet during the period 1881 to 1884.

The transition from family to army life was not easy. Most cadets were from southern Italy, they spoke different dialects, and many of them were sons of Army officers. The separation from my family and the new rigid discipline contributed at first to a difficult adjustment. I was really happy when my mother and sister Gilda came to Naples for one of my first outings. My uniform was too big, my "kepi'" (special round hat) was too large, and my shoes were too tight. But I realized that both my mother and my sister were extremely proud to stroll with me through the crowded streets of Naples. I promised myself that I could stand the change and that I was not going to disappoint them.

Life at the military school was geared on tight schedules and hard study. Slowly I discovered that I could cope with both. In a short time I found myself at the top of my "course" in academic and military achievements. At the bottom was Guglielmo Mileto. He and I were probably attracted to each other because we were so different.

Guglielmo was born in Tripoli, Libya, to a family of Army people, with many high ranking officers on both the father's and mother's sides. The high degree of discipline, punctuality, self control, and inflexibility that both parents tried to impose on him for many years clashed with his artistic, fun-loving, outgoing temperament. Bill, as he was later called, was in fact a Renaissance man typical of 14th century Florence. He was gifted with a great dose of talent, if not genius, and had an incomparable artistic dexterity for improvisation and color. He did not want to follow the career of his father and many uncles. He was not "designed" for the Army. All Bill wanted from life was to remain free from responsibilities that would interfere with his strong desire for

My step brother, Theo, having lunch during the German occupation of
France.

painting and drawing. He liked women and women, all too often, liked him, for he was a nice looking young man, tall and thin with brown, thick curly hair. His face had the expression of a person of distinction in one of Piero della Francesca's paintings. He was definitely a Renaissance man.

Guglielmo and I became very good friends in Naples and we maintained our friendship for a long time in Italy and America.

Naples was heavily bombed by British planes aiming at the destruction of Italian naval forces and sea communication with Sicily. We had to spend most of our nights in shelters, and for this reason, towards the end of my second year, the school was moved to Benevento, a smaller city in the interior considered "safe" from air raids. This proved not to be true: all my belongings were destroyed in a heavy air raid which took place in the summer of 1943, when I was faraway on leave.

By September 8, 1943, when Italy surrendered to the Allied forces, Maria's "soldier boys" were scattered in different places. Umberto and Italo were still in Munich. Theo had temporarily moved to Frascati, where the German troops regrouped before occupying Rome. I was leisurely spending my time in Riccione, a beach resort on the Adriatic coast, where my family used to go on summer vacation. For a short while my mother lost contact with all four of us. I was the first to return to Rome. Unaware of what was happening, and still wearing my elegant uniform, I traveled back to the city on a train crowded with Italian soldiers. These were dressed in all sorts of clothes, having dropped their uniforms and abandoned their units. Weariness and fear were written in their faces. It was an unforgettable sight.

A few days later, Theo returned to Rome. He had lived another of his spirited experiences. As mentioned, his unit had moved to Frascati, one of the towns on the hills south-east of Rome which have terraced vineyards overlooking a flat strip of land that extends all the way to Anzio and the Tirrenian sea. These hills offered the Germans two important advantages: a good strategic area in the event of enemy attack, and a good source of "Frascati" wine in case of no attack. But Frascati wine was difficult to find. Local growers, aware of the latest developments in Italy and in their area, were keeping their good stock under secure lock and key.

Theo found himself walking in the countryside with two other German soldiers. The sun was hot and the thirst was great. Suddenly he had an idea. He asked his comrades to take away his gun and to tie his hands behind his back. He asked them to knock on the door of a nearby farmhouse and to let him do all of the talking. When the farmer suspiciously opened the door, Theo explained in perfect Italian that he was an Italian Army officer likely to be shot by the Germans for wearing their uniform. He was no spy: he had been using their uniform only to reach his family in safety. "Could I, please, have some water to drink?" he asked very politely. The farmer looked at Theo's dusty uniform, his hands tied behind his back, and the panic clearly showing in his eyes. He did not want to see this scared Italian officer shot by the Germans. He had a better plan. The farmer then proposed going down to his cellar, drinking wine and getting the German guards so drunk that Theo could easily escape. The plan was implemented. After some time and much drinking, the farmer realized that Theo did not want to run away. Instead, he sheepishly admitted that he was also a German. The farmer at first thought that Theo had had too much of his wine. Then he realized what had really happened. With great sport and a good sense of humor, he joined the Germans in laughter and more libations!

A phone call from Gitschi, Theo's second wife, informed my mother that Umberto and Italo were safe, but prisoners in a German concentration camp near Munich. For the time being there was nothing that could be done for them. Shortly thereafter, Theo was informed that his house had been seriously damaged by an air raid. He requested and obtained a special furlough to return to Munich. As he was leaving Rome. Allied forces landed in Anzio and the Germans mobilized all their troops in central Italy to stop the invasion. All furloughs for German officers and soldiers were immediately canceled.

Theo took a chance, ignoring this order, and proceeded with his travel plans. When he reached the border, he told the German guards that he was carrying a "special and urgent message" from Field Marshall Kesserling and that he had to reach Munich immediately. The guards believed him and Theo reached his wife. He then went to visit a General who had been a frequent guest at the "Four Seasons Hotel," where Theo had worked before the war. He explained the situation of his two stepbrothers lying idle in a concentration camp while there was great need for German-Italian interpreters at the Transport Command in Rome. Theo suggested taking them out of the camp and, under his own personal guarantee, transferring them to Rome. The general agreed and signed the release order.

Theo went to visit the concentration camp where many thousands of American, British, and other European prisoners were being kept together. By a stroke of luck, he recognized Italo upon entering the camp. The two brothers hugged each other, to the great surprise of the German guards and surrounding prisoners. Italo promptly asked Theo if he wanted American cigarettes and, maybe, some "true" coffee or chocolate. Without hesitation Theo gave Italo his gold watch to trade with the Americans. Meanwhile, Umberto was informed about Theo's visit. Again there was one more embrace in front of many curious spectators. No one could figure out what was going on in that camp between a German staff sergeant and two Italian prisoners.

Theo returned to Rome without his gold watch, but very pleased with his mission. Not long thereafter, Umberto and Italo safely arrived at our apartment. They were both dressed in German uniforms and accompanied by an armed escort. My mother prepared a good meal and offered the former prisoners and their vigilant guard plenty of wine.

The next day Umberto and Italo reported to the German Transport Command, but no one there knew what to do with them since they had not received any instructions. Only Theo knew that the story of a shortage in interpreters was his own invention. After a few days, it was decided that Umberto and Italo were to be hired as civilian interpreters, the first to stay in Rome, the second to be assigned to Viterbo, a small town forty miles to the north. Both could now shed their German uniforms and return to civilian clothes.

The war was still going on, but for my mother it was as if the hostilities had already ended. She was very happy to have all her boys at home. Occasionally, she organized dinners for the whole family just as in pre-war times. On one of these occasions Umberto asked if he could invite a secretary from his staff. My mother agreed. This young lady had been recently courted by Italo in Viterbo, where he had told her that he was "an orphan without a family." Shortly afterwards, when this woman went looking for Italo at the main Transport Command in Rome, she met Umberto and then Theo. At first she could not accept that both of them were Italo's brothers. Then she understood that Italo had not told her the truth. She gladly accepted Umberto's invitation to come to dinner as a challenge to meet Italo, his wife Anna, their sons, and plenty of living relatives.

Italo and his family were late to arrive at our apartment that evening. In the meantime, everybody around the dinner table was informed about this delicate situation. When Italo finally entered the dining room, the young lady from Viterbo was sitting between Theo and Umberto, who very calmly introduced her as his secretary. Italo's face rapidly lost color and his eyes became smaller and smaller behind his glasses. There was also plenty of heat in Italo's eyes and anger in his chest. He coldly requested Umberto to step into another room as he had very important communications for him. But Umberto did not move an inch from his secure and comfortable chair. He continued to smile, inviting Italo and Anna to sit down at the table and to start eating because mother's food was getting cold. And the dinner proceeded with no further incidents other than Italo's lost appetite. This was one of the many memorable events that illustrate how, despite the war, its horror and destruction, there were family occasions which could bring everybody happily together. Of course, in this case, it was all at Italo's expense!

Rome was declared "citta' aperta" (open city). This meant that no further air bombing was to be carried out by Allied forces, in exchange for the Germans keeping their fighting troops and military installations outside the city. This "gentleman's agreement" was reached in order to safeguard the Eternal City's cultural treasures. It was one of the very few civilized decisions of the entire war.

Theo's Transportation Command was not considered a "military installation," as it was only involved with the movement of trains (civilian and military) from northern to southern Italy. Theo himself was not allowed to carry a weapon, nor were the thirty-two unarmed German soldiers who were killed in Via Rasella by a terrorist's bombs. This cruel and unnecessary event triggered one of the most brutal reactions on the part of the German SS. They randomly took 320 innocent men from the Regina Coeli prison and killed them at once at the Fosse Ardeatine. Among the victims were Ottorino Rizzo, my former captain in the Naples Military School, and two teachers from the high school I attended in Rome. The terrorist who did the bombing could have saved all these lives had he had the courage to turn himself in to German authorities. He never did.

The real danger in the "open city" was to run into a "retata", a police net set by fascists and SS troops to round up and arrest men capable of doing physical work for the German Todd Organization. This outfit was responsible for carrying out projects which required plenty of human labor such as digging trenches, fixing railroad tracks, clearing rubble, and so on. By the early autumn of 1944, some seven-and-a-half million foreigners had been rounded up in occupied Europe to work for the Todd Organization. The use of the bulldozer was still unknown to the Germans. It was, however, one of the three machines that Eisenhower reckoned essential to win the war. The other two being the jeep and the Dakota plane.

Most young men avoided the streets and stayed in the homes of friends and relatives. Others joined the Red Cross, special police corps, or even some religious order. Fake German "Ausweiss" (special circulation permits) were appearing all over the city to avoid arrest. Guglielmo and I discovered that the safest place for us was to stay around Via Sistina, where the German Transport Command was located. The street was blocked at both ends by Italian guards, and no "retate" were allowed there. The immediate advantages of this location were the cafeteria in the Internazionale Hotel, run by Theo and freely available to us, and the auto repair garage in Piazza Mignanelli run by Ildo Sarti. Ildo was a veteran of the Russian campaign and a close friend of Umberto. He was known for saying "Get me two hammers and I will repair any kind of car!"

It was in these surroundings that another unusual event took place in the spring of 1944.

Guglielmo and I were informed by Ildo that Theo had arranged a blind date with a young lady, apparently a girlfriend of Umberto. The date was set for a certain day and hour in the small plaza of Trinita' de' Monti at the top of the stairs leading to the Spanish square. The young lady was to wave a flower bouquet so that she could be recognized by Theo. On the same day, Guglielmo and I started looking for some girl willing to go to this appointment in place of Umberto's girlfriend. Our objective was to harass Theo. We purchased a bouquet of flowers and kept looking for the right girl.

By coincidence, in front of Ildo's garage, we met an old friend of ours by the name of Gigliola. We tried to convince her to step up to Trinita' de' Monti and to wave the flower bouquet. At first Gigliola did not want to do it, but then she accepted. The stage was set. Guglielmo and I were hiding to watch the scene. Theo, in his stern German uniform, stood at one side staring at Gigliola but hesitating to approach her. Gigliola, on the other side, kept waving the bouquet. Finally, Theo moved close and started speaking to Gigliola. At this point we came out of hiding and, laughing at Theo, we accused him of being a "dirty old man," taking advantage of young girls. And this girl just happened to be one of our friends. At first Theo appeared very embarrassed, but then he understood the gag and joined in laughing. He explained his hesitation. The girl looked a bit too young for Umberto's taste!

A few weeks later, I was surprised to discover that Gigliola herself was the person responsible for the whole situation. She had phoned me at home and, in my absence, she had talked with Umberto. After a few days, she phoned again looking for Umberto, but she found Theo. With him she arranged for the blind date at Trinita' de' Monti. All this was the cause of much laughter by my mother, who candidly admitted in German that : "Meine Kinder sind alle speziell!"(my children are all very, very special).

In the meantime, just as flowers blossom in the spring, so did the German and Allied troops waking up from their winter-long hibernation. Sixteen hundred artillery pieces had been placed in the Cassino sector alone, apparently undetected by the Germans. On May 11, 1944, the American Fifth and the British Eighth Army maneuvered for their final, strongest assault against their still formidable enemy. It was close to midnight. For forty-five minutes the skies were lit by the fire of the artillery and filled with the roar of many cannons shooting at once, all over the countryside. Then was the time for the infantry to move in. Men from many nationalities kept moving in the dark, hanging on to their rifles and machine guns. Americans, English, South Africans, Indians, Polish, Moroccans, Algerians, French, and even Italians: they all knew this was "their big battle." And they fought in wave after wave across the bloody mountain ridges. The Germans, on the other side, showed an incredible tenacity and determination. On May 18, the Montecassino Abbey was occupied by the Allied forces. So much blood for only a large pile of rubble. Cassino, in the end, did not mean much. It was only the prestige of conquering Rome that was important.

Marshall Kesserling immediately understood that no other line of defense was possible south of Rome or on the Tiber river. What was left of his troops could be easily lost by an Allied landing in Civitavecchia or by a pinching maneuver of the advancing American and British divisions. The Appenine mountains had to be reached right away, without losing valuable time. And in this way Theo left Rome with the other German troops, without fighting and in an orderly fashion. The family lost track of him for several months.

The German occupation quickly came to an end. Tired German soldiers were seen lying on the street sidewalks, dirty in their uniforms and with fear in their eyes. Most of them were extremely young, probably only high school boys sent to war too soon and without sufficient training. Some of them were seen stealing bicycles from civilians to join the retreating troops. What had been hate against Hitler's army now became pity for these young, inexperienced victims of the war, a confrontation that they probably never understood and that they certainly did not want.

On June 4, 1944, the Allied forces entered the city. The Roman population came out in the streets to greet the soldiers, cheering and hugging them in a true explosion of joy. For quite some time the atmosphere remained that of a big, loud, and colorful carnival. Freedom had finally arrived. But with freedom came many new problems. There was no police operating in the city and armed groups of men were roaming around the streets taking advantage of this situation by looting, or even killing. One such group forced its way into our apartment hoping to take possession of suspected food supplies. The group was disappointed to find only a few cans of sauerkraut that were immediately refused because they were only fit to feed "pigs like the Germans." Once again, my mother had outsmarted the "good Italians" she always loved. A number of bags of potatoes and flour, left behind by Theo for the family, had been safely hidden next door in the neighbor's apartment.

A few days later, Italo was arrested, accused of being a German spy. Apparently, somebody had seen him wearing a German uniform and construed all the rest. He was taken

American landing at Paestum, near Salerno. Navy beach battalion men are hugging the shaking beach while debris from a German bomb hit can be seen in the background. (OFFICIAL COAST GUARD PHOTO - from Library of Congress Photo Duplications.)

American light boats are loading gears and ammunition at Paestum. (OFFICIAL COAST GUARD PHOTO - from Library of Congress Photo Duplications.)

first to the Regina Coeli prison, and then to an internment camp in southern Italy where Fascists and suspected "collaborators" were kept under surveillance by the British army.

Shortly after Italo's arrest, we were surprised by the unexpected visit of an American cousin, Richard Chiarappa, from Middletown, Connecticut. Richard was a heavy set, dark-haired man in his mid-thirties. He had a protruding nose and an ever-changing facial expression. He could not speak a word of Italian, nor could anyone in the family understand him as his voice waved up and down like a roller coaster. Richard grew up in Connecticut where he was employed as an accountant by the Internal Revenue Service.

Richard had landed in Salerno on September 8, 1943, with one of the first assault units of Clark's Fifth Army. This landing had taken place under heavy fire from German coastal fortifications and tanks. It was supposed to be a surprise landing. However, the surprise was only for the American troops: they did not expect a rendezvous with three German Panzer divisions firing on to the beachhead from the surrounding highlands.

Many American assault vehicles, heavy equipment and ammunitions could not be discharged by the invading fleet, and for seven days Richard and his comrades were subject to German fire and massive counterattacks. Lacking the needed equipment and weapons, the assault troops became defense units. They included mechanics, cooks, truck drivers, and even a regimental music band. Finally, American B-24's were called in from the air bases in Sicily and North Africa. With their heavy bombing, they were able to force the Germans Panzers to abandon the surrounding hills. The Germans retreated to Naples and Richard safely proceeded toward Rome.

Ever since Richard had landed in Italy he had searched for Italian relatives. In each village, town or city he entered with his unit, he made sure to grab a telephone book to find someone named "Chiarappa." Finally, he succeeded in Rome. Richard remained for nearly a week in our apartment where he could sleep long hours in a regular bed and eat tasty Italian meals with his newly discovered family. He even tried to negotiate with the British Military police to free Italo, but with no success. Once again, it was clear that American parliamentarianism lagged behind that of the British.

By the summer of 1944, I applied to the Naval Academy where I was accepted for a forty-day training period. I reported to Brindisi in the fall. The atmosphere at the academy was totally different from what I had expected. It was depressing because of poor facilities, scarce food, and below-average staff officers. The gloomy prospect of graduating as a naval officer in a country that had lost practically all of its fleet made me soon decide to give up the idea and to return home before the forty days were over. I requested Guglielmo to send a cable to the academy (under my father's name) asking for my immediate resignation. And so, I was back in Rome just in time to enroll in the local university. Having lost all my ambitions for a military career, and having nothing better to replace it with, I decided to enroll in the School of Pharmacology. There was only one reason for this decision. The number of applicants was very small and it took less time to register. I was Italian then and did not like to stand in line!

After a few months, the city of Florence was freed by the Allied troops. The German defense, called the "Gothic line," was then established along the Appennine Mountains to prevent Allied troops from entering the Po Valley. Umberto, who was in Florence, could thus return to Rome where he was immediately informed about Italo's arrest. Without hesitation, Umberto went to the British Military police to plead for Italo's freedom. He explained why Italo had worn a German uniform, he assured them that no spying was involved, and then he dramatically concluded that if Italo was considered guilty, he too, should be arrested. After a few days, Umberto was invited to go back to the police station, where he was placed under arrest, taken first to the Regina Coeli prison and then to an internment camp near Terni, sixty miles east of Rome. All this was done in a smooth and simple way: with no harassment or further questioning. Once again, British police acted deaf and dumb, with the same expressionless faces of marble statues in a museum.

After leaving Rome, Theo moved to Bologna and then to Milan. Here he became the patient and friend of a dentist, who happened to be the leader of a large partisan unit. The new friend suggested that in the forthcoming insurrection Theo should shed his German uniform and join his partisan group. By early April, 1945, the partisan uprising came into full swing in the Po Valley. Part of the German troops in Milan promptly barricaded themselves in the Hotel Regina and were ready to fight to the last man. It was Theo who played a leading role in convincing his commanding officer that the war was over and that he should surrender to save human lives. He finally succeeded. Theo marched his unarmed German comrades out of the hotel and delivered them into the skillful hands of his dentist. In exchange, he was given civilian clothes, a special partisan pass and the job of driving his friend in a bullet-proof car.

Shortly afterwards, Theo had an opportunity to drive his new boss to Rome. This was at the time when communications between North and South were still closed at the former Gothic line. One late afternoon, a dusty car with Milan license plates and carrying a big sign "NLC" (National Liberation Committee), parked in front of our apartment. The car was immediately surrounded by numerous bystanders curious to see the first partisan's car reaching Rome after the bloody uprising in the North. Theo stepped out of the car wearing a red bandana around his neck and showing a fierce smile in his face. He walked confidently into the crowd which quickly split down the middle to let him go through. Without hesitation, Theo rang the doorbell of our apartment. There was complete surprise mixed with joy to see him free and in good health. But soon there was serious concern for his safety. Theo was briefed on what had happened to Italo and Umberto, and in the evening, when it was pitch dark, he was cautiously moved to Irma's apartment in another section of Rome, where no one knew him to be a German soldier. After a few days, Theo returned to Milan.

The war was officially over in Italy but it was difficult for Theo to go back to his wife and son in Munich. He no longer had a uniform or papers to show that he was part of the defeated German army. After various attempts, he succeeded in being accepted in a Prisoner of War camp near Modena. But, if the war was over, the fighting was not.

At the border crossing with Austria, the German POWs met a long column of Italian soldiers heading south. These were the survivors of those units taken to internment camps after Italy surrendered on September 8, 1943. Some thirty thousand of them had died in these camps. When the Italians saw the Germans going in the opposite direction, they started throwing rocks and launching insults. It was a tense and dramatic situation. But Theo promptly intervened to restore peace. In his good Italian he said, "We both have had enough fighting and suffering, and all this for no good reason. It is time to forget the past and to look at our future. The war is over!" Once he re-established peace and order, Theo asked if there were any Romans in the group. When he found one, he requested him to phone his mother Maria to let her know that he was alive and safely crossing the border, going north. With this phone call, made by a civilized and compassionate soldier from Rome, the bloody war that had destroyed most of Europe also came to an end for my family.

Some years later, when Count Carlo Sforza, the Italian Foreign Affairs Minister was asked to define to a group of reporters the difference between the Italians and the French at the closing of World War II, he stated, "Simple. The Italians must forget their defeat. The French must invent their victory. Our task is infinitely easier." As Montaigne once stated, "There are defeats more triumphant than victories." This is exactly what happened in Italy with the end of Mussolini's era.

4

The Post-war Period (1945–51)

*The mere absence of war is not
peace.*

—John F. Kennedy

he Italian economic and political situation in the
years immediately following the end of the war
was tragic, almost desperate. Most cities had
suffered heavy losses due to bombings from the air and the
sea. There was a great shortage of houses and apartments all
over the country. Unrelated families were often forced to
share the available space, creating unending grievances and
widespread dissatisfaction

Transportation within and between cities was functioning
on an ad hoc basis. In Rome, public transportation no longer
existed. Private pickups, taken out of storage or retrieved
from used car lots, were equipped with a few benches and

plywood signs, on which their itineraries were written by improvised painters. Every day, people by the thousands risked their lives on these overcrowded and poorly maintained vehicles. Bicycles surfaced from dusty cellars and storage places to provide some relief in transportation. Their rubber tires were often worn out and needed bulky patches to protect the exposed inner tubes.

Most of the locomotives and freight cars had been destroyed by the war and many railroads were no longer operating. There were no jobs in the cities and no incentives to create jobs. In the countryside, the situation was no better. Agricultural production was virtually at a standstill: there were no machines, farm animals, seeds, or fertilizers. Many fields had been flooded by the retreating German army, and plenty of productive land was lying under water, waiting for dams or dikes to be repaired.

Scars had been left wide open in many villages and rural areas by the passage of the invading armies. Particularly the troops from Morocco and West Africa had left behind a long trail of raped women of all ages, from young adolescents to old grandmothers. This brutality was paid back with violent ambushes by outraged farmers and villagers, resulting in the death of many African soldiers. So destitute were Italian women that some of them eagerly traded their bodies to British or American soldiers for canned goods, a few bars of soap, or just a package of exotic cigarettes.

Food was very scarce, especially in the larger cities. In Rome, where the Allied Forces had nominated an American, Charles P. Poletti, as Special Military Commissioner, graffiti all over the city declared "Dear Poletti, give us less words, and much more spaghetti."

The black market had taken over Rome economy and that of other cities. Naples, in particular, had become the center of these illegal activities because it was the major

naval base supplying American troops in Italy and south
Germany. A good share of these supplies never reached the
troops: they were routed instead to the thriving Italian
black markets. When a large American freighter disappeared from port with its load, the American authorities
decided to ship to Naples only left foot army boots. This
was to discourage Neapolitans from stealing and reselling
boots by the pairs. It was an ephemeral and damaging
economy, with a newly rich class flourishing in luxury
against a background of rubble and destruction.

By mere chance, Nicla's father's office was located in
Borgo Pio, the main center of the Roman black market
area. Vittorio, who was to become the High Commissioner
for Food in the De Gasperi governments of 1947-50, made
the elimination of the black market the top priority of his
post-war reconstruction program.

In the fall of 1945, Nicla went back to the Mamiani to
complete her high school studies. Her family was financially
broke after spending a long confinement in Cortine di Nave
without any income. The family had survived on money
borrowed from friends and relatives, and on the
ingeniousness of mother Gina. (To cope with the cold winter
weather and the lack of heating at Cortine, she made some
warm quilts from used sheets and recycled wool from old
mattresses. She also transformed Vittorio's old underwear
into comfortable woolen sweaters for her girls).

Vittorio was finally cleared by the Ministry of Agriculture for having gone North and he received all of his back
wages. At last, things were getting better for his family.

On the Chiarappa side, I was the only man left at home.
My father lived on the Gianicolo hill with a chorus lady.
Theo was in East Germany, where his family escaped after
the bombing of the Munich apartment. Umberto and Italo
were in concentration camps in Terni and Padula

respectively. It was their turn to face a year-long situation with no income and much debt. Umberto's family (Rosa, Marcella and little Theo) moved in with us in the apartment of Piazza dei Quiriti. Anna, instead, went to Padula with her two boys (Umbertino and Vittorio) to be closer to Italo's prison camp.

The Italian political situation was gloomy and uncertain. The "Action Party," an assembly of people with different political orientations from Communists to Liberals, had served well during the war to bring together and coordinate partisan forces against the Germans, but it was now falling apart. Clearly, this party no longer had a role to play during peace time. Recognizing this weakness, Ferruccio Parri, the party leader, resigned from his post as first Premier of Italy. In this way, he opened the first of many government crises which were to characterize the Italian post-war period right up to today.

For some time after the end of the war a witch hunt operation continued all over Italy. This operation, aimed at all former fascist activists, was politely called "epurazione." The intended "purification" from the remnants of twenty-three years of Fascism also had some very practical objectives: the appropriation by new politicians of all privileges, properties and assets formerly belonging to the Fascists.

Violence and bloodshed still took place in the streets of many Italian cities and the countryside. I personally witnessed one of these events not far from Nicla's apartment. Suddenly someone in the street recognized a man as being a former Fascist. He immediately started screaming to attract other people's attention. In no time a large crowd of angry men and women surrounded the suspected "Fascist" and began beating him to death. They laid his body on the tracks of a street car and demanded the driver run over him. The driver refused. Meanwhile the crowd's anger intensified. A few men lifted the lifeless body and carried it to a nearby bridge. From there they threw it into the rushing waters of the Tiber river. Someone from the mob then dashed down to the river bank, grabbed a boat and went to the point where the body had surfaced. With one of the oars he kept hitting the floating corpse, while the crowd on the bridge, excited by this violence, continued screaming, "Kill, kill, kill the bastard." It was a disgusting and savage scene. The following day, a local newspaper reported that the man killed by the mob was not a Fascist after all; only an innocent citizen who was a victim of mistaken identity.

In this "purging" and violent atmosphere, abuse of power was common. Nicla's family was also affected. One day, a man showed up at the apartment in Via Ovidio to proceed with a "requisition" for himself and his wife. A member of the Communist party, he felt entitled to take over the apartment because "the owner had left it empty to go North with the Fascists." Father Vittorio explained in clear terms that he was no Fascist, that he had been "arrested" to go North, and that he had no intention of yielding to intimidations of any sort. The intruder walked away promising all kinds of revenge.

Understandably, healing the wounds left open by a long and bloody war was not a short-term undertaking for most Italians.

In February, 1946, my family was informed that father Luigi was under arrest at the Gianicolo police station and that he wished to see some of his children immediately. Romolo and I went to the station to find my father in tears. His face was pale, his coat was stained with blood and a finger of his left hand was broken. When the police chief left the room for a few minutes, my father quickly turned over to me a good-sized pocket knife that I immediately slipped into my pocket. My father kept weeping, asking to be forgiven for his blind act of jealousy. A little at a time, he told us what had happened.

Apparently, the chorus lady had found a new boyfriend, a British Army officer. It also appeared that she was another destitute woman who was ready to give up my father's delightful music in order to receive some canned goods, maybe some bars of British soap, or exotic cigarettes. As a result, she no longer wanted to see her old lover. This was enough to make my father lose his head. He rushed to purchase a gun, some bullets, a pocket knife, and then he marched to the lady's apartment to ask for explanations. When she opened the door and saw the pointed gun, she quickly grabbed my father's hand forcing him to lose his balance, and rolling with him down the stairs. The gun went off, but fortunately no bullets entered any human body; they only penetrated the plaster wall. My father's nose began to bleed, staining his coat in several places. People from nearby apartments heard the gun shots, dashed to the stairs and saw the two entangled bodies lying flat on the ground. They immediately called the police. The next day, a leading Roman newspaper reported this dramatic event under a concise and unmerciful heading, "Music, jealousy and gun shots."

This incident gave rise to another painful period for my mother. But once again, she was prepared to forgive and accept yet another difficult situation. She visited Luigi at the city prison, where almost daily she brought him a clean change of clothes and home-made food. I was able to find a good lawyer, who cleverly demonstrated that the whole case was "non-intentional and purely accidental." Italian law is very flexible, especially with love affairs. My father's case was promptly resolved out of court, and Luigi sheepishly returned to his family. When the broken finger healed, he started to play his cello again in the symphonic orchestra. Once more he was the free man and highly regarded artist of former days. It appeared as though nothing serious had ever happened. He never changed his personality nor his exceptional ability to play his most delightful music.

It wasn't until early 1946 that I first encountered the family of Professor Guido de Marzi, colleague and close friend of Vittorio Ronchi. Professor De Marzi had three young daughters: Ida, Raffaella and Anna Maria. These girls were, in turn, good friends of Lisa and Nicla Ronchi. It was carnival time in Rome and for young people, this was also "fun time." In this spirit, Ida de Marzi organized a dancing party at her father's apartment. Apparently, there was a shortage of young men to keep the party balanced, and Ida asked Lina Mazzarella to invite some boys she knew. Lina had recently met Guglielmo and me on one of our weekend skiing expeditions. On the bus to and from Terminillo (a ski resort fifty miles northeast of Rome), we were known for singing mountain songs and for improvising funny sketches. Lina informed us about the party but she warned that this was a very elegant evening affair. Formal dressing was strictly required.

Guglielmo and I prepared accordingly. We went through my father's wardrobe and selected some of his best clothes, those he used to wear at performances. Guglielmo opted for a redingote, a garment reaching to the knees without buttons in front, commonly used by orchestra conductors or concierges of luxury hotels. Its entire front was left open to show a white shirt and a huge black ribbon wrapped around Guglielmo's neck. Unable to find a pair of matching socks, he settled for a long pair of my mother's black stockings. I selected one of my father's tuxedos, even though this was too large for me. My father was, in fact, two feet taller. We both roughened up our hair, squirted on a generous dose of cologne and, pleased with our appearance, we went to the

party. As we entered the apartment, we realized that we were
at a higher social level that we had ever been before. Antique
furniture, expensive crystals and chinaware, beautiful
paintings and art work, and many smiling women in long,
elegant dresses. All men were in their tuxedos, the type that
are personally owned, and not procured at a rental place.
Guglielmo and I were at first intimidated, but then we reacted
with special vigor. Our numerous sketches soon captivated
the general attention and the party turned out to be a great
success. But in one corner of the main dance hall was a well-
dressed young woman, appearing somewhat annoyed and
detached from our performance. This was the first time I met
Lisa Ronchi, Nicla's oldest sister. Soon afterward, she
reported to her family about "two funny" young men who
stole the floor at the De Marzi's gala. It was in these unusual
terms that Nicla learned about my existence: that of a
"bizarre guy" named Gigi.

Nearly three months after Ida's party, her younger sister
Anna Maria organized an afternoon dance gathering. Both
Nicla and I were invited. We met for the first time and
immediately became friends. We danced together with great
pleasure, ignoring everyone else in the room. We definitely
liked each other, but made no attempt to follow up. As we
know, it takes time for big fires to get started. But once the
flames begin to spread, nothing can stop them.

Following the popular elections of June 2, 1946, Italy
became a Republican state and representatives were elected
to draft a new Constitution. There was widespread
dissatisfaction with the electoral results, especially in the
South, where the king and the monarchy were still very
popular. The great majority, instead, voted for the Republic,
mainly to punish a king who had accepted twenty years of
Fascist dictatorship, who had declared war on England and

France, and who, at the last minute, had run away, leaving the country and his army in the hands of the Germans.

Alcide De Gasperi was elected Premier. Born in Trento, De Gasperi had been a subject of Franz Joseph, the Emperor of Austria-Hungary until 1918. Before World War I, he was actually a member of the Vienna polyglot Parliament. He proved to be the best statesman Italy had in the post-war period. In forming his first and second cabinets, De Gasperi could not ignore the political strength of the left wing coalition, the power of labor unions (also controlled by the Communists), and the impact of the left-induced strikes paralyzing Italy's economic recovery. He had no alternative but to let the leaders of these leftist parties become members of his governments. The hope was to douse some water on the many street demonstrations and the outright violence still frequent all over Italy. This decision, however, did not prove to be a solution and times continued to be difficult for all Italians for two more years.

The country was essentially split into two emotional and irrational mass movements. At one side were the Christian Democrats, grouped in the so-called "Center-Left party." The majority of these voters were inspired only by fear: fear of another totalitarian regime headed by the Communists, fear of the future of the Church and the Christian faith, fear of losing individual privileges, and fear of forfeiting Italy's Western values. On the other side was the fanatic, blind loyalty of millions of unreasoning Communists, Socialists, Anarchists, and the like, who still believed in the writings by Engels, Marx or Lenin and trusted their obsolete pre-industrial ideas.

In a country of many intelligent, resourceful, individual-istic people these emotions continued to dominate Italy's politics for many years.

Nicla's father returned to manage the "Maccarese," which had been nearly destroyed by the war. He found it difficult to do his job because of constant problems with the newly established leftist-oriented labor unions and the lack of essential means of production. He was able to overcome both problems, however, and by the end of his first year he was able to show a profit. At this time, Vittorio was also nominated to the Presidency of the Superior Council for Agriculture, a very important position within Italy's postwar economic reconstruction program.

As mentioned before, my father was back with his family, but not entirely so. He relegated himself to his study, where he slept and practiced his cello. Outside of these self-imposed boundaries he maintained a totally independent life of his own.

Italo and Umberto were finally released from their respective internment camps. After many years spent in the army or in prison, the two faced the reality of a very difficult civilian life. They looked at many employment possibilities, but there were no openings in their line of work. Most hotels were out of business because of the bombings or the occupation by the Allied armies. Tourism no longer existed in the country. Italo was finally able to find a job as personal driver of an American major in charge of a Supply Depot near the Saint Paul station in Rome. He quickly recommended Umberto for another driver position, and myself for the Ice Cream Plant. This temporary arrangement helped us to get our feet back on the ground during a very difficult postwar period.

Meanwhile, Theo had fled with his wife and son from the Russian zone in East Germany to Munich. Just as Italo and Umberto had found, there was no work for him, either. The Four Seasons Hotel, where he had worked before the war, had been severely damaged by air strikes. After looking

"Style in dressing and in acting" two of Nicla's most distinctive features.

around for any kind of work, Theo found a temporary job as butler in the house of an American Colonel. His wife Gitschi joined him as a cook and live-in maid. So, thanks to the American occupation forces in Europe, all four of us were happily employed trying to heal our own economic wounds. A fifth "family" member who found a job with the Americans was my good friend Guglielmo. He started working for a unit dealing with American graves in Italy, and he ended up marrying Mary, a lively American girl from Connecticut.

My job at the Ice Cream Plant was one of the tastiest experiences of my life. I was the youngest of a nine-man team responsible for producing ice cream for the troops and American offices in Rome. Production went on day and night (in three shifts) seven days a week. We had the supervision of three young and inexperienced GIs, who essentially oversaw the plant's sanitation whenever they could take a break from reading magazines or working on crosswords. Controls from outside supervisors were instead frequent and rigid. My shift was soon recognized to be the best in efficiency, product quality and sanitary standards.

Peppe and Luigi were my two other companions. They were both veterans, without any particular trade or skill. They represented that part of the Italian working class capable of doing any type of job just by using their promptness, intelligence and imagination. They were both kind and gentle and had a tremendous sense of humor with which they filled our working hours. This was my first exposure to real work with real people. It was a positive experience, one that helped me in the future.

A man who always liked a taste of American ice cream was Manlio Sarra. He was to become a famous Italian painter of open air markets, full of color and movement. Manlio was then part of the unskilled crews pushing around rail cars for loading and unloading. Being an artist, he was always hungry. I made sure that something was done to remedy this. A large can of freshly prepared ice cream was strategically left outside the plant's back door, and it was up to Manlio to take it in time, before my tangible sign of friendship had melted away.

Nicla and I met again in the fall of 1946. This time, our encounter was purely accidental. She was going to school and I was on my way to work. We walked together and I explained to her my latest "technique" for providing my mother with good American coffee. I carried to work an empty bottle in which, at the end of my shift, I would pour some freshly ground coffee. On top of it I added some cold water. At the Depot control gate I would declare the resulting brown suspension as a "left over coffee from the mess hall." At home, my mother promptly dumped the supernatant, added the required amount of water, boiled the mix and enjoyed good, freshly made and inexpensive coffee, something she had sorely missed during the whole war.

The following January, Nicla and I bumped into each other again. This time she was in the company of Anna Maria de Marzi, while I was ready to go on a ski trip to the North of Italy. The encounter was brief, almost impersonal.

The third time we met, Nicla was going to a piano lesson and I had time on my hands to accompany her. While walking, I was admiring her friendly face, the velvety eyes, the long, wavy dark hair, and the fresh attractiveness of her smile. I liked the girl: I had no doubts in my mind. I then took the liberty of suggesting she cancel the piano lesson to go with me to a nearby motion-picture theater. The proposal was risky, but it was worth taking. My suggestion was quickly turned down.

On my lonely walk back, I had time to reconsider the whole matter. It was the first time a girl refused my invitation to see a movie. I was particularly hurt because the reply had come quickly and decidedly. Either I was losing my old charm, or this new girl was different. The matter kept me thinking for some time.

After nearly two months, at the end of June 1947, I was surprised to receive a postcard from Nicla. Her short message from Udine sparked my imagination again. I was happy to see that my offer to trade a tedious piano lesson for a good action movie had not offended her. A long letter was needed on my part to smooth things out.

Upon her return to Rome, Nicla phoned me to let me know that she had appreciated my letter. She then gave a detailed account of her vacation. Phone calls between us became increasingly frequent. One day in October, I found the courage to ask her out for a date. This was set at Ponte Vittorio, the old bridge on the Tiber river connecting Via della Conciliazione with Corso Vittorio.

Nicla came to the appointment ahead of time. She was wearing an old- fashioned hat and a navy blue coat. When I arrived she was calmly peeling a juicy orange. It was evident that Nicla was not used to this kind of appointment. I apologized for the delay and tried to appear calm and normal. Internally, instead, I was in a state of agitation. We then started walking towards the top of the Gianicolo hill, a very quiet city park well suited to young couples at sunset. We arrived at a place in the back of the statue of Anita Garibaldi, the wife of Giuseppe and the heroine of Italy's independence. Here, the first kiss in a chain of many was finally exchanged. The Roman sky was full of stars and our young hearts were filled with emotions. It was the very beginning of our long lasting love.

In early 1947, Italy's political and economic situation was still precarious. Something had to be done to procure financial aid and needed food supplies. Premier De Gasperi decided to travel to the United States to ask for help. He accepted the invitation by Time Magazine to participate in a round table discussion on the theme "What the world is expecting from the United States." He also arranged for an official visit to meet members of the government in Washington. Even though Italy had fought a war against America, this great country had always remained friendly towards Italy and the Italians. Only the United States could provide the required assistance. De Gasperi met with Harry Truman and was acclaimed wherever he traveled. A two-hour-long parade with Italian Americans took place on Broadway through friendly and cheering crowds. Americans were quick to recognize in De Gasperi the first democratic leader who could save Italy from Communism and economic distress.

De Gasperi's tour to America was well timed. In fact, the idea of providing economic aid to Europe had been in Truman's mind for some time. The Italian Premier's visit merely fostered his decision in this direction.

In June, 1947, Nicla's father was requested by De Gasperi to become a full member of his new Cabinet as High Commissioner for Food. Shortly afterward came the announcement of the European Recovery Program, better known as the "Marshall Plan." In this important announcement, the American objectives were clearly spelled out: "Its purpose should be the revival of a working economy in the world so as to permit the emergence of political and social conditions in which free institutions can exist."

Vittorio was immediately engaged in seeing that Italy quickly received wheat, corn and other American supplies. In September when he met with Will Clayton, the American Undersecretary for Economic Affairs, Vittorio clearly indicated the urgency of delivering these food stocks. They were needed within two weeks. Clayton looked firmly in Vittorio's honest eyes, he then glanced at Vittorio's bar graph, showing the commodities Italy required, and with no hesitation he told him, "You have the right to be helped."

Two hours later, Vittorio received a phone call from the American Embassy. "Professor Ronchi," said a friendly voice in a very bad Italian," I wish to inform you that a cable was sent to the State Department with the approval of all your requests." Two weeks later, De Gasperi and Vittorio went to Naples to meet the first two "Liberty" boats delivering wheat to Italy. By the end of December, more than 200 such ships arrived in Italian ports to bring food and other supplies valued at 65 billion lire. "Never before in history," wrote the popular Messaggero paper, "has a gift of this kind and value been given after a war by a winner to a loser." All this happened several months before the Marshall Plan was officially approved by Congress, in April, 1948.

Thanks to Vittorio, to his honest blue eyes and his concise bar graph, Italy was on its way to recovery much earlier than any other state in Europe. For the American people, it was one of the proudest moments in American history. President Truman and the United States did save Europe from Communism and likely starvation.

During this same period, several important events took place in my family. Umberto, after looking in vain for a job in his line of business, came to the conclusion that there was no hope in sight. He had to find a solution outside of Italy. One day, he left Rosa and his children at the apartment of Piazza dei Quiriti and took off for Naples, to get a passage on a steamer for Argentina. He carried with him only an old suitcase with a few personal effects, and little money.

The emigration fever had started again. While at the end of last century nearly five and half million Italians, mostly farm workers from the South, were forced to leave their country to escape poverty, ignorance, malaria, and malnutrition, this time the emigration was different. The postwar emigrants were well educated and qualified people, including technicians, physicians, and scientists, who were looking for countries where their skills could spark a better life.

Umberto was one of these Italians who had been harshly treated by their country. He had spent five long years, the best of his life, in war, in prison, in concentration camps only to discover at the end that his career had been destroyed and that there was no work for him in Italy.

Umberto left Italy with no regrets, but he promised himself never to return. After a few weeks, he wrote that he had a job in a small hotel in Buenos Aires. Shortly afterward he moved south to the Rio Negro province, where greater opportunities existed for tourism. In late 1948, Rosa and the rest of the family also emigrated to Argentina.

I became affected by the same emigration fever and started to consider going to Argentina or some other American country. This made me change my major from Pharmacology to Agriculture, and to transfer from Rome to the University of Bologna.

By this time I was going steady with Nicla. One day, after we had been seen by Lisa entering a motion picture theater, Nicla decided to report to her mother what was happening. As a result, I was politely invited to pay a visit to the Ronchi family. This was not an easy task for me since I had nothing to say for myself. I was a student with a bad record of academic achievements. I was not rich, I was working for hourly wages, I had no prospect for a future career. Mother Gina, being a wonderful and understanding woman, avoided any kind of embarrassing questions, making things easy for all concerned. When I suggested that I could help Nicla in preparing for her examinations, she gladly accepted. This offer allowed me from then on to safely justify my daily visits to Nicla's family. My relationship with her grew stronger with time and so did my worries about the future.

For the first time in my life, I felt inadequate and guilty. I realized that I had been wasting valuable time in my studies. Nicla, instead, was more positive about the whole matter. "Why don't you start drafting a list of courses you need to take and group them together into a feasible time table?" she asked in her typical, practical approach to problem solving.

Drafting the list was the beginning of an unbelievable academic marathon which saw me taking an increasing number of courses at an accelerating pace. From Bologna I transferred to Florence to save on travel time, and from one or two exams per session I was able to take as many as nine. The list was getting shorter, but I was running out of steam.

On one occasion, I traveled by overnight train to Florence to save on hotel expenses, stayed in line from 5 to 8 AM waiting for the exam room to open, took two oral exams in a single morning, and by noon I boarded the return train to Rome. I was very pleased with myself: I passed both tests. Two less on my long list. My mind, however, was functioning below par. I boarded the train, smiled at the passengers in the crowded third class compartment, and, when the train was well out of the Florence station, I rolled down the window and threw away my ticket. The other passengers did not realize what was going on. When the conductor came by, I had no ticket nor money to pay for my fare. I was taken under police escort to the Rome station where Nicla was waiting. But she, too, had no money. Fortunately the Grand Hotel, where my nephew Walter was working, was not too far away and Nicla was able to borrow enough money from him to pay for the lost ticket and my freedom.

Nicla was helping me in every way she could. She even agreed to copy by hand a book on Farm Economics that could not be found in any bookstore. We decided to go to one of the Roman libraries, where each of us took one of the text sections and patiently copied them into our note books. It was tedious work, especially for Nicla who had absolutely no interest in the subject. The lights of the old library were very dim, adding more stress to our work. One day, after several hours of writing, we looked out of the window and saw a downpour outside. It was time to go home, but we had no umbrellas or rain coats, nor money for a taxi. Nicla decided to phone her mother to see if Vittorio's car and driver could come and pick us up. Mother Gina appeared surprised by this request. "I don't understand about this heavy rain," she said, "here we are having plenty of sunshine and not a cloud in sight." After the phone call, we rushed to the library window to look outside again. Sure enough, the sky was clear. We then discovered that one of the exposed pipes was broken and leaking abundant water on the outside of our window. When we arrived home that evening, we were ridiculed by everyone in the family. As they say in Italy, "l'amore e' cieco" (love is blind). Nicla and I were in love and, consequently, sightless.

By December 22, 1947 the new Italian Constitution was approved. Six hundred people had been involved in its drafting, by means of a large number of commissions, committees and subcommittees. At the end of nearly two and half years, all of the components were pieced together, resulting in a bulky, verbose document full of many gaps. A major problem was created by the two contrasting political forces: Catholic on one side and Marxist-Leninist at the other. Both forces, for different reasons, were equally interested in maintaining perpetual weakness and instability in the executive power. Instead all the influence was given to the political parties and the Parliament. This problem has affected Italy and Italians for all these years.

After the return of De Gasperi from America, it was apparent that big changes were in the air, mostly resulting from the international situation. The Cold War between the United Sates and the Soviet Union had just begun, President Truman had already stated his containment doctrine, and the Marshall Plan was getting underway. Italy, with the second largest Communist party in Europe and a large number of left-wing sympathizers in its intelligentsia, was running the risk of becoming another Communist country by legal means: through the popular vote. Political elections were to be held on 18 April, 1948, and in preparation for these, the Communists and Socialists had united in what was called the Democratic Popular Front (DPF).

It was a very critical period, not only for Italy, but for the United States as well. In case Italy folded up, Tito could easily march through the Po Valley giving the Soviet Union easy access to the Mediterranean sea. President Truman called a meeting of the National Security Council to decide what to do in case of a legal takeover by the DPF. Many important decisions, including some of a military nature, were made in preparation for this event. Yet one of the strongest American weapons was still food and economic aid.

In early April, when Vittorio Ronchi traveled to the United States to purchase some wheat, he met the Undersecretary for Foreign Affairs, who clearly indicated the American concern about a victory of the leftist parties in the forthcoming elections. "I do not share your pessimism," said Vittorio. " You will see that the Italian good sense will prevail. Of course, it could greatly help if, just before the elections, we could receive an additional allocation of wheat from America. It could strengthen the Italian government and De Gasperi's position with the voters." By April 14, Vittorio received approval for nearly 7,000 tons of wheat. He immediately sent a cable to De Gasperi, in time for the

Premier to announce the new "gift" from America at his last rally of the election campaign. This was in Naples, the city that knows best the value of wheat for making pane, pizza and pasta.

The Catholic church stepped up its efforts to see that everyone of voting age would cast his or her vote. Hospitals, villages and houses in the most remote areas were visited by Catholic action youth offering to drive voters to the voting booth. Nicla and her sister Vittoria participated in this all-out effort. As a result, an outstanding 92% of the voters cast their ballot. Likewise, the outcome left no doubts: 48.5% of the votes for the Christian Democrats and 31% for the DPF. Italy had turned away from revolutionary utopias and wanted only to work in peace, knowing this time where work, food and freedom could be found.

By 1949, it became necessary for me to stay in Florence for the entire spring quarter because most of the advanced courses required full-time attendance. I moved into a small rented room on the outskirts of the city, and had my meals at the student cafeteria. Food was far from acceptable, but Nicla solved this problem by sending frequent "care packages." On one occasion, she also sent a bottle of brandy to help me fight the low temperatures in my unheated room. Soon I discovered that the level of the brandy in my bottle was dropping unusually fast. After marking the bottle, I learned that the landlady also liked my brandy. Unable to stop her from drinking, I stoically accepted this drop in the spirit's level as a fact of life: just a hidden cost for a cheap rented room.

After a few months, I was informed that Nicla was coming to Florence for a one-day visit. She was accompanied by her father and Dr. Passerini, of the High Commissioner's Food Secretariat. This was an official trip and I was worried about what to expect. I went to meet the train at the station with a small bouquet of forget-me-not flowers. I was very nervous: could I kiss Nicla in front of her father and her father's secretary, both of whom were on an "official visit?" Nicla appeared from the train wearing a beautiful gabardine dress. She looked very happy and beautiful, as usual. I could not resist and I kissed her in front of the two accompanying officials. After all, I said to myself, railroad stations are good places for kissing.

It was soon decided that Nicla and I could take a stroll along the Arno river, while Professor Ronchi attended his meeting with local authorities. Dr. Passerini was given the unappealing task of chaperoning the two of us for the entire afternoon. In the evening, dinner was offered by Nicla's father in one of Florence's fashionable restaurants. My shyness was easily subdued by an extra-large portion of a wonderfully barbecued steak. I greatly enjoyed this departure from the food served at the student cafeteria.

The next day's program called for a tour of Florence's surroundings. An official car and driver were provided, and Dr. Passerini was again assigned to accompany the two of us. On our arrival in Fiesole, Dr. Passerini, with great tact and finesse, pointed out a small hill from where the view of the valley was especially magnificent. The best observation point, he suggested, was from just behind an old church on the hill. Thanks to this old church, some kissing was finally possible. This took place under a clear, blue sky overlooking one of the world's most beautiful landscapes.

By the end of the summer, all the required courses were successfully completed and only my thesis remained to be written.

I had the opportunity to go to work for the Torlonia Farms in the Fucino area, half way between Rome and the Adriatic coast. Fucino was once a large lake situated at an altitude of 2,200 feet in the mountains.

At the time of Emperor Claudius I (41-54 A.D.), the Romans tried draining the lake to reclaim the submerged land for agricultural use. The project involved excavating through one of the surrounding mountains a sloping tunnel nearly 4 miles long and with a cross section of 130 square feet. The water was then to be discharged through the tunnel into a valley at a lower elevation. Historian Svetonio reported that 30,000 slaves and 11 years of work were required to complete this project. In the year 52 A.D., the emperor himself participated in the ceremony of the opening of the gates. The water started rushing away and the people watching the scene cheered loudly. But not all of the water drained. Because of some miscalculations of the tunnel's slope, a good portion of water remained in the lake. A rare fumble of the otherwise superb Roman engineering.

It was only at the beginning of this century that a banker by the name of Alessandro Torlonia was able to secure a government concession to drain the entire lake in exchange for all of the submerged land. The old Roman tunnel was abandoned and a new one built in its place. Completion of the project required eight years of steady work and large sums of money. "Either Torlonia drains the Fucino, or the Fucino will drain Torlonia," the banker repeated to his friends and customers. And finally he succeeded. The princedom of Fucino was officially established and Alessandro, the banker, became its first Prince.

With the disappearance of the water, the hope of the poor people living in the villages surrounding the lake also vanished. Describing the peasantry of the villages, Ignazio Silone once wrote: "God is the head of everything. He commands everything. Everybody knows that. Then comes Prince Torlonia, ruler of the earth. Then come his guards. Then come his guard's dogs. Then nothing. Then more nothing. Then come the peasants. That's all."

For me it was a challenge to work in Torlonia's new "reclamation" project. The Prince at this time was Alessandro's grandson, and the problems were very complex: of a political, social and technical nature. Under pressure by the Communist and Socialist parties, the Italian government was enforcing an agrarian reform throughout the country. The objective was to take away large tracts of land from individual owners, and to divide them into small farms. These were to be assigned to farm laborers, peasants, war veterans, artisans, and even town barbers. All this was in the name of a "new social justice."

Prince Torlonia had many large holdings in Central Italy and he was an easy target for the bureaucratic organizations created to apply the reform. To prevent this from happening, the young Torlonia decided to modernize his farms, starting with those in the princedom of Fucino. His objective was to demonstrate that, through technological innovation and large capital investment, another type of "reform" was possible, one which would increase farm productivity, provide steady work, and improve living conditions to rural populations. A new Director General was hired for this purpose. He was Dr. Riccardo dalla Favera, a top animal husbandry expert, and a former associate of Professor Ronchi at "Maccarese." I was employed as his assistant. For me it was a good experience and a unique opportunity to study old agronomic problems in the light of new technological innovations. As a result of these studies, I was able to prepare my thesis, the title of which was "New Agronomic Problems of Fucino."

Nicla and I were forced to live far from each other during this period. But two people, who understood our hardship were willing to help. They were mother Gina and Dr. Passerini. The first totally ignored the many long distance phone calls to Fucino, and the second graciously paid the costly phone bills (without concerning Prof. Ronchi about their amount).

By the summer of 1950, my academic marathon had come to an end. My thesis was accepted by the Agronomy Department, and had only to be officially presented for discussion at the School of Agriculture in Florence. Nicla traveled to Florence the day before this event and she was hosted by Lisa Frangialli, an old friend of her mother when Gina was a war refugee in that city. I waited in Rome for the usual midnight train to arrive early enough in Florence to shave, change into a clean shirt, and read a few sections of my manuscript. By 6 AM, I was fresh and ready to go see Nicla. It was early to ring Lisa Frangialli's door bell, but I saw that her maid was already up and on duty. She let me in with a big, acquiescent smile. Nicla was soon in the living room. She was happy to greet me with a big hug and a long kiss. We went then to the campus, conscious that we were soon to reach the goal for which we had worked and worried together.

The setting for my thesis' presentation at the School of Agriculture was intimidating. The "aula magna" was a huge hall, with elegant decorations and many large mirrors on the walls, to make it appear many times as large. Around a bulky oval table in the middle of the room sat the School's professors, dressed in their rich and colorful academic robes. In front of them was a podium for the candidate, and on one side several rows of chairs for the public. In the first row was Nicla. Professor Oliva, my major professor, introduced the subject. I then followed with an analysis of Fucino's agronomic problems. The "firing squad," comprising various professors, started addressing question after question. I was able to respond without hesitation: I felt like a gladiator in a Roman arena, parrying blow after blow from the "enemy." The defense was good and solid because I had really lived my experiences in Fucino. Finally, the ordeal came to an end. I passed the test. Professor Oliva congratulated Nicla and me, and we returned to Mrs. Frangialli's house. After lunch, we took a train back to Rome, where Vittorio was waiting at the station. He wanted to be the first to congratulate the new "Doctor," and hug Nicla, the person who made all this happen so well and so quickly.

A few days later I asked Gina for permission to marry Nicla. With no job, no prospect for employment, and no money, this was not an easy request. But once again, Gina demonstrated her total confidence. "Something will come up for you," she said. With a warm smile, full of love and understanding, she agreed to the wedding. This was planned for July of 1951.

5

A Dream Comes Through (1950–51)

*In bed my real love has always been
the sleep that rescued me by allowing me to dream.*

—Luigi Pirandello

t the beginning of 1950, Ronchi, Vittorio left his position of High Commissioner for Food. He did so by maintaining a low profile, as he had when he accepted this important job in 1947. His resignation coincided with two important events which affected the life of millions of Italians. The first was that the black market had virtually disappeared. The second was that food commodities were abundant in the stores and markets. People had thus started to eat and drink more and better than before the war. Ronchi, Vittorio had promised all this in his reconstruction plans and he had succeeded by applying the rules of a free enterprise economy. His strategy obliterated the last residues of a terrible war, allowing the country to recover and achieve what was called "Italy's economic miracle." All this was guided by his Christian faith, great honesty, perseverance and no trace of ostentation.

The summer of 1950 appeared empty to me, with no deadlines or tests to be taken. There was plenty of time for a well-deserved vacation. And this was exactly what Nicla and I intended to do. Nicla was invited to spend two weeks in San Remo, on the Italian Riviera, with the Barozzi family. Dr. Barozzi was an old friend of her father, and his invitation was straightforward: there was room only for Nicla in their rented house. If, however, I could camp out in the backyard, I was also welcome. This was more than expected. After gathering my camping gear, I left for San Remo with Nicla and a little-known family with many small children.

The nights on the Italian riviera were illuminated by many shiny stars. There was no better way to enjoy them than sleeping outdoors, like I was doing. Nicla came out every evening to kiss me good night, and I showed her that our good star was there, mingled with many others in the splendor of celestial space. A phone call a few days later confirmed that our star was indeed there, where we had placed it: halfway between our dreams and our expectations.

Nicla's father, after leaving the position of High Commissioner for Food had become the President of ICLE, a banking institute financing Italian colonization abroad. With funds from the Marshall Plan, he was organizing a number of expert missions to Latin America to identify areas and projects for the settlement of Italian farmers. He phoned to ask if I was interested in a mission to Chile. After a quick glimpse at the good star, my answer was yes: I was definitely ready to go. Nicla and I recognized that this was the break we had been looking for. A chance to explore international opportunities, and save money for our wedding.

Professor Giuseppe Venturoli, a general agriculturist and businessman who had worked for many years with Nicla's father, was the team leader of the mission to Chile. He enjoyed Ronchi, Vittorio's confidence. Other team members included two agronomists, one soil chemist, two civil engineers, one forester, one medical doctor, one attorney, one economist, and one animal husbandry specialist. I was the latter. My experience with dairy and beef cattle at the Torlonia Farms in Fucino qualified me for the job. Several meetings were held to brief the team members on the mission's objectives and procedures. Then we were off flying to Santiago.

On my way to Chile, I made a short stopover in Argentina. This gave me the opportunity to spend time in the field with Nicla's father. He was visiting the area of Rafaela near Rosario, in the northeast of the country, with the objective of identifying land suitable for colonization. I joined in this visit. It was a windy and cold day and I was glad to wear a heavy raincoat to keep me warm in the frigid weather. Vittorio, instead, was dressed in a light brown field suit with tall brown boots and an elegant Borsalino hat. He did not seem to mind the weather. He was earnestly looking at the flat land extending over a large territory and at the nearby Parana' river. He recognized the great potential they both offered for large scale transformation of existing pastures to intensive farming.

Suddenly, Vittorio wanted to take a closer look at the soil structure of a nearby field. This, however, was enclosed by barb wire and its only access was through a chained metal gate. Vittorio did not wait for someone to open the gate. With surprising agility, he climbed over and in no time was on the other side. I could not avoid imagining the young infantry captain in World War I climbing out of a muddy trench and leading his soldiers to a bloody attack on the other side of the enemy barb wire. I recognized the same determination and drive he had had during those hellish days. There was only one difference: he was now forty years older.

Our counterpart organization in Chile was the "Caja de Colonizacion," a government agency helping settle farmers to increase farm productivity. During the first months, our team was directed to the area of La Serena in the North, where the "Caja" had already reclaimed some land along the coast and divided it into small parcels. Each of these had its house, storage and irrigation facilities. However, it lacked equipment, animals and other essential inputs (seeds, fertilizers, and pesticides). It was our job to procure whatever was needed to assist twenty families from Trentino.

It was an emotional experience to meet these families as they came ashore on large barges from the "Vespucci" steamer. Men, women, and children, as they landed, were singing the beautiful choirs of their native country as if they were pilgrims to a promised land. There were many people waiting for them on the pier, including authorities of all kinds, even the President of Chile. Only a very small Italian flag was hanging down unnoticed from a tall mast on the windless, sunny day. For some time, the Italian language spoken by our mission was the only thing these people could recognize and appreciate. It was a thin but still a strong link connecting them to their native places, their beautiful mountains and centuries-old culture. It was not an easy task to transplant so many different people at once. In fact, this was the first lesson we learned. In the beginning the failure rate of these immigrants was high, but as time went by, a process of natural selection took place: the stronger men and women succeeded, while the weaker ones gave up and returned to Italy. I never suspected that in only one year I would be one of them. An emigrant.

A second objective of our mission was to identify properties suitable for colonization. This proved more difficult than expected, since the "Caja" had already acquired whatever was available. When these properties were subsequently found unsuitable, they were sold on the open market. Occasionally their price was so low, that speculators would buy them only to make a good profit. Our mission was trapped in this situation when it decided to purchase Fundo San Manuel one of the Caja's largest estates. The intent was to re-sell this property and invest the resulting profit in land better suited for colonization.

This "fundo," extending over thousands of acres bordering the Andean "Cordillera," looked much like the foothills of California's Central Valley. There was only a limited area of flat land suitable for cropping. This was confined to the low valley floor, comprising only shallow soils. The area was crossed by a small creek. The rest of the estate was hilly countryside covered by trees or thick brush that could be crossed only on horseback. Cattle were left free to roam around and once a year they were brought back to the ranch headquarters for counting and marking.

I was given the responsibility of inventorying the cattle and, later on, to assess the grazing potential of the "fundo." This allowed me to reach faraway places that no one from our mission or the Caja had ever visited before. I performed my job as best I could. I wished, however, I had had more training as a cowboy than as an agronomist, so I could better keep up with the skilled Chilean "capataz" accompanying me on the survey. This, in fact, called for tiring horseback riding in rough and dangerous terrain. During the nights, we would sleep in a small tent, after spending several hours in the open, around a camp fire and under many beautiful stars. There was a great silence around us, only interrupted by the familiar crackling sound of the fire.

My survey report was completely negative. The grazing resources were extremely limited and insufficient to raise more or better cattle. Also negative were the reports by the forester (who indicated that there were no sufficient trees for commercial timber exploitation), and by the soil expert (who confirmed the poor quality of the shallow valley soils, unsuitable to raise crops). This was essentially the situation of "Fundo San Manuel:" no possibilities for more profitable cattle ranching, farming or lumbering. Based on these evaluations, the only conclusion was that the property was "unsuitable for the purpose of colonization", (the same conclusion the Caja had reached many years before).

A "proper utilization" for this large property in the secluded foot hills of the Andean Cordillera was found many years later. In the mid-sixties, Fundo San Manuel was sold to "Colonia Villa Baviera," now known as "Colonia Dignidad." A group of approximately two hundred Germans from around Garmisch-Partenkirchen, in Bavaria, emigrated to Chile and settled in San Manuel. These were mountaineers from an area where Adolph Hitler had his famous "nest of the eagles," a spectacular and almost inaccessible natural fortress with a superb view of the surrounding Alps. These emigrants were all hard working, highly disciplined, totally self-contained, and hostile to people outside their settlement.

No one knows what went on in this German colony. There have been many different rumors, including allegations of sexual molestation and abnormal sexual practices with squatters on the property. There has been also a formal indictment for exploitation of Chilean workers connected to illegal restrictions on their freedom to leave the colony.

Anyone approaching "Colonia Dignidad" was stopped by guards at the gate and firmly requested to leave the grounds.

It was during Pinochet's dark dictatorial period that this German settlement was frequently utilized by the DINA (Dirección de Inteligencia Nacional), the equivalent of Pinochet's Gestapo, to host prisoners or "unwanted" people. It has been suggested that Fundo San Manuel was used, not only as a prison camp and a place of torture, but also as a cemetery for the many Chileans who disappeared during the political struggle. As of today, no one seems to know who financed this operation. After many years, Chilean authorities are still unable to find out what is going on inside the well-protected property. Where Chileans and Italians failed in their colonization plans, the Germans from Bavaria succeeded. In which manner and at what cost still remains to be discovered.

The mission in Chile offered me one more opportunity. I was able to visit Umberto and his family in San Carlos de Bariloche, in southern Argentina. To reach San Carlos, I had to travel by train from Santiago to Osorno and then, by an elaborate boat and bus transportation system, I crossed Chile's lake region, and reached Argentina's Nauel Huapi lake. It was a long and fascinating trip in one of the most spectacular regions of the world.

I finally reached San Carlos where Umberto, Rosa, Marcella, and little Theo were waiting for my arrival. They proudly showed me their Italian Restaurant named "El Barquito" (the little boat). Umberto, with the help of his friend Mario, had salvaged a sunken boat from the lake, using a very elaborate system of ropes, pulleys and oxen. People watching this operation from the lake's shore, could not understand why these two Italians were cussing and sweating so hard only to retrieve a useless wreckage. The boat was dragged out of the lake in an upright position, and then it was solidly anchored to land. With plenty of imagination and many repairs, the boat was transformed into a comfortable and cozy restaurant. For all this, Umberto was called "el gringo loco," which translates as "the crazy foreigner." One more example of what resourceful "gringos" are capable of doing in faraway places of the world.

Unfortunately, my visit had to be cut short: I had to report to Santiago. I was sad to leave Umberto's family and never expected that this would be my last hug to my wonderful nephew. Not long afterward, little Theo died in a bike accident. He was only 14 years old. They buried him in a lonely and windy cemetery near San Carlos de Bariloche. But he was never forgotten: his memory is still alive and deeply enshrined in my heart.

After my return to Santiago, the months of separation from Nicla appeared to go by much faster. There was an intense exchange of letters and phone calls and I was finally able to announce that I had an offer for a steady job in Chile. I was to become the manager of a brand new tomato processing plant. I also informed Nicla that I had enough savings to get married and pay for a small detour on my way back to Rome. Guglielmo, who was living in Connecticut, wanted me to stop over for a few days. No one realized the full implications of this "small detour."

At the completion of my mission in Chile, I flew to New York via Miami. Guglielmo was not at the airport as promised. Instead, a young pilot from a Connecticut flying company was there to take me to Hartford.

It was a beautiful summer morning and New York from the air appeared as a dream city. The surroundings were incredibly green and the freeways, cutting through the landscape, were full of cars moving in opposite directions like busy ants in a garden. In no time the single engine plane landed in Hartford, where Guglielmo was waiting. It was a joyful encounter. I told my friend about my experiences in South America and my plans to return to Chile after my wedding. Guglielmo smiled. It was evident that he was paying no attention to my words and my plans. In a short while we arrived in Winsted, a small town where Guglielmo and Mary lived in close proximity to Mary's relatives. She had a younger sister and many brothers. I spent most of the afternoon shaking hands with one family member or another. Finally, in the evening, when everybody had gone to bed, it was possible to talk to Guglielmo alone. The record "Der Rosen Kavalier" by Strauss was playing, wine was flowing into our glasses and we could freely open up to each other. At one point Guglielmo, who apparently was homesick for Italy, his family and friends, suggested that I forget about going back to Chile. "Come to the United States," he openly exhorted, "this country is bigger; there are greater opportunities and many more resources." Furthermore, Guglielmo reminded me, there was also a good friend in Connecticut who was ready to help me get started in America. Guglielmo's arguments seemed solid, the music was soft and the wine exceptionally mellow. I was nearly persuaded, but there was still a big obstacle: how could I get an immigration visa for Nicla and me? "No problem," answered Guglielmo. "Tomorrow we go to see an attorney in New York City who specializes in immigration laws."

The following day we met the attorney. When he found out that I had a degree in Agriculture, he recalled an old immigration law that allowed preferential visas to "skilled agriculturists and their spouse." After this visit, Guglielmo and I had time to catch a glimpse of New York from the top of the Empire State building. Then we proceeded to the airport where I boarded my plane for Rome. As I flew to Italy, my mind and heart were in great turmoil. I clearly sensed that I was toying with my destiny and that of Nicla.

I arrived in Rome only one week before the wedding. Everyone was very nervous about my delay, as there were many things that needed to be taken care, including the wedding announcements and invitations to friends and relatives. During my absence, Nicla had purchased enough fabric to make three suits, two sport coats and a tuxedo. All these required several fitting sessions with my old tailor, who had been waiting for me since early June.

But what really disturbed most was my announcement that I no longer intended to return to Chile. Instead, I wanted to go to the United States. Nicla's father was especially concerned about this change of plans, as he foresaw difficulties in securing immigration visas and finding work in the United States. For a while, the situation remained tense. Again, mother Gina intervened in her calm and reassuring manner. "Tojo, sposemoi," she said in her Friuli's dialect. ("Vittorio, let them get married.") And Vittorio, knowing his wife's good judgment, finally waived all reservations.

Our wedding was the third of four marriages celebrated in the Ronchi family within a one-year period (Vittoria and Giancarlo married in November 1950, Francesca and Marcello in June 1951, and Lisa and Orseolo in October 1951). Mother Gina was busy preparing the various trousseaus, and Nicla took over her family's management responsibilities. It was a burden, but also a useful experience.

On the Fourth of July, Independence Day for America, a late afternoon reception was given at the "Casina delle Rose" (Little House of Roses). This was a stylish restaurant overlooking the city of Rome from the top of the Pincio park. The setting was most impressive: a beautiful view and green surroundings, with many tall and fragrant pines, a perfect orange-reddish sunset, many elegant people talking and laughing in the garden, and a gorgeous buffet. Nicla was most exquisite in her pale blue lace and silk organdie dress,

Our wedding at the Santa Sabina basilica.

which she was wearing in an easy and uninhibited manner. I was very comfortable in my last-minute-made suit. Everybody appeared to enjoy everyone else. And the party went on well into the night with a sky full of shining stars. No doubt, this was offered to us as a personal gift by the Eternal City, the same old, wonderful Rome which saw us grow into loving adults.

The next morning, only a few friends and relatives were present at the wedding ceremony. This took place at the Santa Sabina basilica on the Aventino hill. This church, one of the oldest in Rome, was dimly lit but decorated with many light-colored flowers. As I waited near the entrance, time seemed to stop. Finally, Nicla appeared, radiant in her long, flowing white lace wedding gown, her soft face framed by a simple cap from which the veil cascaded to the floor. Her father walked with her through the atrium and the long nave all the way to the high altar, while music filled the basilica with echoing resonance. Nicla smiled and her eyes carried a simple message: "We finally made it!" The ceremony was short; rings were exchanged and a few tears were shed. Kisses and handshakes were shared with friends and family outside the church. Then we were driven to Via Ovidio, where we quickly changed into travel clothes and left for the train station.

Ideally, honeymoons should last forever. Those who best qualify for long honeymoons are jobless and homeless people. This was exactly our case. We had no employment and no house. We had good reasons to ensure that our honeymoon be extended for as long as possible, at least as long as hosting relatives and friends could bear us.

The first stay in our honeymoon was to be in Munich. Since the trip to this city was too long, we made an overnight stop over in Bolzano. My major concern was not to appear a typical honeymooner. But, as we checked in at the Hotel

Grifone, we were immediately congratulated on our wedding by the concierge and the bell captain. Of course, all our luggage was fresh from the store, as was my suit and Nicla's stylish outfit (a silver gray jacket and dress, red shoes, a red Gucci hand bag, and a most attractive red hat). I realized that to appear older and well-traveled takes experience and, certainly, well aged baggage.

After a splendid overnight, I was ready for a good breakfast, while Nicla could only sip a cup of coffee. We were served on the outdoor patio under a clear blue sky and a crown of magnificent mountains. We boarded the morning train to Munich, where we were met by Theo, Gitschi and a large bouquet of red roses. Together we proceeded to the Four Seasons Hotel where the owner, Mr. Walterspiel was waiting.

Life magazine once published an article on the world's most famous restaurants. The Walterspiel Restaurant in Munich was one of them. Mr. Walterspiel was also Theo's boss. As a wedding gift, he wished to host us in one of his best suites. A trail of bell boys escorted us and our brand new luggage to the presidential suite, where famous kings and presidents had lodged. Everything appeared like in the imaginary realm of the fairies: the magnificent bedroom with silks and expensive carpets, the huge bathroom with shiny marble and many mirrors. And flowers, many delicate flowers in precious vases, were scattered all over. This was the welcome Theo had organized for his step-brother and the young, beautiful wife.

In the afternoon, a welcome party was scheduled at his apartment. French champagne, pink salmon, and filets of lobster were served with whipped sour cream and an asparagus salad. We happily shared the many photos of our reception and church ceremony. Gitschi promptly suggested that we leave these photos "unguarded" in our presidential suite so that the hotel staff could see them and spread the word about the elegance and importance of our Roman wedding. All this, of course, to give her some glory.

A full program of visits to Munich and surroundings was arranged. In the morning, the hotel phone would ring and Theo's pleasant voice would wish us, "Buon giorno," from his work desk. This was followed by a "ceremonial breakfast" consisting of two carts full of food delicacies pushed into our room by two waiters. A maitre d'hotel would follow to see that the service was given with due elegance. Theo's work schedule allowed us to spend some time with him in the afternoons and evenings. A week went by rapidly, and the presidential suite had to be vacated for the arrival of some other "important" guests. Mr. Walterspiel was informed that we had plans to leave Munich to continue touring Germany and other cities in Europe. He arrived at the hotel as we were ready to board a taxi for the station. We expressed to Mr. Walterspiel our gratitude for his wonderful hospitality, gave generous tips to the porters, and finally departed in high style. As we turned the corner from the hotel, the taxi driver was re-routed to a small bed and breakfast place not far from Theo's apartment. We were going to pay for this place with our own money.

We stayed in Munich for another two weeks. When Theo was working, we continued to take tours by ourselves, visiting famous places such as Garmisch, Oberammergau, the Castle of Ludwig the Second, the Chiemsee, and so on. Both of us enjoyed the beautiful countryside, the small houses scattered on the mountain slopes, the window boxes full of flowers, and the fairytale atmosphere that makes Bavaria unique. On weekends, Theo drove us around for more sightseeing. On one such occasion, he arrived early to pick us up at our bed and breakfast. He patiently waited in his car, finally honking the horn to inform us that he was ready to go. From the street below, Theo saw our room's window open, but all he could see next was a pair of trousers waving at him. This was my way of sending him a message of explanation, pleading for more time and indulgence.

All beautiful things come to an end, and our wonderful stay in Munich was nearly over. A few more evenings spent drinking beer at the Hofbrauhaus, a few more mornings eating white sausages, a few more lunches in cozy Bavarian restaurants, and it was really time to return to Rome. But not before Theo could organize another of his many surprises. The last evening in Bavaria he invited us to one of the most elegant dining places, about fifty miles from Munich. At a certain hour the "Queen of the Roses" beauty contest was announced. The lady receiving most complimentary roses would be elected queen for the evening. Many of the ladies in the hall were blonde and German-looking. The only pretty dark-haired lady was Nicla, who received one hundred red roses and was elected "queen." Most German men, like Johann Wolfang von Goethe, love Italy and Italian women. Many men in that fancy restaurant must have contributed flowers to Nicla's cause, but Theo, for sure, spent most of his money to win her election.

Upon our return, we stayed in Rome long enough to change into lighter clothes and repack our suitcases. Nicla and I then headed for Parma. This is a city located in the southern part of the Po Valley, famous for its prosciutto, Parmesan cheese and operatic music. Parma is also known for tomato processing. Most of the tomatoes for the Italian canning industry are grown around this city. In Parma there is also an experiment station devoted to tomato processing. As mentioned, prior to my departure from Chile, I had been offered a position to manage a new tomato processing plant. I was no longer interested in this offer, but I still wanted to get the training in processing technology in case the US entry visa should not materialize.

The honeymoon in Parma lasted almost a month, long enough to learn something about married life. We rented a one-bedroom, one-bathroom furnished apartment, and we shared the kitchen and dining facilities with our landlady. We were happy to live together in a modest environment, quite different from where we had been raised.

There were three memorable things during this period of married life: the height of the bed, the heat of the summer and the abundance of the food.

The average bed height in the western world is about 18-19 inches from the floor. The bed in Parma was at least 30 inches high. This height was excessive when climbing into bed at night, and very unsafe when getting out of bed in the morning. In addition, unexperienced honeymooners could easily crash down from such an altitude. We had to be careful as we were still jobless and with no medical insurance.

The second problem was the summer heat. The Po Valley is cold and foggy in the winter and hot and humid in the summer. No air conditioning was available, not even a plain refrigerator to keep our food at a decent temperature. I solved this problem by placing, each day, two large ice blocks in the bath tub after the morning showers. Food and drinks were kept on this ice until the next morning or next shower, whichever came first.

The third problem was not really a problem until I discovered that I could no longer fit into my newly-made suits. When Nicla took over the management of her parents' house, she cooked for a family of six. In Parma, she maintained the same quantitative standards. Naturally, I said nothing: I enjoyed her excellent food too much.

After Parma, it was time to travel again. I had learned all I needed to know about tomato processing, hoping that I would never use this knowledge. I proposed that on our way back to Rome we take a detour through Riccione. This is a very elegant beach resort on the Adriatic coast where my old friend Luciano Albanese was vacationing. I decided to play a trick on him. Since Luciano had not been informed about our wedding, I introduced Nicla as my travel companion. The three of us went sailing and Luciano, as expected, started flirting with her. This went on until I told him to leave "my wife alone." Luciano's face changed color and expression. He could not decide whether I was telling the truth. After landing, I showed him our hidden wedding rings. This was sufficient to receive his apologies and congratulations at the same time.

Upon our return to Rome, we found a letter from the New York attorney indicating under which chapter of the US immigration laws a preferential entry visa was granted to "skilled agriculturists." He further suggested that we personally visit the US Consul in Naples to explain our case. September was still a fine month to spend some free time at the coast, so we decided to go first to Naples for the interview, and then to Capri for another bit of honeymoon.

The American consul was a nice and friendly person. He patiently listened, and then candidly admitted that this was the first time he had heard about this kind of preferential quota. He walked out of his office and returned with a big book where he had found a special clause on this matter. The consul did not see any problem with the visa and he invited us to fill out some forms to start the necessary action.

Happy about our interview, we boarded the ferry to Capri. This island, located in the bay of Naples, is world-famous for its beauty and year-round tourism. I had a relative in Capri, "zio Antonio," my uncle who was a night concierge in one of the island's first class hotels. He was my father's youngest brother, who had been raised with Theo by my mother in the early period of her marriage. Antonio remained very close to Theo, with whom he had shared his adolescence and hotel career. Antonio's approach, however, was different from that of Theo. He was satisfied to work at a much lower level, where the money was less but so was the pressure.

I phoned Antonio to inform him about our visit, and when we arrived at his hotel, he hurriedly wrote on a piece of paper the address of a private house where he had made reservations. We went to this address and met a smiling landlady. She had the unmistakable appearance and manners of a brothel manager. After looking around in the apartment, I had no more doubts about her background or profession. When I asked for a room with a king-size bed, she was nearly offended. She snapped back, saying that in many years of renting rooms to male customers, this was the first time she had had such a silly request. Fortunately Nicla did not realize what was going on. The hospitable landlady placed two small beds together, and our honeymoon continued as happy as ever before. The next day, we went swimming near the famous Blue Grotto and greatly enjoyed the crystal clear water. After a long and enjoyable swim, we departed from "zio Antonio," beautiful Capri and our "rent-a-room by the hour" lady.

We spent a few weeks in Rome and then returned to the American consulate in Naples for our medical tests. Things were getting serious about the visa and our American adventure was just about to start.

PART TWO

The American Dream

6

The Emigration Story

*Let us then, be up and doing, with a
heart for any fate; still achieving,
still pursuing, learn to labor and to
wait.*

—H.H. Longfellow 1839

On January 3, 1952, the transatlantic steamer
"Saturnia" was departing from Naples for New
York with stopovers in Genoa, Lisbon and
Halifax. The "Saturnia" was an old passenger ship without
air conditioning or stabilizers. Thanks to Nicla's father, it
was possible to purchase two third class tickets for a cabin
actually located in second class.

A few days prior to departure, Nicla got sick with the
flu. Everyone was worried about her. The family doctor,
however, authorized her departure, provided she would take

certain medicines and vitamins. While Nicla was in bed taking care of her illness, I used all of my good health and imagination in packing and repacking our belongings. There were a total of eleven trunks and eight suitcases in which everything had to fit. The contents were extremely varied: there were many wedding presents, including a set of silverware for twelve; Nicla's trousseau with many finely embroidered table clothes, sheets and towels; a brand new Necchi sewing machine with a built-in desk; a large number of books, and two pairs of skis. Everything was finally packed, the trunks and suitcases were properly labeled, and our possessions were ready to go.

Vittoria and Giancarlo accompanied us to the railroad station with Vittorio and my father. They were all sad to see us leave and concerned about our future. Yes, we were young, adaptable, and with many personal resources. The step we were taking, however, was still very risky. Emigration in Italy was considered a solution for peasants or second class citizens, for people who had no alternatives and were so desperate that they had to find elsewhere what they could not have in their own country. Emigration has always been the safety valve for crowded countries with an overabundance of brains and human bodies and with chronic scarcity of economic and sociological resources. All these thoughts were going through their minds as our train slowly moved away from the crowded station.

Lisa came with us to Naples and worried all the way about Nicla's health. Soon after checking into the hotel, she called for a doctor. After a thorough medical exam, we were given the same diagnosis and prescriptions already received in Rome. The next morning we went together to the pier. After the usual formalities, Nicla and I boarded the "Saturnia" and took possession of our cabin. It was a beautiful sunny day in Naples and the port was bustling with

Leaving Rome by train. Vittoria is crying in her father's arm. In the background: father Luigi, Mrs. Mileto, Giancarlo and Orseolo.

A pensive good-bye from the train window.

activity. In one section of the harbor there were many American warships lazily basking in the sun. Opposite them was Mount Vesuvius, majestically overlooking the bay and the city and discharging into the air what appeared to be a white smoke signal. It was time to depart. Lisa on the pier waved her hands and a scarf until the boat moved away and she was only an indistinguishable speck. We stayed on deck for a while. Nicla, bundled in a heavy coat, was wearing a soft angora hat which protected her from the chilly breeze. She looked back at Naples fading away in the distance, but had no tears in her eyes. She was definitely ready for our adventure.

The overnight voyage to Genova was pleasant. The sea was calm, and the ship's motors could be clearly heard through the silence of the night. Another beautiful sunny day was waiting for us. Mother Gina and father Vittorio, were at the pier when the "Saturnia" arrived. They were in Genova on official business to wish farewell to a large group of Italian emigrants who were leaving for Australia under the auspices of Vittorio's banking institute. We spent the day touring the city together, enjoying each other's company and avoiding any reference to our impending departure. It was clear that no one wanted to show feelings of sadness or concern. All of us knew that it was going to be a long separation, and this alone was cause for melancholy. That evening, we kissed Nicla's parents good-bye and, with our hearts full of emotion, we boarded the "Saturnia" for our new life in America.

The weather was fine during the crossing of the Mediterranean and we enjoyed the blue sea water more as cruising tourists than as emigrants. In Lisbon there was another stop-over. New passengers came aboard, while those going to America were allowed to go ashore. Lisbon is a pleasant city, rich with seagoing traditions. We took

Boarding the "Saturnia" with self-confidence.

advantage of the beautiful day to tour the city and returned to the ship by late afternoon.

We had a very comfortable cabin, with a well-decorated bedroom, a bathroom with a good-sized tub, and a small private veranda. We also had a special pass to enter the first class area and use their facilities. Everything appeared to be in perfect order, except for the weather. Wind, heavy rains, and huge waves characterized the entire Atlantic crossing. The "Saturnia," without stabilizers, rolled up and down and rocked sideways like a toy ship in a vast ocean. There was no air conditioning, and a stagnant odor, like burnt tomato sauce in a canning plant, was present everywhere we went. Most passengers and a good number of the crew were seasick. Nicla did not feel like eating and did not appear in the dining room, which was always nearly empty. In one corner a lonely waiter, with a colorless face and a big menu under his arm, was ready to receive orders that never came. I was the only passenger in the room. I felt fine and was ready to eat regular meals. Occasionally, another passenger would quickly appear and disappear. He was an old man, an Italian American for sure, maybe a tailor or a shoemaker. His rapid appearances followed the same pattern: he tottered to his table, grabbed a flask of red wine, turned around, and after smiling to the lonely waiter in the corner, briskly retreated to the security of his cabin.

After a few days, Mr. Luca, the head waiter, asked me about Nicla's condition. He worried about her not coming to the dining room and insisted that she should eat plenty of solid food, even if she had no appetite. He wanted to make sure that she received all sorts of well prepared sandwiches in the cabin. A little at a time Nicla started eating and gaining back all her strength.

As for myself, I was fine. I took long walks on the ship's deck and enjoyed the sight of the surrounding stormy ocean and the huge waves. In my mind, I thought that this could have been my way of life, had I remained in the naval academy. This reassured me of the correctness of my decision to leave the academy and choose a career in agriculture, safely anchored to land.

After each walk on deck, my preferred pastime was to go back to the cabin and climb into a tub half-filled with warm water. I would soak for a long time, lazily watching the water level moving up and down with the rolling of the ship. By lounging in the water most of the time, I was probably the cleanest passenger on board and one who could later claim to have been able in mid January to float across a stormy Atlantic, all the way to America.

Halifax is a seaport in Nova Scotia, southeast Canada. When the "Saturnia" arrived, after nearly a week-and-a-half at sea, snow covered the coastline and the temperature was extremely cold. It was a great contrast to Naples! No more blue skies or blue waters. Everything was either grey or white. Many passengers were allowed to disembark except for us and a few other Italians and Germans without Canadian visas. We spent the day watching the coastline and the porters unloading the ship. They were big, tall and extremely silent men. These giants moved slowly, carrying no more than one or two small pieces of luggage at the time. Maybe their union did not permit heavier work at a greater speed, but to us they appeared more like ghosts than men. Unequivocally, we had landed in a New World!

Only a few days were left before our arrival in New York. For this occasion the "Saturnia's" captain wished to organize a farewell gala ball for first-class passengers, and he kindly sent us an invitation. For Nicla this was a good occasion to wear her black evening organza dress made by a fashionable dressmaker in Rome, and her beautiful evening sandals by Dal Co. (An old American lady, who approached Nicla, openly confessed that in all her life she had never seen such a small and beautiful pair of feet!) I wore my trusty tuxedo. We entered the first class hall like two movie stars on Oscar night. Everyone turned around to watch us. It was evident that none of the passengers had seen us before in either the dining room or on deck. It was also evident that everyone was curious to know who we were and why we had escaped their notice during the entire crossing. We were too eye-catching and rich-looking a couple to have been overlooked. The captain himself had to explain to some of the curious ladies that we were a wealthy, newlywed couple honeymooning in New York. Winking to these ladies, the clever captain further explained that honeymooners at sea prefer the intimacy of their cabin to the crush of curious crowds.

Nicla's graceful dancing attracted additional attention and admiration, especially when she was delivered a cable from Italy wishing her a "Happy Birthday." It was at midnight of the 15th of January. In no time we had the entire floor to ourselves under the scrutiny of the amazed passengers. The captain himself enjoyed playing his part. He came to us, and with much gallantry, he bowed and kissed Nicla's hand. No one suspected that we were third class passengers, and emigrants in search of a better destiny.

Upon our arrival in New York on a bright sunny day, there were two smiling faces waiting for us. The first was the Statue of Liberty on Long Island. For all emigrants arriving from Europe this statue remained the symbol of acquired freedom and the embodiment of hope. Nicla stopped for a moment to look at the statue and a tear came rolling down her cheek. The other smiling face was that of Angelo Lucia, waiting on the pier. Before landing, we had to go through the U.S. Immigration Service. We were both carrying large manila envelopes full of forms, medical reports, X-rays, and so on. Immediately we attracted the officers' attention with our special visas. Apparently, no one had ever seen a preferential visa for a "skilled agriculturist." One of the officers took both passports into another room and then came back shaking his head. He asked Nicla to turn her hands up to show the presence of calluses on her palms. Somewhat disappointed to find no hardened skin, and still shaking his head, the officer finally applied his "admitted" stamp on both passports. There were no more doubts: we had landed on American soil.

The first reality we faced was going through customs with eleven trunks and eight suitcases. The inspectors were trying to clear all passengers as fast as they could. For some reason, however, they were also avoiding our bulky luggage. Close to us, three inspectors were carefully examining a passenger's suitcase. They opened his shaving kit, squeezed out the tooth paste from its container, and slowly inspected any item that could be shaken or sniffed. The passenger was clearly nervous and so was I, thinking that the same process would be applied to our luggage. A porter had already volunteered to take our baggage outside the customs area, but nothing could be moved without official approval.

Soon most other passengers were cleared from customs, but we were still there, like ducks sitting on a pile of trunks. We began bargaining with the porter about his fees. "Seventy dollars, mister, and this is a real bargain, I guarantee it," the man said. And there was no way to lower his request. Finally, one of the officers came by, asked if there were valuables or agricultural products to declare, and receiving a negative reply, he stroked all items with a yellow chalk. He then invited the porter (the only one left in the area) to move the baggage out. All this happened in a matter of seconds. The porter loaded his trolley, walked a few yards and, just around the corner, he dumped everything on the sidewalk. "Welcome to New York" the porter said, and with a grin on his face he quickly counted the seventy dollars he did not deserve. Angelo was there watching this transaction. With an understanding smile he explained that the long wait on the pier and the high porter fees were likely to be interconnected. The officer and the porter must have had some sort of arrangement for taking away money from dumb and inexperienced immigrants.

After leaving the trunks and some suitcases in a public storage, we went to Angelo's apartment in Times Square. This was a tiny bachelor's nest in the heart of bubbling New York City.

The city was beautiful and Nicla, seeing it for the first time, was immediately taken by its special charm: the magnificent Central Park, the tall, elegant skyscrapers, and the unique atmosphere that only a big metropolis can offer. People in the streets appeared to move at a rapid pace, without looking at each other or even at the windows of the many beautiful stores. Everyone seemed to be in a great hurry.

Angelo also moved at that same speed. He was determined to show us all of New York City in the shortest possible time. He did not realize we had been at sea for nearly two weeks, and that we were still floating with our heads in the clouds as we walked on the firm and opalescent surface of the city sidewalks. It was a remarkable feeling, probably the same which sailors experience when they reach land after a long stay at sea. At night things were even worse: we had the impression that one side of the bed was going up and down, just like on the boat. It took several days and nights to overcome this feeling and to become adjusted to the traffic, lights and sounds of New York City. Nicla and I were considering how our feelings compared with those of other emigrants who came from small European towns and villages to this huge metropolis. It must have been a shocking experience.

After a few days, we were invited to a welcome dinner by Aldo Giurgola, an Italian friend of Angelo's and a promising architect. This type of welcome was something that previous emigrants probably never experienced: a tasty, homemade spaghetti dinner with a large group of charming friends. The beginnings of our "American dream" could not have been better.

It was soon time to come out of the clouds and start facing reality. Each morning we scrutinized the newspapers to see if there were any farming jobs in the state of New York. Angelo had seen an advertisement for a job on a dairy farm located about half way to Winsted. A stop-over was therefore arranged.

The place was in the hilly countryside off the main road, where a small house and a large barn were surrounded by scenic pastures and abundant trees. Everything looked old, dirty and trashy, especially around the buildings. The owners were two elderly ladies in desperate need of a robust, experienced dairyman to take care of their twenty cows, the farm, and, possibly, the house. For all this, a young live-in couple would have been ideal. We took a quick look at the house, the large barn, the cows, and the two elderly ladies. In no time, we reached the same conclusion: not to get stuck in what appeared to be a full-fledged rest-home for old people with plenty of extra activities to be performed. The job offer was quickly turned down and we proceeded to Connecticut without further delay.

Mary and Guglielmo were happy to greet us in Winsted. Supper was prepared right after our arrival, and there were plenty of lively discussions around the dining table. Guglielmo, who was working as a draftsman for an architect in Hartford, wanted to get an American degree in architecture to improve his position. He enjoyed discussing with Angelo the current problems of their profession. Another topic of discussion was what kind of work would be best for Nicla and myself. It was agreed that possibilities were to be explored first in Connecticut. After all, agriculture was a very important activity in that state. There was also the possibility of working for the Connecticut Agricultural Experiment Station, one of the finest in the country. A third "important" subject was skiing: Guglielmo and I both loved to ski, and January was the best time of the year to practice this sport. Why not organize a ski trip before any job could come around to upset our plans?

Angelo proposed a trip to Vermont, where he and one of his brothers owned a cabin, and plenty of good snow was always available in the winter. Plans were made for the following weekend. Angelo was to drive to Winsted from New York City, and then all together we would proceed to Vermont.

One detail remained to be resolved: our skis were stored in New York City along with our boots and other ski gear. Since I had a number of interviews scheduled for the next few days, it was decided that Nicla should go alone to New York to collect our belongings. She could take the early morning train, then a taxi to the storage place, retrieve whatever was necessary for the trip and then come back to Winsted in the evening. One detail left out of our discussions was that Nicla did not speak a word of English and that she had been in the United States for only a few days. This, however, did not seem to worry her.

The next day, she did exactly as planned. That evening, Guglielmo and I went to the train station to meet her. We were both concerned for her safety. But there she was, stepping down from the train and smiling, as if nothing had happened. Nicla had the skis and all the rest of the gear we needed for the Vermont trip.

Mary and her many brothers could not believe that a young lady, fresh out of Italy, was able to accomplish a task of that kind without any problem. This was something they probably could not have done by themselves. Admittedly, some of them had never been to New York City.

The first week in Winsted was busy with interviews and job hunting activities. We stayed in Guglielmo's house and slept on the floor of his living room. We felt, however, that we had to find some other accommodation. In fact, the situation in our friends' house was rather tense. At night we could hear Mary and Guglielmo arguing for many hours. We realized that our stay in their house was not helping smooth matters between them.

As planned, on Friday night, Angelo arrived from New York City and everybody proceeded to Dresden Station, Vermont. It was a long ride, but finally we arrived at the cabin. The night was extremely cold and there was plenty of snow on the ground. Once in the cabin, we discovered that the house was still under construction, it was dirty and without a bathroom. We also found out that all the firewood had been used by some previous guest. If we wanted to survive the night, we had to go out into the woods to collect anything that could burn in the fireplace. This was, in fact, the only source of heat in the cabin. Accidentally, I spilled some brandy on a table and it froze after a few minutes: a convincing demonstration of the need to collect firewood. The better part of the night was spent doing just this. Finally, exhausted after a long trip and an unexpected night of work in the woods, we bundled up near the fireplace and tried to get some rest. Angelo, however, did not get any sleep. Like a Roman vestal, he kept the sacred fire alive all night long.

The next day, all of us had fun skiing on the fresh snow that whitened Vermont's most beautiful countryside.

On February 11, we saw an advertisement in a local newspaper for a job opening on a poultry farm. This was located near Watertown, only 30 miles from Winsted. We immediately arranged for an appointment to meet the owner and learn about the job.

The owner was an old, soft-spoken gentleman who looked much like Colonel Sanders of "Kentucky Fried Chicken." He did not fry his chickens, however. He specialized in breeding pedigreed baby chicks that were sold all over the country and even abroad. The old gentleman appeared friendly and interested in hiring us. Our work required ten hours of labor a day, seven days a week with Sunday off every other week. Free housing was provided and the proposed salary was $180 a month. Having considered the alternative of milking twenty cows three times a day and, possibly taking care of two old ladies in their filthy house, this offer appeared favorable. After all, chickens are smaller and easier to keep clean than dairy cows.

Before moving to the poultry farm, we requested that the eleven trunks and few suitcases still stored in New York City be shipped to Watertown. The rest of our belongings, including two beds, a stove, a small refrigerator, a kitchen table, and two chairs, that we had purchased in Winsted, were loaded on an old truck that Guglielmo had borrowed from one of Mary's brothers.

After securing everything with heavy ropes, we were ready to hit the road, like "Okies" in one of Steinbeck's novels. In many ways, we were worse off than the "Okies," as the driver's cabin of the old truck had no bottom and we had to lift our feet to avoid hitting objects left on the road.

The farm house where we were to be lodged was a two-story building secluded on the top of a small hill. At night it looked spooky, like one of the mystery houses in Hitchcock's movies. On the ground floor lived a man who worked with dairy cows. He had a family of three, owned a car, and once a week he would take us to town for grocery shopping.

The inside of the second floor appeared run-down, filthy and in need of repair. In the center of a large family room stood a kerosene stove, an old fashioned open flame heater serving the entire floor. It was a nightmare to light it and to let it run day and night, alongside a large refill container. But we were happy just the same. Finally we had our own house, even if it was in the middle of nowhere and there was nowhere for us to go.

Shortly after our arrival, the owner came by to inform us that all our trunks had arrived in Watertown and that we had to pay over one hundred dollars for the shipment from New York City. Also we had to go to the railroad station with a truck to transport everything to the farm: they would not deliver to the house. We went to town, paid the fee, loaded the cargo, drove home, unloaded the trunks, and then, one by one, Nicla and I carried them up the very narrow, steep stairs to the second floor. We had our first good taste of "do-it-yourself America." This was then followed by the cleaning and painting operations that we started right away and continued every night after work.

It was necessary to cover the mish-mash of colors used by the people who had lived in the house before: greens, reds, yellows combined with huge pink flowers on the wall paper. Something even Picasso would have considered excessively bold.

The owner agreed to purchase white paint, and we did the rest of the work to restore the interior to a snowy whiteness to match that of the surrounding landscape. The owner only argued about the installation of our electric range. He wanted us to use bottled gas so that we would pay for its consumption. I objected, saying that Nicla had never cooked on gas. He finally gave in, installed a 220 volt outlet, and paid the cost of the monthly bill.

It was time for me to report to work, but my Italian-made wardrobe did not include work clothes. Fortunately, Angelo had left an old army coat and a fatigue cap which he had worn as a service man during the war. I welcomed both and completed my attire with an old pair of pants, an old sweater and my heavy ski boots. I was ready to start to work in America.

The center of the farm was only a few hundred yards away from our house, and to get there took just a short and refreshing walk in the snow. Two other men were working in the poultry section. The first was Harry, a loquacious but pestering individual; the second was Joe, a reserved and cold person. He looked much like Bing Crosby, but he never sang or engaged in long conversations.

My work consisted essentially of cleaning chicken pens, feeding baby chicks and older hens, collecting and labelling eggs, unloading feed bags from supply trucks, and fighting the roosters. These were kept in separate compartments with small groups of selected hens. Collecting those eggs was always an uncertain battle. The roosters attacked whoever walked in the compartment and these attacks could be quite painful. As mentioned, I was wearing heavy ski boots. When I was attacked, I had to kick back as if I were playing in a soccer game. Thanks to the heavy boots, my kick was so powerful and well centered that the rooster was thrown against the wall where it remained stunned. Occasionally, as I turned my back, the rooster would attack again. As time went by, collecting eggs from these pens became an increasingly risky affair.

Feeding young hens in the open range.

Packing baby chicks for shipment.

Joe did not have any of the above chores or problems. He looked after the incubators, ascertained the sex of newly-hatched baby chicks, and did the gassing of those unfortunate ones who happened to be born males. After a few weeks, Nicla was called to work as Joe's part-time assistant at $150 a month. In short order, she learned how to handle the job in a professional way, as if she had been doing this kind of work all her life. However, it was hard for her to accept the killing of innocent baby chicks by gassing them in barrels. So, when Joe was not in the incubator room, we activated a rescue operation. We placed twenty-six baby chicks in a box and took them to safety in our house. We had a large attic where these chicks were given "political asylum." They were then raised with all the attention required by small animals of their age. Feeding them was not a problem. Everyday I carried in the pockets of my bulky army coat two packages of feed "borrowed" from the farm. As the chicks grew bigger, there was need for extra food and more space. The twenty-six survivors were transferred to an abandoned barn and they were fed with all sorts of left-overs. Occasionally, they also received a share of wine. Judging from the way they drank that wine, and by the quantity they ingested, the growing chicks showed an appreciation for this type of drink that, even today, is denied to minors all over America.

Another matter Nicla and I could not stand was to see old hens being killed and thrown away only because they no longer laid eggs. Coming from Italy, and having experienced hunger during the war, we were not prepared to accept such an incredible waste. So, another rescue was organized that we called, "operation old hen." This meant that after Harry had killed some of the older chickens, we promptly intervened to make their bodies disappear. These were taken to our house, where they were quickly cleaned, cut, boiled, and frozen. In this way, we always had an ample supply of excellent chicken soup.

Life without days off could be hard on most working people, but Nicla and I accepted this situation philosophically. We had our love to share, we enjoyed each other's company, and we knew that things, in the long run, would change for the better. We even smiled when Harry would needle us about having a good time as immigrants from Italy.

Occasionally, Guglielmo would come to visit us. Since he liked eating raw eggs, it was always a great pleasure to satisfy his good appetite right in the chicken pen and, sometimes, with valuable "pedigree" material.

On week-ends we also enjoyed visits from Angelo. He knew that we liked fresh oysters, and, when possible, he would bring a good quantity of them to satisfy our craving. On his way to Watertown, Angelo would stop several times along the highway to collect clean snow and make sure the oysters remained under refrigeration.

On one of these excursions Angelo was accompanied by Aldo Giurgola. It was a good occasion for Nicla to prepare a fine Italian dinner, starting, of course, with a first-class chicken broth. At the end of the meal, the conversation shifted to our future. We realized that "Love Among the Chickens," the humorous book by P.G. Wodehouse, could not apply too much longer to our situation. Aldo informed us about a large fruit company that might represent a viable alternative. He suggested that a letter of inquiry be sent to the Di Giorgio Company to see if they had any openings in their agricultural operations in Florida or California. He would provide us with their address in New York. Once we received this information, I arranged for an interview with Mr. Philip Di Giorgio, one of the Company's vice-presidents.

Chianti to the Italians.

I went to New York City and had a long meeting with Mr. Di Giorgio. I was told that living conditions on the farms in California were difficult, that married men were housed in separate buildings from their wives, that the average wage for unskilled labor was 95 cents an hour, and that no moving expenses were paid by the Company. I was also warned that any offer of employment would have to come directly from the San Francisco main office.

With these "good" news stewing in my mind, I took the train back to Watertown. Prior to this, I stopped in one of the many Italian grocery stores to buy a jumbo flask of Chianti wine and a large piece of provolone cheese. In their company, I was better prepared to face Nicla and to report the outcome of my interview. It was a very long evening on the second floor of the farm house near Watertown. I described in detail the discussion and my impression of the interviewer. Philip Di Giorgio appeared to be a very nice person, but the job conditions he pictured were disappointing, no better than we already had on the chicken farm in Connecticut. Eating provolone cheese and drinking Chianti wine softened things up for that evening. And the two of us continued talking until late into the night. Our situation at that point was easily summarized. We had no assets other than our eleven trunks and a few household items. We still had a $500 bill hidden somewhere in Nicla's wallet (to be used for emergencies only). We had no car, no telephone, no bank account, and no insurance of any kind. On the positive side, we had two good friends (Angelo and Guglielmo), our youth, a high dose of optimism, and a strong desire to move ahead.

We had been working at the poultry farm for nearly four months. Other than a one-day trip to Winsted, we had not been away from our house during this entire period. It was the end of May and we had great expectations for some nice spring weather. One morning, we opened the blinds of our bedroom windows and all we could see was a countryside covered by snow. We both felt frustrated by an impossible winter that never ended.

Our frustration increased a few hours later when Nicla was notified that she had been laid off and that her last, undated check had been cut in half. She asked the owner about this reduction in wages, and his explanation was that "things had slowed down at the farm and a pay adjustment was necessary." When I was informed about this, I could not contain my anger. I went immediately to see the owner, and told him that if "things had slowed down at the farm" he should have warned Nicla before and not after she had put in 15 days of work. The owner did not expect this type of reaction. He continued looking at me and his eyes behind the gold rimmed glasses showed amusement. I could no longer stand his smile: I took Nicla's check and tore it in two pieces which I threw on his desk. "From now on," I said, "you better look for another couple of suckers. We are through with you as of this moment."

Shortly afterwards we had a visit from Richard Chiarappa from Middletown, Connecticut. We told him what had happened and he became so upset that he was ready to go to the owner to rescue the full amount of Nicla's salary. But Nicla stopped him from doing this, just to avoid something worse happening: a heart attack. In fact the owner was a frail old man, and Richard was a tough looking auditor in the Internal Revenue Service. Richard smiled at Nicla's request. "You Italians are too soft and sentimental about business matters," he said. "If you want to succeed in this country, you must set aside these feelings and adopt our way of thinking." It was a good lesson that we never forgot.

Richard complied with Nicla's wishes, but promised that he would take a good look at the farm's income tax returns.

Who knows, he might still retrieve the undated check which was never cashed. A promise that Richard very likely kept.

After this visit, we killed and cleaned all our pullets and then packed our belongings into crates, trunks and suitcases. We found a farmer in the neighborhood who, for only twelve dollars, helped us move the trunks, the refrigerator, the stove, and other furniture into a storage place in Waterbury. I then called Guglielmo to come and pick us up with the old truck. We still had our suitcases, many ready-to-eat pullets and a few crates to be left in Richard's cellar in Middletown.

We boarded the truck with great relief, and, as we went through the farm gate, I could not refrain from saying: "That's for the birds." There was a roar of laughter as the three of us rode the bottomless truck to Middletown and Winsted. It was raining cats and dogs, and we were getting wet from the bottom and the sides. The truck windows could not be rolled up, either.

Hartford was a city that appeared to offer a large number of work opportunities due to its many industries. For this reason, we decided to relocate to Hartford. The next day we left most of our luggage in Winsted, and with only a few suitcases, we took a bus to the city. Here we found a room in a furnished rental house. The other bedrooms were leased to couples or single individuals who shared a bathroom and a refrigerator on each floor.

Our room was small and had a sloped ceiling which fell at a sharp angle over our bed. Before getting up, we had to be careful not to bang our heads against the ceiling. There was also a small hot plate provided by the landlady to warm up coffee or some fast food. The other couple on our floor seemed to be respectable people. He worked night shifts and slept (with an open door) during the day. She worked during the day and slept (with a closed door) at night. It was nearly impossible to see the two together (either awake or asleep), just like Castor and Pollux of Greek mythology.

The refrigerator was small, and it became even smaller once it was stuffed with bulky vegetables or fresh fruit that Italians seem to appreciate so much. It was amazing what Nicla could do with the small hot plate. The odor of her simmering spaghetti sauce could be smelled all over the building. The landlady downstairs did not know what was happening in her house. She asked Nicla what she was cooking and Nicla offered her a generous sample of tasty sauce. This was the beginning of a solid friendship between the two.

Nicla found a job almost immediately. This was with a garment factory, where her talent as a seamstress was greatly appreciated. In fact, she was liked even "too much" by one of the supervisors. This man, in admiration for a capable and good-looking Italian woman, asked her to go and see him on a Saturday morning when no one was around. That evening, when Nicla met me at the apartment, she was in tears. She had never been exposed to this type of proposition and she did not want to go back to that factory. It was our first encounter with sexual harassment in America.

Shortly afterwards, Nicla found another job. This was in a section of a large department store where they repaired fur coats during the summer. June is particularly hot and humid in Hartford, and it was very unpleasant to work with furs, especially when the air conditioning was not operating. Nicla complained about this with her landlady friend who suggested that she apply to the Royal typewriter factory. "I am quite sure that wages and working conditions at Royal are much better," she said. Nicla applied, and shortly after, she was hired.

At Royal, Nicla was given many jobs in short sequence. Supervisors kept her moving from machine to machine, and from operation to operation. However, she was so good, precise and fast that she was soon assigned to do piecework. And Nicla succeeded also in this. Many of the ladies working at the factory were curious about Nicla, probably because she was the youngest on the assembly line, and she could hardly speak English. During coffee or lunch breaks they would assemble around her to catch a closer glimpse of this Italian girl and to exchange a few words. Nicla was pleased with this attention. One day she addressed one of these smiling ladies to let her know that she looked like her uncle. The lady's smile suddenly disappeared and Nicla realized that she made a serious error. She wanted to say her aunt. She apologized for the mistake due to faulty translation from Italian. The lady promptly understood and started to smile again. On another occasion, on her way home, Nicla was telling a work companion about her success in beating minimum piecework requirements. The lady looked at Nicla and told her without hesitation, "You keep quiet about this, especially with your fellow workers. You could stir up some really serious problems with our Union."

Meanwhile, I was not able to find any work. I went from interview to interview, including one with the Connecticut Agricultural Experiment Station. I explained my situation to the Director, gave him all the details of my training and experience, and pleaded to be associated with one of their projects. I was bluntly told that I did not have a Ph.D., and that my Laurea Degree from the University of Florence was not sufficient to be hired even as a field technician. I felt that I was snubbed by the Director and resented this for many years.

The feeling of being jobless in opportunity-rich America was frustrating. After all, I had come to the United States to work and start a productive career. Not to sit on a bench in a public city park, feeding birds and reading classified ads. It was my first encounter with jobless America.

Finally, after several days of looking for "any" type of work, I was able to find a job in a dairy processing plant. My functions consisted of feeding pasteurizing vats with milk from cold storage. This meant taking individual milk containers out of cold chambers, transferring them to a steam room, lifting the containers and dumping their content into the pasteurizers. This operation required much physical effort but it also involved considerable overtime. I soon discovered that I was putting in an average of 13 hours of work a day, seven days a week. The physical stress, however, was so great that I was no longer able to get enough rest during my short nights.

One evening, I felt so tired that I was ready to "throw in the towel." I unveiled my feelings to Nicla and asked her if our American dream should not be considered finished, and if we should not consider returning to Italy. She looked me in the eyes and her answer was a clear, "NO! The American experience has been far too short to give up so soon," she said. "And furthermore, I do not want to go back to Rome with our tails between our legs." She then added, "I would like to give you more time before a decision of this kind. If, after five years, you will not have succeeded, then you are entitled to go back and I will join you." The five years went by, but the decision to return to Italy was never taken. Once more, Nicla was right.

Not long after this conversation, we received a letter from the Di Giorgio Company in San Francisco with an offer to work at their "Sierra Vista Ranch" near Delano, California. There was an opening for an "Assistant Entomologist" which involved a monthly salary of $275 and free housing on the ranch. With no hesitation, the offer was accepted and plans were made to move west to the Golden State. We sold the furniture in storage at Waterbury and with the money earned in the dairy plant and at the Royal factory, we were able to purchase our train tickets and pay for the shipment of our belongings.

Angelo was the first person to receive the news about the Di Giorgios' offer. He met us at Grand Central Station in New York City to wish us a good trip and help us transfer from one train to another. In the confusion, the typewriter Nicla had purchased for me at the Royal factory, was swiftly stolen. Once again, a toll had to be paid for going through New York City.

Crossing the United States by train was an unforgettable experience. The country was so large and varied that there was always something spectacular to admire: the endless plains, the rugged mountains, the harsh deserts. It was a continuous symphony of music and colors, just as in Dvořák's magnificent "New World Symphony." The tunes of this music were constantly in our ears as we traveled west.

Our train, named "El Capitan," was to arrive in Bakersfield, Kern County. However, an earthquake had seriously damaged the rail tracks in the Tehachapi area, and passengers had to be transferred to buses, driven to Barstow and then to Bakersfield. The arrival was scheduled for the late morning of August 15, 1952.

When we stepped off the bus, a loudspeaker was paging our names. We reported to the central office where we were met by a sheriff waiting for us. He was dressed just like we had seen in many western movies: a big revolver hanging at his side, shiny boots with high heels, and a large Stetson hat. The man was one of the two security officers of Sierra Vista Ranch, where we were headed. His name was Hershall, and immediately he appeared to be a kind and helpful man. He was our first pleasant encounter with the Golden West.

After leaving most of our luggage in storage at the station, we were driven north to Delano, California and then to the ranch. The landscape around us was totally different from that of Connecticut. We were in the Central Valley, one of the world's great depressions, structured like a giant cucumber flat between two mountain ranges. The valley floor was covered by vineyards, olive groves, almond orchards, and many cotton and alfalfa fields. All of the land was under irrigation. The temperature outside the car was hot and there were no clouds in the blue sky. We recognized at once the flowering oleanders planted as dividers between the south and northbound lanes of the highway. They were also of Mediterranean origin. Grapes, olive trees, oleanders, and beautiful blue skies. For the first time in America we felt very close to home.

Hershall parked his car at the ranch headquarters, where hundreds of trucks were loading men to go back to the fields after a lunch break. The sight was most impressive. In a cloud of dust there were thousands of workers and a huge fleet of trucks and pickups on the move. I reported to an office where Hershall introduced me to the head of personnel, a man who appeared cold, almost hostile. I had the impression that I was only an "outsider" sent to Sierra Vista by the San Francisco office, possibly without consultation or request from the ranch superintendent. This was sufficient to generate suspicion and the subsequent unfriendly welcome.

Following this introduction, Nicla and I were taken to our house which was not really a house: only a freight car that had been taken off the tracks, stripped of its wheels, and aligned with other cars, like barracks in a military compound. In fact, our compound was called the "Italian Camp." Other than the two of us and Sam Cimino, the local janitor, there were no other Italians in the camp, nor anywhere in sight.

The appearance of the boxcar was depressing. The grass on a small front lawn was all dried out and the upper roots of a lonely mulberry tree had spread around the lawn like a huge spider web. The inside was not any better. There were only two small windows cut on the north side of the car, one in the bedroom and one in the living room. On the south side, a small addition had been built to include a kitchen, a bathroom and a storage area. There was also a little garden in the back yard, covered by weeds except along the fence where Sam Cimino had already planted, for his own personal use, a surprising number of fava beans.

While we were still taking stock of the house, trying to identify what was needed to make it liveable, a man knocked on the door. He was the former tenant. Before leaving the ranch, he had come to see if he could be refunded the money he had spent for installing linoleum and a desert cooler. I looked at the man to see if he was really serious about his request. When I was sure that he expected money, I invited him to take both items away. I firmly told him that I would never spend money on something I did not order. The man argued for a while, but when he understood that he could not get any money, he walked away grumbling and cussing about "these damn foreigners."

Hershall stopped by to see how things were coming along, then he took us to town to spend the night in a local hotel. He also offered to take care of our bulky luggage left at the Bakersfield station, and to drive us to the city for any shopping we might require.

The trunks and crates had arrived safely and it took a Company truck to deliver them to the "Italian camp." What was still needed was a bed, a refrigerator, a gas cooking stove, and a dining set with four chairs. All this was purchased in a furniture store in Bakersfield. The agreement with the salesman was that all these items had to be delivered to the ranch that same evening. Since we did not have a bank account, nor any form of credit, we made our down payment with the five hundred dollars from our emergency fund. We were thus left without cash nor any reserve.

That evening, after the hot sun had disappeared from the horizon, there was only darkness and anxiety in our empty house on the ranch. We decided to sit on the doorstep while waiting for the furniture to arrive. We were aware that with this last move we were three thousand miles farther away from Italy. But we had the apparent security of a job, a boxcar all for ourselves and the comfort of our great love. This was sufficient to stay on the course Nicla and I had charted together. The delivery truck interrupted our thinking. It was time to unload the furniture, put the beds together, and try to get a good night's sleep.

Sleeping in a new bed and a new environment is not always easy. In our particular case, we had additional difficulties. A few hundred yards away there were several locomotives working all night long and making a harsh noise. They assembled and moved around long lines of freight cars loaded with fruit going to the East. Fortunately, our boxcar could no longer be moved. It had no wheels. With this reassuring feeling of stability, we smiled and kissed each other goodnight. We fell sound asleep in our new and unusual house, under a California sky full of twinkling stars.

The next morning I reported to work. I met "Doc" Osner, my new boss, as he was stepping out from the bunkhouse where managers, foremen, and top office personnel had their meals. George Osner appeared old, fragile and shy. He was a small, lean man wearing gold-rimmed spectacles. His eyes suggested a high level of intelligence. He was, in fact, a well-educated gentleman with a Ph.D. in plant pathology from Cornell University. For health reasons, Doc Osner had moved from the state of New

York to California soon after graduation. He had then joined the Di Giorgio Company in the early years of its West Coast operations.

George, as he was commonly called, was highly respected for his seniority, knowledge and experience. Although his Company title was "Entomologist," George was actually responsible for all activities requiring scientific or technical training. He was responsible for the control of diseases, insects, rodents, birds, and weeds. He also supervised the functioning of water wells on the ranch and maintained close monitoring of water supply and management. Furthermore, he was on the board of the local Irrigation District. All this made him a perfect boss, with only one exception: he was extremely shy and did not easily communicate with the people working under him. When I introduced myself, I saw in him the same suspicion I had recognized in the head of personnel. Again, I was an outsider and George most likely had never requested my services.

For nearly four years George treated me with sparing words and always at a respectable distance. In fact, I was not even given office space or a simple desk to write my reports or keep my records. Instead, I was left "outdoors," practically assigned to work under his three field foremen. These were Al, jack-of- all-trades, capable of doing all sorts of chores, but extremely allergic to hard work; Slick, manager of spraying operations and a big talker; and Elby, the nicest of the three, responsible for night dusting operations. These men had been at Sierra Vista for many years. They had come either from Oklahoma, Arkansas or Tennessee, and they had worked their way up through the ranks from common laborers to foremen. Having reached the "top," they felt entitled to certain privileges. These included driving around in Company pickups for conducting their private business, spending many hours of Company time drinking coffee at the local cafeteria, or playing cards during "long" lunch hours.

My first job was to hoe vineyards to control morning glories. This came under Slick's supervision. He drove his crew to the edge of a vineyard, assigned each man to a row, handed him a hoe, and quickly disappeared with his pickup to take care of some undetermined business. He later returned in time to move his crew to the next vineyard and start the cycle all over again. It was extremely hot and humid in the vineyards. Weeds were knee-high between the vines and walking through them on the rough terrain was very tiring. Occasionally, irrigation water was standing at the end of the block, causing me to sink deep into the mud. I forced myself to continue walking and hoeing, even though I could not relate this work to that of an "entomologist."

Another of my early jobs was to drive a sulphur rig at night to control powdery mildew disease. This work came under Elby's supervision. It involved loading sulphur dust into the hopper of a dusting machine and starting its noisy blower while entering a vineyard. The challenge was to drive an old model "A" in the dark and at the same speed as other rigs running in nearby rows, making sure that at the end of the row the proper turn was taken in synchronization with the other drivers. For this operation it was necessary to wear goggles to avoid sulphur burns to the eyes. However, due to the humidity in the air and perspiration, the goggles always fogged, making the driving difficult. This form of practical experience cost me some sleepless nights. Regardless of how long I showered, sulphur particles remained in my eyes, causing great discomfort when I tried to go to sleep.

My third early experience at Sierra Vista Ranch was to assist in the connecting of long metal pipelines to deliver water from a well to an underground distribution system. This work was under Al's direction. He was the handyman who managed the operation and bossed all others. "God damn, Louis, get me a hammer and a long screwdriver," cursed Al without looking at me, but chewing a little harder on the cigar constantly stuck in one side of his mouth. I immediately obliged, running to the tool box on his pickup and bringing back the needed hammer and long screwdriver.

At times, I was directed to harvest oranges, prune olive trees, paint vines with zinc sulphate, and haul dirt to fill holes in Company roads. This was the type of practical experience I received as a "green" assistant entomologist, waiting for something better to come along.

Shortly after our arrival, Nicla was hired to pack grapes. She was one of the many women doing this work at the packing house, not far from our boxcar. This work consisted of clipping defective berries from grape clusters, and tightly packing these bunches in shipping boxes. The fruit was then refrigerated, fumigated and loaded on trucks or trains for shipment to the market.

To perform this work, Nicla had to stand on her feet eight to ten hours a day. However, she mastered this new job as quickly as those in Connecticut. She could pack five boxes an hour, while the average was three to four. Nicla was praised for being someone who would waste no time talking to others. In fact, being not yet fluent in English, she could avoid the conversation and easily focus on defective berries and tightly packed clusters. In no time, however, the sound of other women talking around the packing tables, and the need to answer many of their questions, forced her to speak and quickly refine the new language.

By the end of September we received a letter from mother Gina announcing a detour through California on the way back from Argentina, where she and father Vittorio were on an official visit. Their arrival in Los Angeles was scheduled for early October. We were happy about this news, but also somewhat concerned for we did not have a car to meet them, nor a decent house to host them.

A special effort was immediately directed at decorating the interior of our boxcar. I decided to hang new wall paper, something I had never done before. I purchased many rolls of paper, glue and brushes. I borrowed a ladder from one of my neighbors, and I started my work with enthusiasm and great expectations. Everything proceeded well, as long as the paper was glued to the walls. I could keep the joints straight without making serious mistakes. The problem started when the paper had to be glued to the ceiling.

On a Saturday afternoon, while Nicla was working at the packing house, I tried hanging the paper on the living room ceiling. I started in one corner and proceeded with the entire roll to the opposite side. When I got there and turned around, all I could see was the other end of the roll flat on the floor. I quickly ran back to pull it up, but then it was the other end of the paper that came down. I soon gave up in frustration and waited for Nicla to come to my rescue. With her help, and with the right amount of glue, I was able to complete the "Saturday afternoon project" very late into the night.

In the days that followed we continued with our decorating endeavors. Crisp white curtains were placed on the windows, and a large yellow drape, with a very light fern design, was hung on the far end wall of the living room. This gave the impression that the room continued behind the curtain. The trunk containing our silverware was opened, and after much cleaning, elegant artifacts were strategically displayed all over the room. Some extra chairs and a sofa were borrowed to fill part of the empty space. In a matter of weeks the place looked incredibly cozy, elegant, and unusually "rich."

Our transportation problem was easily resolved by informing Roy Boone, the ranch superintendent, about the expected visit. He called the San Francisco office, which immediately authorized him to place a car and a driver at the disposal of Professor Ronchi and his wife. Mr. George Solari, a vice-president of Bank of America responsible for International Activities, with whom Nicla's father had business contacts, had already informed J.S. Di Giorgio, the President and Chairman of the Board, about the visit. Through these high-level contacts, a large Cadillac and a driver, the ranch sheriff Leon Ragsdale, were placed at our disposal to go to Los Angeles.

Meeting Nicla's parents at the airport was a true joy. They had followed our progress in America with great anxiety and they wanted to see with their own eyes what was really going on. Nicla's father, Vittorio, had already written numerous letters to banks and other institutions in the United States trying to help pave the rough path we had taken. Also mother Gina had been concerned, but, as usual, she was able to mask her anxiety. It was wonderful seeing them in California and traveling with them through Los Angeles to Santa Monica. After an overnight in a motel near the ocean, we went back to Delano. We had beautiful fall weather, and Highway 99 was full of speeding cars. The gas stations bustled with customers. Gina watched all this in fascination, and at one point she could not resist saying "Toio, i se' fora de modo!" In her dialect from Friuli this meant: "Vittorio, they are really out of proportion." In fact, to anyone coming from Europe or South America, it was a unique show to watch California motorists in full motion.

The Sierra Vista's boxcar was not a disappointment to Nicla 's parents. They liked it. They saw the good side of the coin and were impressed with the progress we had already made.

Also impressive to Vittorio were the efficient ranch operations, the well cultivated vineyards, the good quality of fruit produced, and, above all, the cotton harvesters in action. After a few days' stay on the ranch, Vittorio and I left for San Francisco. Leon Ragsdale drove us again in Mr. Boone's Cadillac. It was a nice trip, which provided an opportunity to see more of the Central Valley and its outstanding agriculture. In San Francisco, we made two visits. One was with Mr. George Solari, who greatly helped us in finding work in California and also wished us full success in our "second Italy." The other was with Mr.Robert Di Giorgio, Vice President of the Di Giorgio Fruit Company and member of the Board of Directors of Bank of America. It was useful to meet both of these important men.

After one week Nicla's parents returned to Italy satisfied with what they had seen. The two young "immigrants" were doing fine. But the very best was yet to happen.

7

A California Melting Pot

The land has a common cast of characters. Their biographies, their resources and destinies are so closely bound together that each is ineradicably woven into the fabric of the whole.

—Irving Stone, 1956

ierra Vista Ranch was a microcosm of immigrants brought together from many parts of the world by a single common denominator: the growing of grapevines.

Joseph Di Giorgio, the owner and founder of the Di Giorgio Fruit Corporation, was an immigrant himself. He came to the United States in 1889 from the small town of Cefalu', not far from Palermo, in Sicily. He emigrated to

America when he was not yet 15 years old. Joseph 's father had sent him to New York with a cargo of lemons produced in the family orchards and other groves scattered in the Cefalu's countryside. "Peppino" worked first with a fruit importer and jobber at $8 a week. A few years later, Joseph was busy in the streets of Baltimore selling lemons and vegetables with a small pushcart. This happened at the time when most fruit and other agricultural products were still imported by boat from Italy or other foreign countries. Joseph was a shrewd salesman who knew his fruit and his business quite well. Occasionally, he procured his merchandise by going directly to the piers to meet freight boats as they arrived. He always kept abreast of what was going on at the docks and what kinds of cargos were being delivered.

One day young Joseph was told that a cargo of lemons had just arrived from Sicily. He quickly went aboard to meet the captain. "Is it true that you are carrying lemons to New York City?" he asked with an incredulous expression. "Don't you know that the city is flooded with Florida lemons? You better be prepared to take your cargo back to Palermo," insisted Joseph. The captain was obviously alarmed. He explained that he had to load other commodities in New York City for the return voyage. However, he would be prepared to reduce his price considerably if someone wanted to buy his lemons.

Joseph was quick to make an offer many times lower than the originally requested price. The captain accepted this offer and Joseph suddenly remembered he had no cash to pay for what he had just purchased. With a youthful and innocent smile he added that he needed a few hours before closing the transaction. He went ashore, walked into a nearby bank, and asked to see the manager. He was able to convince this man that he had a "terrific bargain" on his hands, for which he

Mr. Joseph Di Giorgio. At 19 an immigrant from Italy. At 72 the largest
grape, plum and pear grower in the world.

needed a quick loan. Joseph had no collateral to offer, only a very honest look. This, apparently, was sufficient to convince the chancy manager, borrow the money, buy the cargo, clear a profit, and in a short time, return the loan plus interest to the bank.

At age 21, Joe became director of the Monumental Trust Company, a bank in Baltimore, which was very popular with Italian immigrants. He then acquired his first corporate enterprise: The Monumental Trading Company. This was the beginning of a fruit marketing enterprise that saw Joseph Di Giorgio move into the banana importing business in successful competition with United Fruit and other large companies. It was a rough battle against these giant competitors. Joe Di Giorgio admitted later that during those years he "fought United's $300 million with nothing but my good-looking brown eyes and curly hair." He had great courage and a clear vision of ways to expand his business. Soon, he created a number of companies to handle fruit auctions in Baltimore, New York and other large cities on the Eastern Seaboard. These auctions allowed perishable fruit to reach retailers and consumers in the shortest possible time and at the best level of maturity.

The auction innovation led to further expansion of activities. Joseph purchased several fruit shipping companies and, later on, he proceeded with the acquisition of land in California and Florida to produce his own fruit. In this way he created a diversified company that was solid, well managed and highly competitive. Di Giorgio's slogan, "Oh, yes, we grow the best!" clearly defined Di Giorgio Fruit's ability to provide high quality fruit for highly competitive markets.

Joseph Di Giorgio is an outstanding example of an Italian immigrant who contributed to the improvement of life in California and elsewhere in America.

In contrast with Joseph Di Giorgio, there was another Sicilian immigrant at Sierra Vista. Sam Cimino was the same age as Joseph and also came from Cefalu'. He was the only Italian living in the "Italian camp" before we arrived. An extremely nice man, Sam resembled a Roman emperor, with a very pronounced nose, an open, forceful smile, and short white hair crowning a large forehead. Instead of riding a two-wheeled chariot, as he deserved to complement his striking appearance, old Sam moved around the camp pushing a two-wheeled cart in which he collected all sort of junk. He had a fine memory, one that would have served a highly educated librarian. From his extremely crowded storage, Sam could quickly retrieve any object that had been thrown away years before, which he had saved and kept well preserved.

Sam liked children and loved to produce his own wine. But he had no luck. Throughout his life, he accumulated little fortunes that he lost as fast as he could make them. At one time he operated a large saloon in Colorado, which someone burned to the ground. He had no insurance, no money to rebuild, and no friends to help him out. Sam was terribly alone in a country so big and so difficult to understand, where his only faithful companion was his own misfortune.

Sam clearly lived in a world of his own. He also spoke a language that only he and his wife could understand. It was not English, not Italian, and not even Sicilian. It was a mixture of all three, plus what Sam was capable of inventing on his own. It was almost like Etruscan, the extinct language of Etruria, not known to be related to any other language. It was a challenge for me and others to comprehend what Sam was saying. After a while, however, I was able to interpret his mysterious, unwritten language. To achieve this, I pieced together sounds and logic. After all, I had studied Latin and ancient Greek. I knew German, French, Spanish, and Italian. I also had had many Sicilian friends at the military school in

Naples, and my father was a musician. I could deal with languages, dialects, jargon, and sounds of any kind. I was also equipped to deal with logic. Philosophy was one of my preferred subjects in high school.

When Sam repeatedly referred to "cappucci cans," no one understood what he was talking about. After some time, I found the correct interpretation. "Sam intends to refer to "garbage cans," I explained to Nicla and to some skeptical friends. "This is because Sam cannot differentiate between the phonetics of garbage and cabbage, and because in Sicily there are some cabbages called cappucci. Sam must have linked the word garbage to "cabbage," cabbage to "cavoli"" and cavoli to "cappucci." In the end, he came out with his "cappucci cans." Sam and I were both right.

Sam 's destiny and achievements were at the opposite end of the spectrum from those of Joseph Di Giorgio. In his mid-seventies Sam was still working for hourly wages as a janitor in the Italian camp. He never made it to the top. Instead, he had a hard time surviving at the bottom. In fact, he was the despair of the chief of personnel, who openly disliked Sam and tried to fire him at every possible occasion. But Joseph Di Giorgio was always present to protect Sam from being fired. Just a phone call from Joe was sufficient to reinstate Sam in his old job. After all, Sam and Joe were both good Sicilians, both were immigrants from Cefalu', and both had encountered different opportunities in their adopted country. The only difference between the two had been their very different fate. One had become a successful businessman and a generous philanthropist. The other had remained an unsuccessful Roman emperor with an exceptional librarian's mind.

A third Italian immigrant, whose fortune and achievements fell somewhere between those of Joe and Sam, was Tony Perelli-Minetti. He no longer lived at Sierra Vista when we arrived. He had already moved to Delano after succeeding in building himself a wonderful house and a very large winery. Tony had been a wine processing consultant for the Di Giorgio Company at the time when Sierra Vista Ranch had its own winery.

Tony had lived a long and adventurous life in California and Mexico. He was born in Barletta, Apulia, in 1882 to a family of winemakers. He graduated from the school of Viticulture and Enology of Conegliano, where Nicla's father had also studied and taught for a few years. When father Vittorio visited us at Sierra Vista, he also met Tony. The two enjoyed talking about their old school. Tony assured Nicla's father that he and his wife would look closely after the two of us, a promise they maintained until they died.

There were many stories at Sierra Vista about Tony Perelli Minetti. One of these, repeated many times over by "Slick," my field supervisor, was about the construction of Tony's house. Apparently, Tony had complained to Joseph Di Giorgio about not having proper lodging on the ranch. He then received from Joseph the agreement to build a house for his own use. Tony built the house, but later it turned out that the house (financed with Company funds) was standing on one of Tony's lots.

Another story about Tony was how he made money during prohibition. He had just purchased a small winery in Ukiah, shortly before the new law was enacted on January 20, 1920. While most other wineries were forced out of business, Tony managed the adverse situation very well. He simply placed grape juice concentrates in gallon containers on which he applied a large, beautifully lithographed label. This clearly stated: "CAUTION! When diluted, do not keep in a warm place because it will ferment!" The marketing of Tony's product (at $ 2.50 a gallon) was an unbelievable success throughout thirsty America.

After repeal, Tony started his own wine company, and with his family he operated the California Wine Association. His large winery in Delano and his wine business were top-rated in the state. Recognized as the dean of California winemakers, Tony died in an auto accident at the age of 95. He was the driver of the car.

A special type of immigrant in the Sierra Vista microcosm was Benny, the Chinese cook. He had worked on the ranch for as long as anyone could remember. He had a wife and many children somewhere in China, but he had never gone back to see them since his arrival in California forty years before.

Benny had no car, nor desire to leave the ranch. He was known to save every penny and to be "rich," according to those who lived in the bunkhouse. One of the reasons Benny did not go back to visit his family in China was that he had no legal immigration status in the US. The story was that Bennie, serving as a cook on a Chinese merchant marine vessel, entered the San Francisco Bay in a very unusual way. He jumped overboard and swam ashore. This long, cold swim had never been forgotten by Bennie. He had good reasons not to repeat this type of natatorial experience.

Marcel Auger was probably the most unique immigrant we encountered at Sierra Vista. As his name suggests, he was French, but from Canada. Marcel grew up in the cold province of Quebec where, during his early life, he disliked the snow and the cold weather. During this time he only had one dream: to live in Tahiti or on some other little island in the Pacific, where he could enjoy warm sea breezes and do some sailing on the side. He considered warm and sunny California only a second choice. At a certain point in life, Marcel had no more hesitations. He had to emigrate from Canada. He closed his photography business, said good-bye to his parents, kissed his gracious girlfriend Suzanne, and headed south with no uncertainty or regrets.

Marcel's target was Hollywood and his specific goal was to do photography for some movie studios. He tried his best, but apparently no one appreciated his talents. His savings did not last very long and Marcel had to find work outside of Hollywood and far away from photography.

He started picking lemons with a group of Mexican "braceros" in Ventura county. The surroundings were nice, the fruit was beautiful to touch and to smell, the company of the Mexican workers was cheerful, but the income from piecemeal work was very disappointing. Marcel soon realized that he had neither the skill nor the "bracero" speed required to harvest a crop before it deteriorated on a tree. He had to find a more appropriate line of work.

One day Marcel was told that in the hot Central Valley there were large fruit companies that could always accommodate one more man in their large and diversified operations. For a daring French Canadian coming from a cold province such as Quebec, the heat of the Central Valley was not a challenge: it was heaven. And so, Marcel migrated to Di Giorgio Farms, near Bakersfield, where he was hired as a time keeper. He liked the place and decided to share it with Suzie. He flew back to Canada, married her, and quickly returned to "The Farms." Their further migration, some years later, was only a few miles north to Sierra Vista Ranch, where Marcel worked in the office of the local packing house. This was far from Hollywood, but Marcel was just as happy, because the weather was hot, and from his air-conditioned office he could easily observe most of the women packing grapes, as if they were on stage for him. Oh, yes, Marcel also liked women, especially if they were young, well shaped, with dark, shiny hair, and from far away, exotic places. From his observation point he could not fail to note that in the middle of the busy packing lines there was a "new arrival" corresponding to his taste and requirements. This "new arrival" was Nicla. Marcel wanted to find out more about Italy and this Italian immigrant. He drove to our camp in his Ford coupe, accompanied by his wife Suzie. It was the beginning of a long-lasting friendship.

We were never able to determine what brought Ted and Madeleine Dirkzwager to Sierra Vista Ranch. They were both from the Netherlands, had spent many years in Indonesia, and had been prisoners of the Japanese during the war. They had suffered a great deal in the concentration camps. Madeleine, an elementary school teacher, was ten to fifteen years older than Ted. Not a beautiful woman, she had great charm and displayed a European cultural refinement. Ted was a graduate of the University of Agriculture in Wageningen and had experience with tropical crops. His interests, however, were in the social and political sciences. He loved to argue with anyone who had the patience to listen. The only person Ted did not wish to argue with was Madeleine. He was her respectful servant, barman, cook, driver, lover, and all the rest. The two were good company and they soon become attracted to us and to Marcel and Suzie. A little at a time, we discovered that the French, Italians and Dutch were forming a cultural European Common Market within the boundaries of an incredible California melting pot.

There was another "European" who also had access to our group. This was Joe Lopes, whose parents had emigrated to America from the Azore Islands. He was actually a second generation Portuguese American, but Joe always felt like a recent immigrant, since he had been transferred to Sierra Vista from another Di Giorgio farm in Marysville. As such, he was also looked upon with suspicion. Like me, he was definitely an outsider.

Joe had a good tenor voice. To attract people to his singing performances, his name was quickly changed to

"Giuseppe." This made him automatically part of our group, even though we always placed him at a different artistic level from Caruso, Gigli or Pavarotti.

Joe worked as assistant office manager. He was married to Marian, a nice looking, red-headed school teacher with great talent in the arts and art appreciation. Together they formed a very nice couple. They, too, were to remain friends for many years.

The microcosm of immigrants at Sierra Vista also included other ethnic groups working on the ranch. There were essentially four groups: the Japanese, the Filipinos, the Mexicans and the so-called "whites." The first three groups lived in their respective camps run by second generation Americans of either Japanese, Filipino or Mexican descent. The "whites" were, instead, either lodged in a bunkhouse, or lived in Delano or nearby towns.

The Japanese were all very old. Although it was difficult to tell their age, my impression was that they were well into their seventies. They were very quiet people and did not mix with others. They were first-class workers. The best fruit was, in fact, packed in the field by Japanese crews. Apparently, the palms of their hands did not perspire. This allowed the bloom of the grape berries to remain intact, something much appreciated when selling grapes to retail stores.

Filipinos are cheerful people. They had only two major problems: they liked to gamble and they loved blonde women, especially those across the tracks on Delano's west side. The Filipinos also liked big cars, which they would buy and share in large groups. Cockfights, illegal in the state of California, were regularly organized in their camp on weekends, and everyone knew it, including the Delano police. It often happened that a man who had worked hard all week long was ready to go to town on a Saturday afternoon. When he stopped for a moment to watch the ongoing cockfight,

Dr. George A. Osner, my new boss at Sierra Vista.

Japanese worker pruning a Thompson Seedless vine.

rather than resisting the temptation of gambling, he had to bet all of his weekly salary on one of the fighting roosters. He picked the wrong bird and lost all of his money. Quietly, as if nothing had happened, the man went back to his barrack, slowly undressed from his city clothes and patiently prepared for another week of hard work. The blonde women on the other side of the tracks also had to wait for another week to go by.

Mexican workers had the reputation of being lazy. This was not the case for the Mexicans at Sierra Vista. In fact, Mexican crews on the ranch were used for the most tiring work, such as stripping vines after the best fruit had been harvested. The grapes from stripping went to the winery where they were fermented into alcohol.

For the stripping, a bulk container on wheels, called a "gondola," was slowly pulled by a tractor through the vineyard. A crew of men harvested the grape clusters in buckets or boxes from nearby rows, dumping their contents into the moving gondola. This work was usually contracted to individual crews on a piecemeal basis. The more fruit these crews were able to harvest, the more money they would make and share. It was a sight to watch how fast these Mexican workers could fill one gondola after another. They had the greatest stamina and speed, and deserved to the last cent the good money they could make off their strenuous work.

The so-called "whites" were a very heterogeneous group of people. They could essentially be divided in two subgroups: residents and migrants. The first group was mostly composed of "Okies," people from Oklahoma, Arkansas and Tennessee. They were also immigrants in their own right, having left their Southeastern states during the depression years, attracted by better jobs in California. John Steinbeck, in his book The Grapes of Wrath, described this situation and these people. After much moving around, these workers were able to settle in the farms of the Central Valley, where steady work was available almost year-round. They became tractor and truck drivers, store keepers, plumbers, mechanics, and so on. They specialized in their jobs and soon became the core of California's work force.

The second group was mainly formed by hoboes or other vagrant people. These men never wanted to stay in one place. They had to travel, usually in groups of two, using freight cars to move at no cost from one point to another. They worked sufficient days at any single location to get enough money to continue this endless odyssey. When one of these men was asked why he was quitting so soon after starting his work, the answer was a clearly surprised, "Don't you know that quitting is contagious?" Evidently, his travel companion was already on the road and the man had to join him without further delay. Other workers in the same group were men running away from the police, from their families, or from society in general. At the lowest level were the old "winos," those working only for a bottle of sweet wine with a high alcohol content and a low price, a wine especially made for these derelicts by a rich and complaisant industry. Understandably, this branch of the work force was not always dependable.

In one way or another, even these people could fit under the "immigrant" label. At different times and for different reasons this varied human surf would break upon the Sierra Vista shores looking for the calm waters of this protected port. Its beacon would guide a few to safety. But, more often, the multitude of shipwrecked persons could never make it.

Sierra Vista Ranch was located six miles east of the city of Delano. The town itself, like many others in the Central Valley, was divided in two separate sections by the railroad and Highway 99. Both of these also run north to south. Soils, business and people seemed to be divided longitudinally. On the east side were the best, deeper soils, with the greatest fertility, easiest to irrigate and cultivate. Most of the best vineyards were planted on this side. On the east side was also the town's "Main Street," with all the best shops, the main drugstore, the banks, the post office, and the only movie theater. The nicer homes were on this side as well, so that the police could better keep a watchful eye on them. On the west side were the low-income housing, most of the repair shops and storehouses, the bars and, of course, the blonde women practicing the oldest profession in the world. Soils on the west side were not as good as those on the east. They were more difficult to work, having a high clay content and salinity problems. The field crops, such as cotton or alfalfa were grown on this side. This type of urban, agricultural and social arrangement, with a few exceptions, seemed to run the length of the Central Valley, all the way from Bakersfield to Sacramento.

Delano was a typical Central Valley town. Its main income was derived from the payrolls of surrounding ranches growing table grapes. In addition to the Di Giorgio Company, there were many "Slavonians" and Armenians who owned large properties in this area. Only a few wineries specialized in the production of distillates or of bulk wines.

Medical services in Delano also appeared to be divided in two sections, like the rest of the town. Within the same medical office, one of the doctors dealt with Mexicans, Filipinos, and other low-income patients. The other doctor, took care instead of the rich clientele, including ranchers, white collar workers or wealthy business people. Our friend Chuck Keagy took care of the first group, which included our family as well. He was a special kind of person and doctor: a unique combination of a humanitarian and a Renaissance man. He could always find time for helping people and for displaying a wide spectrum of knowledge and cultural interests.

Passenger trains no longer stopped in Delano, as the town was too small to afford a regular station. Instead, there was Greyhound bus service connecting with other cities. Taxi service was very limited and often unreliable.

Sierra Vista Ranch took its name from the view that was once possible of the Sierra Nevada mountains. In recent years smog and other air pollutants have rendered this "vista" impossible.

The ranch consisted of over 4,700 acres of land divided between Kern and Tulare counties. Many deep wells had been drilled in strategic places to provide water for irrigation and domestic use. The Central Valley Project, started in 1935, added an additional source of irrigation water, through the Kern-Friant Canal, which crossed the ranch north to south.

The vineyards, usually laid out in solid blocks of 10, 20, 40, and 80 acres, were planted with the most popular table grape varieties. Fruit produced at Sierra Vista was regarded as being some of the best in the world.

As for infrastructures, the ranch had a good-sized office building, an old packing house, various labor camps, a bunkhouse, and what was called the "foremen road." This consisted of a string of cottages assigned to key ranch personnel. Mr. Roy Boone, the ranch superintendent, was entitled to a very large house surrounded by a mature park, a swimming pool, and, in one corner, a small chalet hidden by palms and other thick vegetation. It was here, that Marcel and Suzie had carved out for themselves a piece of Tahiti in the heart of California.

In October of 1952, Nicla started experiencing signs of an incipient pregnancy. We had to find a doctor. After much inquiring, we decided on Dr. "T," considered by most people on the ranch "the best doctor in town." Both Nicla and I were excited about this important event. It was Katherine, Leon Ragsdale's wife, who took Nicla in her car to the doctor's office for the first visit. Nicla's mother also went along. Everything appeared normal and Nicla continued packing grapes with only an increased appetite for oranges and polenta. After one month, another visit took place and the results remained the same. Thirty days later, Dr. "T" started worrying because Nicla had not yet felt the baby kick. After consulting with his head nurse, he came out from his laboratory with a grim look. He asked Nicla to bring me with her to his office on the following day. He had something important to communicate.

The next day Nicla and I reported together to the doctor's office. It was then that Dr. "T," without hesitation, announced: "I must inform you that your wife is not pregnant." I was caught by surprise and asked him to repeat what he had just said. I was not an expert in pregnancies, but I knew that Nicla had gained weight, that her tummy had grown rather large, and that she was craving large amounts of oranges and of polenta. But Dr. "T" was sure of himself and of his diagnosis. He simply added that Nicla might have a tumor. "Do not worry," the doctor kept saying. "The tumor can be easily removed." The following night was full of tears, anxiety and many unanswered questions. "How could the doctor be so sure? What kind of tests did he run to confirm his diagnosis? What will happen if he was right? Where could the money be found to pay for surgery of this kind?" All these and more thoughts kept us tossing and turning in bed until the pale light of the new day came through the windows of the boxcar.

After a good cup of coffee, we decided to go see the Perelli-Minetti's to have their advice on the matter. When Tony found out who the doctor was, he became angry. "That

Expecting mother and a kiss to last for life.

man does not know what he is talking about. He is an incompetent person and he should not be allowed to practice in Delano. You should go immediately to see a good gynecologist. We can provide you with a name and address in Los Angeles." These words had the effect of lessening most of our worry. But some concern still remained in our minds.

It was not until New Year's Eve that the last apprehension completely vanished. We had organized a small party for a few friends, including a good Italian dinner, champagne and even some dancing. At one point, Nicla felt the baby move. It was no illusion, she had really felt some kicking. When the party was over and we went to bed, there was again some unmistakable movement. The unborn child was politely but firmly trying to communicate, "Please, no longer worry about me!"

To make sure, we decided to take the Greyhound bus to Los Angeles and see the gynecologist. This was a very nice man who inspired immediate confidence. He looked at Nicla, asked a few questions and then started to smile. "Lady, you have nothing to be alarmed about. You look to me as pregnant as any woman could ever be." And his reassuring statement was followed by a very detailed visit. There was no doubt: the baby was to be expected in mid-May. We were relieved and happy. Our bus trip back to Delano seemed as comfortable and pleasant as if we had a fancy limousine all to ourselves.

The following spring, I was assigned a pickup truck, probably the oldest and most run-down on the ranch. But I loved it because with it I acquired my mobility and no longer had to depend on Al, Slick and Elby for my transportation. I needed this little truck for conducting field surveys of pests and diseases. During the summer, I was assisted in this work by a crew of high school students. Walking for nine or ten hours in the rows of tall vineyards was not a pleasant job.

Temperatures, in the absence of ventilation and in full sun, were as high as 120 degrees Fahrenheit. Humidity was also high, due to irrigation water and abundant grass vegetation. We were given salt tablets and plenty of drinking water. Occasionally, however, one of my helpers had to be rushed to the nurse at headquarters for heat prostration.

I had a sun-burnt face, since my African-type sun helmet was not sufficient to protect my face from heavy tanning. However, it was useful for "air-conditioning" my brain. I frequently immersed my head in the water flowing from irrigation pipes, and then promptly covered it up with the helmet. The subsequent evaporation process worked quite well, like a desert cooler.

Soon I devised a survey method to secure reliable and timely information on pest and disease outbreaks. This called for counts and observations in the same vineyard within a seven-day period. Before quitting in the evening, I reported to Doc Osner my daily findings and he instructed the dusting crew to intervene with control measures that night. Everyone appeared satisfied with my pest detection system, but no one openly recognized its value. My method prevented the loss of valuable fruit and the unnecessary use of pesticides.

Doc Osner was a very reserved man who spent no time teaching or discussing technical matters. However, he allowed me to become a member of the Southern California Entomological Club so that I could attend their meetings in Riverside. This was an opportunity to meet researchers from the University or private industry interested in new products and technology. Other valuable sources of information were the two Farm Advisors from Kern County (A.N. Kasimatis) and Tulare County (F. Jensen). Both were experienced viticulturists and both became good friends. Through these contacts I was able to establish a good liaison with the

Departments of Plant Pathology and Entomology of the University of California at Davis.

Thanks to the friendship of Joe and Marian Lopes and of Marcel and Suzie Auger, our life on the ranch was becoming increasingly enjoyable. Ski trips to the Sequoia National Park were organized with Joe in the winter and early spring. During the warm season, most weekends were spent at Marcel and Suzie's cottage, where the ranch superintendent's swimming pool was used to cool off and have fun.

Time was passing quickly and Nicla was getting increasingly round. She had found a good gynecologist in Dr. Hall Ramirez, who practiced in Bakersfield. Suzie would drive Nicla to his office at regular intervals. On these trips they were speaking to each other in a mixture of French and Italian, with only occasional English. There were no language barriers between the two, nor lack of subjects for their conversations. They had fun discovering each other and comparing their different backgrounds and cultures.

Sam Cimino and his wife felt that Nicla's pregnancy was a matter of their own personal concern. They were good neighbors and frequently visited us in the boxcar to provide advice, special food, or to return our laundry that Mrs. Cimino had washed for Nicla free of charge. The conversation always centered on the baby to be born. According to Sam, the position of the baby shown by Nicla's pointed stomach was a sure indication of a baby boy. He was so convinced of this that he made a bet with me. Our bet was a bottle of "good" wine. It must be said that Sam was producing his own home-made wine using the culls of grapes that he procured at the packing house or elsewhere. He produced and maintained this wine in a type of grotto that he had constructed by excavating beneath the center of his boxcar. But either from the high temperature or the primitive technology (or both), his wine tasted no better than pure vinegar. Thus it was agreed that the bottle of "good" wine had to come not from his cellar, but from a reputable store.

In the early morning of May 16, 1953, Nicla and I took the bus to Bakersfield. It was time to induce the baby's birth. We went directly to the Mercy hospital only to discover that there was no room for Nicla. The hospital, damaged a year earlier by an earthquake, had no facilities for labor induction cases. Accordingly, Nicla was left unattended in a bed placed in a busy corridor. Dr. Ramirez, informed about this situation, recommended transferring her to a small private hospital in another section of the city.

This was done right away and finally Nicla could have a room with the privacy she deserved. Labor was induced in the late morning and I was given the job of watching her to prevent her from getting up. My watch lasted fourteen hours. Throughout this time Nicla appeared drowsy and in a world of her own. I sat patiently holding her hand, and trying to communicate something I can no longer remember. It was my first experience of being a father, and I did not know what was going on in that hospital room and in Nicla's body. Finally, the nurses came in and took her to the delivery room. I was left all alone, waiting with great anxiety and pacing up and down the incredibly shiny hospital floor.

Suddenly, Hall Ramirez, who had been called in from a party he was attending, appeared through the hospital door wearing his white tuxedo, no necktie and holding in his arms a healthy- looking baby girl. Victoria Alexandra, our first daughter, was born. I looked closely at her and noticed that she was smiling. Yes, she was aware she had contributed to my victory in the wine bet with Sam Cimino.

Hall was kind enough to take me to the Greyhound station to catch the first bus to Delano from where I was able to find a taxi to drive me to the ranch. The night was nearly over and some early morning light had already appeared in the sky. I walked to the nearby packing house and asked the night watchman if I could use his telephone. It was time to wake Marcel and Suzie and announce to them and the entire world this important event.

Life in a boxcar was an experience that cannot be easily forgotten. From April to November, dust was always in the air, due to lack of rain and heavy traffic of trucks and tractors in nearby fields and unpaved roads. The dust penetrated the boxcar through unsealed windows and doors, leaving a heavy coat on everything and everywhere. We did not own a vacuum cleaner and we had to fight a constant battle to keep the house clean. Furthermore, we were without a back door that could be shut during sand storms or cold winter nights. The head of personnel, who was responsible for house maintenance and repairs, did not want to install a regular door. In his opinion, the existing screen was more than sufficient. He did not want to spend extra dollars on that house. Fortunately, Victoria was a strong baby and she could easily overcome the many colds she was catching in her "over-ventilated" house. Our request for better housing was ignored during the entire stay at Sierra Vista

With a new baby in the family it was also necessary to buy a car. This was especially needed to bring Victoria to the doctor whenever necessary, and also to secure our independent mobility. Delano was not the best town in the world to shop for a used automobile, but with the assistance of Joe Lopes (and a little luck) we were able to find a blue 1950 Ford coupe that met our requirements.

The newly acquired mobility made life much easier. It was now possible to become closer to Hall and Charlotte Ramirez in Bakersfield, to visit more frequently with the

Sun helmet and an old truck. Ready to walk the vineyards.

The boxcar in the Italian camp. White curtains and green geraniums.

Perelli-Minetti's, and to play a more active role in our newly
established "European Common Market."

The car also allowed us to take our first vacation in
America. Thanks to the Perelli-Minetti's generosity, their
beautiful villa on Balboa Island near Newport Beach,was
made available to us for a ten-day period, right after
Christmas of 1954. We did not need to worry about
groceries: there was an ample supply of food and wine in the
refrigerators and in the cellar. The name of this beautiful
villa, located in the most fashionable section of Balboa, was
"La Huerta." In Spanish this means "The Orchard." Tony
was the only person in this very exclusive neighborhood who
had enough land to grow fruit trees in his backyard.
Considering the high value of real estate on the artificially-
created island, Tony's Huerta was probably the most
expensive orchard in the world.

In spite of substantial improvements, our life on the ranch
still remained difficult. We were probably experiencing the
pain other immigrants have felt before us: an undefined
mixture of isolation, frustration, bitterness, and anxiety.
While we were trying our best to acquire new habits and
customs to swiftly blend into the adopted country, we had
the feeling that we were far away from all others. It was a
distance that could not be easily eliminated, one likely created
by our own education and background. We were facing a
wall of ignorance built by less educated people in a small
farming community. Ignorance about our country, our
families and schools, our traditions and history. We were
seen as "Aitalians," from a faraway place, somewhere in
Europe. They did not know that in our culture, having
neither a car nor a television, nor a vacuum cleaner, nor a
back door in our boxcar were not signs of poverty or
weakness. We had come from a poor country, yes, but one
rich with many talents. We were also nurturing within

ourselves a strong desire to work and to succeed. We had
decided long before to accept all sort of sacrifices. We knew
that these, when accepted with love, could only become a
source of success and spiritual fulfillment.

I was especially concerned about our future. Although
no one spoke to me, I felt that the Company wished me one
day to step into Doc Osner's position. However, I was not
sure that I liked this prospect. In fact, it would limit my entire
career to Sierra Vista Ranch. I felt that I needed more training
and an advanced degree from a good university to broaden
my experience and move forward in California or elsewhere.
To this effect, I arranged for an interview with the Chairman
of the Soils Department in Berkeley. I wanted to find out
what the requirements were for graduate studies leading to a
Ph.D. in Soil Science. The interview was brief and
disappointing. The Chairman was only interested in how
many children I had, and how much money I could invest in
an advanced degree. One baby, he considered, was still
acceptable, but not having financial resources to maintain
my family and pay tuition for three to four years totally
disqualified me from Graduate School. It looked as if the
door for further training was tightly closed. There were no
alternatives other than to stay put at Sierra Vista and wait
for something to happen.

One of the Davis researchers who frequently visited the
ranch was Dr. William B. Hewitt, of the Department of Plant
Pathology. He was a world authority on grape diseases, with
a special interest in grape viruses and a disorder called "black
measles." The causal agent of the latter was still unknown
and Dr. Hewitt had a plot at Sierra Vista, where for six years
he had been carefully mapping individual vines for disease
symptoms. During the winter, he also used this plot to test
various chemicals in search of a control.

Dr. William B. Hewitt, an outstanding scientist and a humanitarian.

I liked Dr. Hewitt because I saw in him a first-class scientist who was not afraid to get his boots dirty in the field. He knew too well that plant disease problems cannot be studied in the laboratory only. They require plenty of field observations and experimentation.

Dr. Hewitt was in his mid-forties when I met him for the first time. He was well built, with wavy hair, blue eyes and a pleasant expression. To those who did not know him too well, he appeared intimidating and somewhat abrupt. Deep down, he concealed a surprisingly high dose of kindness and generosity. He was a keen observer of natural phenomena and of human behavior.

It was close to Christmas of 1954 when Dr. Hewitt came to Sierra Vista for one of his trials. It was a cold and foggy day, typical of the Central Valley during winter. I assisted Dr. Hewitt in the field. When it was time for lunch, I informed "Bill" that the bunkhouse was closed for the holidays, but that I could take him over to my house, provided Nicla was given a little warning. I rushed home in my old pickup to inform her about this last minute invitation. "Try to put something together," I said. "I will be back in half an hour." Nicla did not clearly understand who the guest was going to be. She thought he probably was one of the Farm Advisors who frequently visited the ranch. Nevertheless, she wasted no time, and with her usual speed she had a "lunch for three" ready in less than half an hour. When Dr. Hewitt entered the house, everything was nicely prepared. The table was set with finely embroidered linen, shiny silverware, flowers, and wine decanters. Nicla's tasty Italian food did the rest. After one hour I was ready to return to the field, but Dr. Hewitt was not. He was enjoying his visit and wanted to know more about Nicla and myself, our background, our life in Italy and in Delano.

When finally we returned to the field, Dr. Hewitt asked me if I would be interested in working for him in Davis. Having received my affirmative reply, he added, "Maybe the Di Giorgio Company is willing to put up a grant with the University to finance your training. Let me think about it. I must first find the necessary funds." His words sounded so wonderful that I wanted to drop everything and rush back to Nicla to inform her about the outcome of her good lunch.

That same evening she and I discussed at length what appeared to be a great opportunity. Christmas was just around the corner, and the offer to go back to school was the best gift we could have received. We decided that for the first time since we had arrived in America we could afford to buy and decorate a Christmas tree. We placed the tree in a corner of the boxcar and our good star also appeared to be there, shining brighter than ever before, at the top of all the other ornaments.

8

Back to School

*The good life is one inspired by love
and guided by knowledge.*

—Bertrand Russell

For several months there was no word from Dr.
Hewitt about work possibilities in Davis. This was
mainly due to the time required by the Graduate
Division to check my academic credentials with the
University of Florence in Italy. Other difficulties arose: to
locate the necessary funds within the University budget, and
the problem of my Italian citizenship. Apparently, no State
funds could be used to support foreign students. In the
meantime, life at Sierra Vista proceeded as usual.

Marcel and I established contacts with a diving club in
Bakersfield that specialized in making "dry suits" for member
divers. We obtained a pattern from them, and with the

assistance of an experienced seamstress like Nicla, we started making our own suits. Soon the Sierra Vista boxcar was transformed into a mini-factory. "Aquafun" was the name given to our new company, and the product we sold was a kit with all the pieces of rubber sheeting cut to size and ready for assembly. Advertisements were placed in a diving magazine and many orders were soon coming in. After supper, we would cut the various pieces, carefully assemble the kits and package them for shipping. The heavy smell of rubber, solvent and glue would fill the air of our boxcar and confirm that once more we were in business.

Shortly afterwards, we founded a club for people interested in diving. The name of the club, "The Delano Wetbacks," called for young people to get wet in the cold Pacific waters and had no reference to the illegal immigrants crossing the Rio Grande from Mexico.

The club immediately became popular with local high school and college students who wished to take part in abalone diving expeditions to the coast. Leon Ragsdale, the sheriff at Sierra Vista Ranch, also joined the club and became a partner in "Aquafun." He was a remarkable diver.

The existence of the diving club came to the attention of local farmers and fishermen, who needed our assistance for entirely different reasons. Farmers who derived irrigation water from the Kern-Friant Canal occasionally could not get the water they had paid for. This was because their pump inlets had become plugged by water weeds. To solve this problem was a complex and costly operation. It involved cutting the inlet pipe, lifting it above the water level, removing the weeds, and placing the pipe back after welding it. The Delano Wetbacks could do the same simply by diving under water and removing the plug when the pump was still running. We received many requests for this type of work, for which we charged very little. After all, we needed the exercise.

As for the fishermen, at times they dropped valuable objects in the canal which they needed to retrieve. One of these men lost his precious dentures. He was fishing on the edge of the canal when he had to sneeze. The sneeze was so powerful that the dentures flew out of his mouth and landed on the bottom of the canal. The poor man phoned the Delano Wetbacks to ask for help. His voice sounded desperate and he was willing to pay a good fee for the recovery of his dentures. It was cheaper and quicker for him to pay one of the divers than to have the dentures replaced by the dentist. And the Delano divers were always willing to help.

By June 1955 Dr. Hewitt informed me that we had to postpone our plans to work in Davis for one and a half years. I could not be hired by the University without my American citizenship. It was a blow to our expectations. Nicla and I felt that we were stuck forever at Sierra Vista. I had no alternative than to continue with my work. George Osner had already reached retirement age, but he continued in his activities as in the past: using his brain and only...my legs.

One day Doc Osner received a phone call from J.S. Di Giorgio, the Chairman of the Board in San Francisco. He had had a visit by Dr. Hewitt who had proposed that the Company make available a grant to the University for work on "black measles" disease of grapes. This involved sponsoring a research assistantship for at least one year at the cost of $2,500. I was to be the candidate for this assistantship. What was the opinion at Sierra Vista about this request? Should the Company invest in such an undertaking? At this point, Doc Osner dropped all his shyness and came forward endorsing Hewitt's proposal. "J.S., you can be assured that the Company could not make a better investment than that proposed by Dr. Hewitt. I support it without reservation." These were the words of George Osner. They came out strong and clear after four years of nearly complete silence. Thanks to his support, there were no more obstacles to my going back to school. All the required documentation was submitted to the registrar of the University, I was duly accepted, and school was to begin in the spring quarter of 1956.

The first problem to resolve was finding a place to live in Davis. For this purpose, Nicla and I left Victoria with Marcel and Suzie, and in early January we drove north to look for an apartment to rent. It was a difficult drive because it was very foggy in the lower San Joaquin Valley, and it was raining cats and dogs in the Sacramento Valley. I knew my way around since I had already visited Davis during grape field days. What I did not realize was how little lodging was available for people with a limited budget. The University still managed the so called "Aggie Villa," a number of barracks put together for emergency housing during World War II. Most graduate students lived there, but when we arrived there was not a single vacancy available, only a long waiting list.

Established in 1906 as a "site for agricultural study" for the U.C. Berkeley students, the college had grown to be internationally recognized as one of the best for agricultural and environmental studies. Downtown Davis had remained instead nearly unchanged from the days when the city was called "Davisville." In 1868, the California Pacific Railroad completed a line from Vallejo to a junction located on the farm of Jerome C. Davis, who gave his name to this small settlement 15 miles west of Sacramento. When we arrived, the only hotel in town was at the corner of "G" and Second streets. The only barber shop was that of Leo, right across the street, and the Davis Lumber store was running parallel to the railroad tracks where it had been built many years before. The rest of the town was pleasantly buried in thick vegetation.

Looking for a house in heavy rain could be very unpleasant. Nevertheless, we were determined to resolve our problem as quickly as possible to return to Delano the same day. Right after lunch we found what appeared suitable. This was one of four duplexes in Wyne Court on East 10th Street. The rent was eighty dollars a month. This cost had to be weighed against an expected income of one hundred and fifty dollars a month. But economics were not to interfere with opportunity. We signed our lease, paid a deposit, and drenched as we were, we were ready to leave for Delano. Nicla, however, suggested to phone Dr. Hewitt first. Only later I appreciated the wisdom of this suggestion. Dr. Hewitt and his wife Maybelle were in fact waiting for us at their house.

Our visit lasted two hours, more than we had expected. The Hewitts had a beautiful house, which had been built to maintain a pollen-free environment. They had no children and everything in the house was spotless and well organized. They were both glad about our lease and looked forward of having us back in Davis in a fortnight. Maybelle was a gentle lady in her mid-forties, with a sweet smile and deep, penetrating eyes. She was particularly interested in Nicla and, while slowly sipping her tea, she studied her very carefully. It was evident that Maybelle had many questions she wanted answered. Through personal contacts, and "nightly reports" that Bill must have provided, she knew everything about the lives of the Plant Pathology graduate students. We also talked about our future in Davis. Dr. Hewitt promised to let me work on a very important grape disease. This would then justify the scholarship he was going to get for me in 1957.

Weather conditions had improved for our return, and after a six hour drive we were back in Delano. Victoria had been very good with Suzie, who appeared to have Nicla's fine Italian hand in dealing with a growing girl. We described our trip and revealed our expectations for the future: living in a better environment would also be good to strengthen our courage.

The date for the move to Davis was set for January 27. I started packing our belongings and soon I discovered that the number of trunks and crates had nearly doubled from when we arrived from Italy. The Company was to provide a truck for the move. They would also keep me on the Company's insurance plan and pay me a full salary for the month of February to "offset relocation expenses." A nice, supportive gesture by an understanding and humanitarian Board of Directors. As a result, our submerged savings account promptly rose to the surface.

We said good-bye to the Perelli-Minettis, the Dirkswagers, the Lopes, the Augers, the Ramirez, the Keagys, the Ciminos and to all the other good people who had helped us in our four difficult years at Sierra Vista. Special thanks were given to Doc Osner and his wonderful wife. On the occasion of our departure, both were particularly moved. They must have felt that, by then, we were no longer "outsiders." We were family. A new chapter of our life was to begin, and all these friends wished us good luck on our new and important venture.

The owners of the small duplex apartment in Wyne Court were the first to notice the arrival of two extra-energetic tenants. Before the arrival of the truck from Sierra Vista, we had engaged in an all-out floor scrubbing exercise. This took care of left-over dirt from previous tenants. Layers and layers of wax accumulated over time were stripped and the resulting effect was impressive: the floors appeared as if they had been newly installed.

New curtains were placed on the windows, and the two-room apartment acquired a fresh and cheerful look. The owners, who lived across the street, were extremely pleased with our "energetic approach" towards improving their investment.

Their parents also lived in the same complex. They were both old and could no longer take care of the house and of themselves. They belonged to some Baptist church, and at night they often complained about lack of alcoholic drinks. The walls were so thin and the insulation so bad that we could hear all that was said on the other side. "Yes," said the old man. "Someday I'd like to become a Catholic, and for only one reason: Catholics do not mind if their people take a good nightcap before going to bed." Feeling sympathy for this kind of philosophy, I was tempted to drill a hole through the thin wall and let the old man have a glass of my wine. But only on one condition: that he lowered his voice and let me go to sleep!

On my first day of work at the Department, I reported to Dr. Hewitt's office at 7:30 am. I knew that Bill always arrived at work early in the morning. For the occasion, I dressed somewhat formally with coat and tie, mainly to show respect to my major professor. As I entered his office, Bill was busy writing and he barely lifted his head to observe me. He only said: "Take off your tie and coat and start to work. Your desk is in that corner. Clean it and be sure to keep it clean." This was the only message I received. It was then up to me to go around the Department and introduce myself to the administrative office staff, the chairman, and the other graduate students.

Erna Thompson was the department's Administrative Assistant. Right away I recognized in her an energetic, efficient and cordial person. She knew all about me and the grant from the Di Giorgio Company, since she had taken care of all the paper work. She smiled as I entered her office and welcomed me to Davis. For many years Erna was to remain a most helpful friend.

Dr. J.B. Kendrick was the Plant Pathology Department's chairman both in Davis and Berkeley. He was an authoritative gentleman, tall, with round-rimmed glasses and a deep voice: the type of person who commanded immediate respect from others. He was very proud of his Department and his graduate students. Frequently he was heard saying that he was happy to pay the highest electrical bill on campus because his "boys were there working late into the night." Jim Kendrick was always ready to offer his personal assistance and often repeated that, "Should there be any problems, the door of my office is always open."

The number of graduate students was rather limited when I joined the Department. Joe Eckert and Bill Schnatorst had already given their qualifying examinations and were completing their research work. Both of them were somewhat snobbish toward me as they learned that I was coming from a ranch somewhere in the Central Valley. They must have assumed that no practical man could ever make a "good scientist." Catch words and complex language were frequently used by both to emphasize their higher scientific status, and, probably, to intimidate newcomers.

There was a larger group of graduate students who were only one or two quarters ahead of me. With them it was easier to communicate and become friends. The group included Tom Shalla and Al Weinhold, both from Colorado, Arthur McCain and Dick Hine from California, and Erika Sholtzmetner from Germany. They were all outstanding young people and their companionship was much appreciated during our stay in Davis and long afterwards.

Graduate student life is hectic because it is geared toward the completion of an assigned course program within a

Graduate students of the Plant Pathology department at UCD.

limited time framework. In addition, above-average grades must always be maintained. During the initial course program, two foreign language exams were to be taken. Once these were passed, and the course program was completed, there was the dreadful "Qualifying Examination." This was the greatest obstacle to overcome. Following this, graduate students only needed to concentrate on their research, which had to meet high academic standards, and produce a thesis of recognized scientific value.

In many regards, this type of life was easier for people who continued their studies without interruption from undergraduate school. In my case, things were complicated because I had been out of school for many years, and my training in Italy had been based on a completely different academic system.

My course program involved a number of lower and upper division courses in other disciplines in addition to all those offered in Plant Pathology. After my arrival in Davis, I registered for a course in quantitative analysis in chemistry. I had not dealt with a chemical formula or reaction since the time I attended chemistry classes at the University of Rome in the mid-forties. This meant that I had to compete with bright young students fresh from high school or college juniors and seniors. Lectures were given in a vast auditorium designed to accommodate several hundred students at a time. Practical exercises were conducted in crowded laboratories.

My first quiz was a total fiasco. I simply could not understand what was going on. I did not get any credit for my answers, even when I was convinced that I had followed the right procedure. I approached one of the Teaching Assistants to ask about my problem. I then discovered that by writing all my calculations on a piece of scrap paper, and reporting only the numerical results on the test sheet, I was doing the wrong thing. My hurried calculations were usually mistaken and there was no way to find out what I had done wrong. Accordingly, I was given no credit.

Having learned this simple detail, my subsequent tests were all increasingly better, and my analytical lab work was not bad at all. Finally, after a long struggle, the chemistry course ended with a "C." This was more than I had expected for a subject so remote in time and interest.

Another obstacle was waiting for me. This was a course on Plant-Water-Soil Relationships, also scheduled for the first quarter. Most students were majors in Water Science or Soils. They had a good knowledge of soil physics and chemistry, as well as of engineering aspects of water movement in soils. Furthermore, I had no background in plant physiology (a course scheduled for a future quarter). I had difficulty in understanding such things as nutrients and water uptake, transport in plants, evapotranspiration, and so on. To complicate matters, the course was given by a young graduate student from Israel, with no teaching experience and a peculiar English accent. I barely survived the course, and, again, I was most happy when it was over.

After the spring quarter, I tackled the foreign languages. I was probably the only graduate student to take French and German examinations three weeks apart. I was familiar with both languages, and it was not a big effort for me to translate half a page of a foreign scientific text into English. The word spread about my successful achievement. I noted that almost overnight, my reputation had grown considerably.

One more advantage I had over other students was with my research. This had been already defined when I entered graduate school: I had to work on grape black measles. I knew the odd symptomatology of the disease in mature grapevines, I already had a wealth of records by Dr. Hewitt. I could freely use field plots at Sierra Vista, and I could start my work without delay. And this is exactly what happened. During that first summer, I was already engaged in my investigations. One of the first matters to study was the possibility that the disease was caused by toxins produced by certain root pathogens. Dr. Hewitt had suggested this possibility after having seen some slides by a German plant pathologist which showed foliar symptoms similar to those of black measles. These symptoms were on young sugar beet plants whose roots had been severely damaged by water molds.

This first phase of my research involved sampling soils and grapevine rootlets with a known history of measles against those in the same vineyard without a disease record. Isolations were made from samples collected at Sierra Vista, and pure cultures of the isolates were grown in test tubes in Davis. Each organism was subsequently tested on grape seedlings grown in sterile soil in the greenhouse. After a while, all the tables of a lecture hall (not in use during the summer) were covered with test tubes containing an incredible array of soil organisms. It was an impressive display, but most pathogenicity tests proved negative. Likewise, there were no visible differences in the organism populations from diseased and healthy vines. A few water molds that could damage the root system of grapevines were detected, and further research was conducted on them. For the rest, the results of my first summer's work were very disappointing.

Because of some administrative technicalities, the Di Giorgio grant to the University was delayed. As a result, I did not receive a salary for the first three months in Davis.

Dr. Hewitt kindly offered to lend us some money, but Nicla and I preferred to struggle through this situation, using our modest savings and the income she could generate. One day Dr. Hewitt showed up at our house with a case of wine. "I thought this might cheer you up and help you forget your financial problems," he said. "I have more Napa wine in my cellar. Let me know when you need some more." The wine was not only good, but a blessing for two thirsty Italian immigrants living on a shoe string budget. Some extra food was sent to us from Delano. All our friends, knowing about our difficult situation, asked Suzie and Marcel to deliver to us their "care packages." A demonstration of affection that we never expected.

It was soon evident that some additional income was necessary. Nicla then started to iron for other people, to make alterations and to create new garments. Her business was slow at the beginning, but after a while it began to boom. Her income showed a steady increase: from eight dollars in February to $60, $110, $150 and $220 in the following months. All this required hard work from early morning until late at night. It also required speed. On one occasion, she discovered that in only two and a half hours, she was able to iron sixteen starched man's shirts, four blouses, and one skirt. And everything to perfection.

Most ladies in Davis had the tendency to buy cheap fabric, often on "sale" in local stores. When they later discovered that Nicla charged twenty-five dollars to make a dress, they complained about what they considered an excessive fee. They admitted that they had purchased inexpensive fabric to save money, not realizing that the labor to make a dress was the same whether the original fabric was cheap or expensive. Mrs. Virginia Eckert was an exception. She was a well educated and sophisticated lady who could easily grasp the difference between high and low quality materials. She had good taste, which made her appreciate expensive things, including art objects and fine embroidery. She was a tall, large woman with a very pleasant face and dark brown eyes. Virginia had married Dr. J.E. Eckert, a world famous entomologist, who had specialized in bee diseases. They had three daughters: Peg, Sarah and Jean. Virginia became Nicla's best customer, once she discovered that "Nicky" knew exactly which colors, material and design best fitted her size and personality. Thanks to her sweet character, generosity and admiration for Italy, we became part of this outstanding family.

House cleaning for other people was another of the activities Nicla took on. All this, in the name of "Ph T," an abbreviation for "Put the Husband Through." This was not only a message of hope, but also a statement of reciprocal trust.

After three months of delay, my salary and arrears were paid by the University. On top of these, we received in August a "bonus" of 60 dollars a month directly from the Di Giorgio Company. I had met Mr. J.S. Di Giorgio on one of my collecting trips to Sierra Vista. At first I did not want to accept this generous offer. But J.S. with his usual easy-going manner insisted: "This way your wife can go to bed a little earlier at night." This was followed by one of his roaring laughs and a check for 300 dollars (for the five-months' bonuses already past). Things were getting better for us and our economic recession appeared to be over. Nicla's business, in full swing, now required a helper and more space. Accordingly, we started looking for a house with an additional room.

In mid-September 1956, Nicla found a house for rent in East Davis. This had the extra space we needed and offered the advantage of being next door to A.N. Kasimatis, the Kern County Farm Advisor. He had also moved to Davis to become the Extension Specialist in Viticulture. It was nice to have a good friend behind a dividing hedge: we could easily talk "grape business" while gardening on either side.

The agreed rent was only 80 dollars per month because the house needed considerable painting as well as the replanting of a good part of the lawn in the backyard. So, we rolled up our sleeves and started doing what needed to be done. Out of our limited budget we squeezed money for buying cleaners, brushes, paints, seed, and whatever was needed for the project. And this was very successful. The finished interior looked beautiful with soft pastel colors that made the rooms appear twice as large. The backyard was no longer a muddy ravine, but lovely with the light green color of the new grass and the beauty of added shrubbery. It was the first time since our wedding that Nicla and I could enjoy a real house. One that was clean, and sufficiently large to meet our requirements.

In mid-January the landlady stopped by for a short visit. She admired the finished product and continued to say that the house never looked so beautiful. The next day she sent us a registered letter with the request for $300 a month to rent the same but "embellished" house!

We were at first surprised, then greatly disappointed. We consulted with friends on what to do, but their answer was pretty much the same: "There is nothing you can do. Either you pay the increased rent, or you find another house." We learned again something we had known in Italy all the time: with a landlord (and often with other people!) "Fidarsi e' bene, ma non fidarsi e' meglio." (To trust is good, but not to trust is better!)

Fortunately, our good luck struck again. While I was on a field trip, Nicla saw people around the corner loading a truck as if they were moving. She stopped to inquire if the house was for rent. "Yes," said the owner, who was standing by. "But the house requires some painting." "Never mind the painting," answered Nicla, "as long as you do your part and pay for all materials." The rent was set at $95 a month, and Nicla promptly signed a six-month lease renewable for one year. One hour later, she started transporting our possessions from one house to the other. She drove the car back and forth with little Victoria sitting in the back on top of boxes, clothing and toys. That evening, when I returned, I discovered that I had a new address in Davis. With the help of three graduate students, a small trailer, and no ropes to tie the load, we moved the rest of the household to the new place. Once this was done, we had plenty of beer for everyone. All the noise we were able to make did not disturb Nicla's sleep. She was dead tired from her "soloist" performance in moving. The next day, the keys of the old house were mailed to the greedy landlady in place of the $300 she surely expected.

Things were considerably better for me during my second year of residency. The courses were more interesting, and competition with other students boosted my performance. A string of "A's" accumulated during this period, and by May of 1957, the course program was successfully completed. All my professors were satisfied with these results and so was J.S. Di Giorgio, who congratulated me and asked me to inform Dr. Hewitt that the Company had already paid the grant for another year.

The date for my "Qualifying Examination" was set for August 14. This was a half-day oral examination aimed at demonstrating my "critical ability, powers of imagination and synthesis, and broad knowledge in my field of study." Conducted by five professors in different disciplines, it was also a one-shot deal. If I failed, I could be given one more opportunity, but no more. Then, all the efforts and sacrifices of two or more years could go down the drain forever.

Preparing for an examination of this kind was difficult because of the unforeseeable nature of the questions. Of course, one must be acquainted with the publications of the examining professors, in expectation that they might ask what they know best. Also, the scanning of scientific review papers might prove useful. Probably the most productive way of preparation was by way of question and answer sessions organized by the students themselves. Tom Shalla, Al Weinhold, Art McCain, and myself reserved one section of the Department library and every night we played the question and answer game. Occasionally, Art brought some popsicles he had personally manufactured. These were appreciated by everyone, especially when we discovered that they were made with wine. By the late 1950s, no alcoholic beverages were allowed on the Davis campus, even though the entire Department of Enology was exclusively devoted to wine production. Oleander bushes were allowed to grow very tall around the enology building to soothe this incredible contradiction!

I brought home large quantities of books and reprints that I wanted to abstract. A large table, built especially for this purpose, was placed in the bedroom and my literature was scattered on it and on the floor below. It was a real mess, but Nicla, understanding how secure I felt being surrounded by so much written knowledge, turned a blind eye on the whole matter.

A record by Paganini was kept playing over and over again to keep me company in my study. It was the Concerto No.1 in D major, op.6. This record belonged to a German veterinarian who frequently came to our house to share good Italian food and classical music. The violin concert stirred deep emotional cords in me. Somehow it gave me strength and perseverance. After several weeks, I felt I was ready for the big exam. Never in my life I had stored in my brain so much information.

The night before the Qualifying Examination, Dr. and Mrs. Hewitt invited me, Nicla, and the Shalla's to the Sacramento Circus. "I do not think you should study tonight," Bill said, with a smile. "What you know by now is all you really need tomorrow. Let's have fun tonight." And he was perfectly right. A relaxing evening was the best medicine to be mentally prepared the following day.

The next morning, the examination started at eight o'clock in the library of the Plant Pathology Department. The beginning was very smooth. One of the first questions was about my research. Of course, I knew more about this subject than anybody else in the room. I realized that this question was kindly formulated to let me have a good start. However, the following questions became increasingly more difficult.

Somehow, I had in the back of my mind the magnificent music of Paganini, and, like Paganini, I was ready for a "crescendo." Like a virtuoso, I was most anxious for the more difficult part to come. Then I could exhibit the best of my talents. I formulated my answers in a rapid, precise and direct manner. I then glanced around the audience and felt that the professors appreciated the tune of my music. One of them, who had stressed before that, "no one in this world knows everything," wanted to demonstrate his point. He asked two questions that he felt were nearly impossible to answer. It so happened that I had the correct answer—to both!

By noon, Nicla and Victoria were parked outside the Department building waiting in the car to hear something about the examination. One of the professors, just coming out of the library, saw them there. He approached the car, saying, "Luigi is still in the library. I need to tell you, he is getting stronger and stronger. Congratulations!"

I finally emerged from the building, smiling and evidently pleased with my performance. I had passed the big test. Two surprises were waiting for me at the house: all the books and the table in the bedroom had disappeared, and in their place was a new record of Paganini's Concerto No.1 played by Zino Francescatti. A dedication on the cover read: "To Gigi on the most successful day of his student's life. Bravo! Mamma and Vicky."

Soon afterwards, all of my time was directed toward my research. As mentioned, the root decay hypothesis had not led to usable results. Instead, during the winter of 1956-57, I was able to establish a strong correlation in Dr. Hewitt's plot at Sierra Vista between occurrence and extensiveness of internal wood decay and incidence of symptoms. I split in half several vines and those with long and consistent appearance of symptoms all had severe internal decay. At the same time, vines with no symptoms for the entire six-year period showed no or only light decay. This observation called for a new direction of research. There was a need to demonstrate that the cause was not in the soil or in the roots, but in the upper portion of the vine itself. A number of experiments were conducted for this purpose. Among these, one was directed at vines with consistent symptoms over six years. These were cut at the soil line and a new shoot was raised the following spring from the old stumps. The results were very encouraging: none of the young vines showed disease symptoms any longer. This clearly demonstrated that the problem was in the trunk and that it was probably due to internal decay.

Some months before, Nicla helped me make another important discovery. I had brought back from Sierra Vista some trunk specimens out of which I tried to isolate the organisms involved in the decay. But for a long time this was impossible: there were too many fungi in the decaying tissues and most of these could outgrow those I was looking for.

One Sunday afternoon I asked Nicla to come with me to the Department to help me water the plants in the greenhouse. I had left a large grape trunk under a bench in one of these greenhouses. I had also covered the cut in the crown with some waxed paper tied with a rubber band, just to keep it clean. Suddenly Nicla called my attention to that trunk. "Look at what is growing out of your dead vine," she said, indicating a profuse brownish fungus mat under the waxed paper. "This is it," I shouted. "This is exactly what I have been looking for all these months." I modified the artificial growing medium and isolated my fungus in pure culture. As Jonathan Smith once said, "A stander-by may sometimes, perhaps, see more of the game than he that plays it."

This finding opened a new series of studies on the organisms associated with the internal rot, their morphology, physiology and pathogenicity. By working late into the night seven days a week, I was able to secure sufficient experimental data to write a thesis. But this was not enough for Dr. Hewitt. "If you want to get out of this place," he said, "you must have all your thesis material written and accepted for publication in a scientific journal." And so, by extending my working hours further into the nights, I was able to write two papers for Phytopathology, the official journal of the American Phytopathological Society. This was the last hurdle of my academic marathon in Davis. All my Ph.D. work was completed in record time: two years and eight months.

A number of memorable events took place in Davis while the marathon was still going on.

In April of 1957, Nicla and I took the oath to become American citizens. This simple and meaningful ceremony had been organized in the Sacramento Courthouse. There were probably forty people assembled for this purpose, the majority from the Orient or Latin America. They had come to America, a country of immigrants, from different parts of the world. They brought with them different traditions, different ambitions, and different levels of education. Like those who preceded them, they wanted to become "Americans." The judge, wearing his black robe, spoke very slowly. He knew that many in the audience could hardly understand him. While he was speaking, emotions were running high in that courtroom. Nicla and I could not avoid thinking of what we had left behind in Italy, and what we had already accomplished in America. All this only with our courage, love and boundless confidence.

For us, American citizenship was an important milestone. It sealed the decision we had already made to give up our plans for returning to Italy. These plans had been conceived in a moment of depression in Connecticut. On that occasion, Nicla had allowed a five-year period before returning to Rome. The five years were just over, but there was a new and bright light shining at the end of our tunnel. Together, we had succeeded in overcoming many difficulties and together we were now beginning to savor the sweet taste of success. Yes, we wanted to go back to Rome, but only for a short visit. We had elected to stay in California for the rest of our lives.

The afternoon following the citizenship ceremony, we organized a big party for all the graduate students and young staff of the Department. Our celebration was the first large party we had attended since our arrival in America.

Another important event took place toward the end of 1957. Nicla was expecting a new baby in late December. The day before Christmas, feeling that the baby was ready for delivery, she was taken to Mercy Hospital in Sacramento. But nothing happened. It was only a false alarm. The next day, I drove her back to Davis. We were both silent and annoyed as we crossed the Yolo causeway. The burden of carrying a baby was still with Nicla, while I was thinking about the $160 dollars they had charged us for an unnecessary overnight in the hospital.

Five days had to go by before Nicla again felt the contractions announcing the baby's arrival. It was late at night. I was sound asleep and Nicla, this time, wanted to be absolutely sure of what was happening. Finally, she decided to phone Dr. Kennedy, and then she woke me up. It was a foggy night but just the same, Dr. Kennedy was able to find his way to our house. He promptly visited Nicla, and then he turned to me. "Luigi, you better hurry up and have some hot water ready for me," he said with a sibylline smile. Only later I realized that this was just one of his dry jokes. I took the car out of the garage and rushed Nicla to Sacramento. The fog was getting thicker on Highway 80 east, and I was getting increasingly worried about the drawbridge over the river. Was it going to be open? If not, what was I going to do? Fortunately the bridge was open and, not far away, on the other side of the river, was Mercy Hospital. As I walked into the entrance with Nicla under my arm, another pregnant woman came through the same door. It was already early morning, and a sleepy nurse at the reception desk had the nerve to ask, "Are you three together?" I declined to answer. There was no time for discussion or clarification: Nicla was ready for the delivery room. One hour later, as I was once more pacing the very shiny hospital floors, I was informed that another beautiful baby girl was born. Marina Laura had sailed swiftly into this world on December 28, just in time to give us another tax deduction.

Soon after Marina's birth, J.S. Di Giorgio stopped by our house for a short visit. He was on his way to Marysville and wanted to find out in person how things were coming along and what plans we had for the future. J.S. had a unique, fascinating personality: he was an executive in the real meaning of the word. He was quick in reaching decisions, he had a strong and intimidating personality, but deep down he was very understanding of people and situations. He was a true humanitarian.

The Di Giorgio employees called J.S. "Major." This was not only because he had been a Marine Major in the Pacific throughout the war, but also because they recognized him as a leader deserving the greatest respect. I was amazed to see how promptly J.S. could understand our situation, the status of my studies and the progress of my research. He was also aware of the new financial constraint that came with a newborn baby in our family. "Well, Luigi, I am glad I stopped by for this visit," said J.S., walking back to his car. "You give me a call in San Francisco whenever you are ready. In the meantime I am requesting our administration to increase your monthly check to one hundred dollars. You have another girl and you must take good care of her." This was Mr. Joseph S. Di Giorgio: a truly fascinating boss and a wonderful man.

We finally wound up our business in Davis and prepared to leave town. I had been offered a job with the Di Giorgio

Mr. J.S. Di Giorgio, Chairman of the Board, a great executive and
benefactor.

Company to work on plant protection problems in a newly established Research Department. A good house and a satisfactory salary made this job particularly attractive. The Company again took care of moving our furniture to Di Giorgio Farms, near Arvin. It was time to say good-bye to the professors and the many friends who had helped make Davis a truly wonderful experience. Chairman Kendrick was the first to be visited. He looked at me and said, "Well, Luigi, you return now to the Di Giorgios with all your good training. Be prepared to do a good job. If they should not treat you well, remember I am still here and ready to find you some other employment." This statement proved that my work at the Department had been appreciated. As events developed in following years, there was never any need to go back to UCD for help of this kind.

9

Return to the Vineyards

We are what we repeatedly do. Excellence, then, is not an act, but only a habit.

—ARISTOTLE

eaving Davis, after nearly a three year stay and much intense work, gave us the reassuring feeling of returning to a more normal life pace. Having obtained a Ph.D. degree also fueled the sensation of having made a gigantic step forward in our life. All the furniture was loaded on a Company truck, and some of our other belongings were crowded into our little Ford. Nicla was sitting in front with me, while Victoria and Marina were in the back. Great expectations filled our compact car. It was a very hot August day and we had no air conditioning. This meant that frequent stops were necessary along the way to refresh ourselves and keep the children from "wilting." The trip south on Highway 99 was monotonous as usual: Manteca, Modesto, Merced, Madera. The names of these towns all started with "M," and the towns themselves looked all alike. Finally, Fresno was in sight. This was a signal for us that Delano was not too far away.

A small stopover in Delano was planned, to pay a short visit to Suzie and Marcel and to say hello to Tony Perelli-Minetti and our friends at Sierra Vista. Just a few miles before Delano, I had to pull off the highway because I was not feeling well: I had nausea and cramps. Nicla took over the driving and drove us directly to Marcel's house. From there she called Dr. Montgomery, who requested that I go immediately to his office. After a thorough visit, Dr. Montgomery announced that he had to perform surgery for what appeared to be serious appendicitis. In no time, I found myself in a hospital bed arguing with a young nurse, who wanted to shave me where I never did!

Without hesitation, Dr. Montgomery proceeded with surgery. The operation was timely and successful, but I had to remain confined to a hospital bed for a few days. Meanwhile, I worried about our furniture and the people at Di Giorgio Farms waiting for our arrival. Nicla decided to go to the Farms to meet these people and make the necessary arrangements for placing the furniture in our new house. Marcel volunteered to accompany her on this visit and the two went in his car. On return, they stopped briefly at the drugstore in Delano where Suzie was working. There they met Dr. Montgomery who, after seeing them together, candidly inquired: "Have you been up to the mountains?" At first this question seemed rude and insinuating, but, when we later gathered at Marcel's house, it became the source of great laughter.

The Di Giorgio winery. On the right corner, the Company houses (ours
was the second from the top).

The new house at Di Giorgio was a great improvement
over the old boxcar at Sierra Vista. It had three good-sized
bedrooms, a very spacious living-dining area and a large
backyard bordering a bearing vineyard. The house was
located on what was called "Winery Lane:" two strings of
five houses each facing each other and aligned like soldiers
in a parade. Nearby was the massive concrete structure of
the ten million gallon winery. Most of the people occupying
these houses worked in the winery, and only three families
were associated with the newly-established Research
Department.

On the whole, this neighborhood consisted of young
families with many small children. This was convenient
because it encouraged all the children to play together and
thus it reduced the isolation of living so far out in the
country.

The laboratory facilities were also satisfactory. However,
most of the available equipment was for the analysis of soil,
water and leaf tissue samples under the supervision of Robert

S. Ayers. I promptly designed a small greenhouse and, prior to my departure for Italy, I ordered the equipment needed for my plant pathology work.

Seven years had gone by since Nicla and I had left Italy to come to America. Many changes had taken place during this period. Now we had two beautiful daughters, a Ph.D. degree, an American citizenship, a nice Company house, a responsible job, and plenty of love and harmony in our married life. Of course, our bank account was still severely depressed. This, however, was not considered important. As Eduard Bordet had recognized, one must chose in life between making money and spending it. There is no time for both. We decided to spend our money (and that of Nicla's father) to purchase airtickets for a four-month vacation in Italy.

Arrangements were made to meet Sarah Eckert, who was to accompany us, at the Los Angeles airport to fly together to Rome. The flight was long and uneventful, especially for Marina (nine months old), who slept the whole time in a tiny basket.

At our arrival, all the members of Nicla's family together with many friends, were waiting on the balcony of Ciampino's airport. When we appeared from the airplane, there was a roar of applause, many hands waving, and even the loud sound of a ringing cowbell. All together, a reception usually reserved for heroes, popular singers, soccer players, or shrewd politicians. A long motorcade followed this happy and noisy reunion.

Most impressed with this unusual reception was our friend Sarah. She did not understand a word of our language, did not know anybody in the crowd, and could not figure out why everyone was talking loud and at the same time. On top of this, she was very tired after a long intercontinental flight

The least impressed was Marina. She was well rested and happy to be kissed and hugged by so many people. She crawled into grandfather Vittorio's arms, kissed him repeatedly and went back to sleep.

A wonderful lunch was served on arrival at Via Ovidio. While eating, it was easy to look around and observe the many changes that had occurred to the people sitting around the table. Changes were visible in children who had become teenagers, and in grown-ups who had reached middle age. For some reason, older people seemed to have escaped this natural aging process. With older people it was easier to connect the past to the present: there was continuity. After lunch, my mother and sisters joined the crowd. In this manner, festivities and confusion continued for a long and pleasant time.

Changes were also visible in the streets of Rome. Thousands and thousands of cars had invaded the city and were disorderly parked in the streets, squares, or wherever there was a bit of empty space. The city, famous for its beautiful "piazzas," unique fountains, impressive "palazzi" and wonderful churches, appeared to have changed into a huge, shabby and chaotic parking lot. Double and even triple parking was frequent in most streets. Sidewalks had been invaded by cars placed so closely to each other they forced pedestrians to make incredible detours. Under these conditions, the cleaning of streets and sidewalks was no longer possible, and Rome, the beautiful, appeared abandoned to itself, sinking under a hopeless sea of trash and disorder.

The warm September weather was still holding up very nicely, and we went for a week at the beach near Terracina. This is a small fishing town on the coast, about halfway

between Rome and Naples. Nicla's father and sister
Francesca had purchased two bordering lots (for a total of
about 2.5 acres), and a house had been built on Vittorio's
lot. The house, designed by Nicla's sister Lisa, had been
constructed under her direct supervision. At the time of our
visit, this was one of the major changes that had taken place.
We greatly enjoyed the stay at the beach, which enabled us
to swim again in the warm, blue waters of the Mediterranean
Sea. The girls played at length in the fine, white sand under a
warm sun like that of the Central Valley.

After returning to Rome, I made preparations for a trip
to Sicily. I had been asked by J.S. Di Giorgio to conduct a
feasibility study for establishing a frozen citrus concentrate
plant in Sicily. I visited Palermo, Cefalu', Catania, and a large
number of other citrus production districts, where I collected
information on fruit quality and availability, production costs
and delivery systems, marketing, and possible constraints. All
this information was compiled in a confidential report sent
directly to J.S. in San Francisco.

On return from this assignment, I found an invitation to
give a seminar in San Dona' di Piave, the city near Venice
which had been destroyed and rebuilt after World War I.
Father Vittorio was the president of a local growers'
association which was very interested in advances made in
California agriculture and in interactions between university
and farmers. This was a broad subject to present in only one
hour. I was willing, however, to meet this challenge, knowing
how much interest father Vittorio had had in this subject
ever since his visit to California. The seminar was held in the
large hall of "Consorzi di Bonifica" (Land Reclamation
Association), which was completely sold out for the occasion.
I could see in the eyes of those sitting in the front rows a
genuine interest in what I was saying. This was followed by
many questions. Definitely, the seminar was a success.

From San Dona', Nicla's father drove me to Mestre to meet the Rome-Munich train. Nicla and Sarah were on this train and I was to join them on the trip. Victoria and Marina had been left in Pisa with Vittoria and Giancarlo's family. The train arrived on time in Mestre, but there was no trace of Nicla or Sarah. We walked repeatedly up and down the entire length of the train, but we could not see their familiar faces. We were ready to phone to Rome to find out if they had boarded that train when, all of a sudden, Nicla and Sarah appeared smiling and giggling. There was no time for explanations. The train was ready to leave and I had to board. Father Vittorio was informed through the train window that the girls had had to use the restroom when the train arrived in Mestre. Since they were unable to verify the name of the station, they remained inside while we were outside worrying about them. One of those things that happen to inexperienced passengers.

Munich is a beautiful city, attracting visitors to see its monuments, meet its cheerful people, and enjoy its majestic surroundings. On this occasion, one more reason for visiting the city was the presence of Walter, Theo's only son, and Dora, his wife. Walter was a handsome young man in his late twenties. While working at the Four Seasons Hotel with his father, Walter had met Dora, a nice looking young guest from Venezuela. She also happened to be the daughter of one of the wealthiest men of that oil-rich country. Love at first sight characterized this encounter. When Dora had to suddenly return to Caracas, she tried to communicate with Walter, but unsuccessfully. This was because Theo had advised his son to forget about his love affair, and to pay more attention to his work. One day, the consul of Venezuela marched into the Four Seasons Hotel and directed himself to Theo's concierge desk. He approached him, saying that he had been formally instructed by his government to present a note of complaint. This was because Dora had not received any reply to her many letters and phone calls. This was interpreted to be a "serious" diplomatic issue which required immediate resolution. The easiest way to solve the crisis was to allow Dora and Walter to be married.

Theo was surprised at first about the diplomatic problem he had caused. Then he smiled to the consul and explained that he had been responsible for the crisis which could be easily resolved. And this was exactly what happened in the following weeks: with plenty of publicity in local and international newspapers and magazines, Dora and Walter finally got married. The story of a millionaire girl marrying a penniless but handsome concierge appealed to teenagers all over the world.

We spent nearly a week in Munich enjoying Theo and Gitschi's hospitality and Walter and Dora's company. At the end of the week we left for Switzerland, while Sarah proceeded to northern Germany to visit some of her friends.

The purpose of our trip to Switzerland was strictly business. Again, on the request of Mr. Di Giorgio, I was to make contact with a large Swiss company producing equipment for fruit conservation under modified gas atmospheres. J.S. wanted to know more about this company, and the effectiveness and practical use of these new methods in Europe.

Our first stopover was in Basel, where I had an appointment with the president of the company. He was a typical Swiss businessman who wanted to show how important and efficient he was. He made several phone calls, at the end of which he proudly announced that a complete itinerary was set for the "American visitors." We had, however, to travel to Martigny, in the French-speaking Valais area, where we would be met by local representatives.

When we arrived in Martigny we were met by two individuals who did not look too reassuring. They were both big men with dark mustaches, wearing black berets down to their eyes. They spoke nothing but French, and they were driving an old, dilapidated Renault. It was already late in the evening, and I suggested going directly to the hotel, leaving the tour for the next day. The two said, "Oui'," but instead, they made an endless number of stops at wine shops and cellars, where they ingested large quantities of wine. They continued laughing and chatting among themselves. I was getting nervous, not being able to understand the intentions of the two men. After a few more stops, however, they left us safely at one of the local hotels. The next day, the two showed up late in the morning. They took us on a tour of the valley with numerous additional visits to wine cellars. Surprisingly enough, not a single modified atmosphere plant was ever seen. Either the two had received a wrong message, or the demonstration plants did not exist in that valley.

When we returned to Pisa, to our astonishment, we found that Victoria could no longer speak English. Instead, she was fluent in Italian (with a strong Tuscany accent). We were pleasantly surprised with this change, which enabled our first daughter to speak a new language in less than two weeks.

Our vacation in Italy was rapidly coming to a close and it was time to return to California. At the end of December, 1958, a second parting from family and friends was to take place. This seemed more difficult than the one before. In particular, my mother saw my family leave for America with great sadness. She was getting old and suffered with heart problems. She strongly believed that she would never see us again. I was, however, much more optimistic and promised to return soon. With this sadness in our hearts, we left Rome for Paris, where we boarded one of the first jumbo jets to cross the Atlantic.

This was at the time when Modugno's song "Volare" was popular in Italy and elsewhere, and it was with this same song playing on the radio that Marcel, Suzie and Doc Osner came to Los Angeles to meet their flying friends returning from a wonderful Italian vacation.

As already mentioned, the Company house at Di Giorgio Farms was bordered on one side by a vineyard. Likewise, my research laboratory was surrounded on three sides by grapevines. Although plum orchards and asparagus plantings occupied a large acreage at Di Giorgio Farms, vineyards prevailed throughout. For this reason, we called this period a "return to the vineyards."

Di Giorgio Farms was the largest producing unit of the Di Giorgio Fruit Corporation. It had been purchased in small lots beginning in 1920, when one of the railroad companies, which owned many sections of land in Kern County, started disposing of its properties. The area was essentially a desert, mostly flat, with some rolling hills on the east side towards the Teachapi mountains. At the end of the winter these hills were a tourist attraction for the beautiful wild flowers growing in a symphony of colors as far as the eye could see.

Following the purchase of the land, the original desert on the southeast side of Kern County was transformed by Di Giorgio into highly productive farmland. This happened after water was found deep in the ground, and powerful pumps were installed to lift it for irrigation and domestic use. Joseph Di Giorgio took upon himself the financial risk of creating one of the largest and best organized farming operations in the world. From a modest beginning, Di Giorgio Farms grew to nearly 11,000 acres of first-class vineyards and orchards. The property was equipped with a most advanced air-conditioned packing house and cold storage, a ten-million

Aerial view of Di Giorgio Farms.

gallon capacity winery, 200 homes for personnel families, a private landing strip, and police, fire, medical, and research departments. Where once was only an unproductive desert, as many as 2,700 people now enjoyed good living conditions.

"Return to the vineyards" was probably the most comfortable period since our arrival in America. A good salary, excellent working conditions, and friendly neighbors all contributed to this improvement in living standards. In line with this, we were blessed by the arrival of a third beautiful daughter. On the 6th of October, 1959, an unusually hot day, Cynthia Lisa was born in Bakersfield. She smiled at us, displaying two well established front teeth. This smile was meant to be a warning signal: Cynthia Lisa knew, from the very beginning, how to make good use of those teeth!

The weather at Di Giorgio was warm to hot from March to late October, and this made it easy to raise children outdoors. A few bathing suits, a small plastic pool in the backyard and a running sprinkler on the front lawn were all that we needed to keep our children growing and happy for most of the year.

It was on the occasion of Professor Baldacci's visit to Di Giorgio Farms that a demonstration of these three values (weather, water and wetness) was offered to an astonished Italian professor from the foggy city of Milan. Being a very conservative man visiting California for the first time, he was overwhelmed by what he called "the great contrasts of the Golden State." "See, Luigi," he patiently explained, "if you go to a supermarket in a hot summer day, inside it is so cold that you must wear a sweater. If you go to a restaurant, inside it is so dark that you do not see your food. When you come out, instead, the sun is so bright that you are blinded if you do not wear sunglasses. If you ask for food, they serve you first a glass of water full of ice so cold it freezes your stomach. Then they serve you coffee. It is so hot that it burns your lips. Your meal, which follows next, is so greasy they must call it a... submarine!"

When Professor Baldacci came to our house, he and his family were faced with more California contrasts. They first saw our neighbor Frank Moller cleaning the bottom of his pool while having supper. He would take a gulp of air, dive to the bottom with a big brush, scrub the bottom the best he could, and then return for more air and a bite of spaghetti from a poolside dish. He would then rapidly disappear under water with this food in his mouth to start the cycle over again. They later saw our three girls jumping into the pool immediately after dinner, quickly change from bathing suits to their pajamas, and go directly to bed for a good night's rest. The three wet bathing suits, left behind on the clothes line, waited all night to start the daily routine the next morning.

There was plenty of work to keep me going for the next four years of employment with the Di Giorgio Company. I was responsible for disease and pest problems of all crops produced by the Corporation in different locations from Marysville, in Northern California, to Borrego, in the Anza desert in the South. Crops included pears, apricots, plums, grapes, potatoes, asparagus, cotton, and peanuts. This work was not entirely confined to pests and diseases. It also extended to horticultural and viticultural problems, some of great economic importance.

One of these concerned chemical spray thinning of plums. During the 1959 season at Di Giorgio Farms there was nearly a total loss of this crop. Apparently, this resulted from late insecticide spraying, followed by an untimely application of a blossom-killing agent. No bees or other insect pollinators were active in the orchards at the time of bloom, and all viable pollen was killed by dinitro sprays before the fruit had set. This incident could not be allowed to happen again, and J.S. Di Giorgio requested that I take over responsibility for the whole operation.

It was not an easy task to take care of so many variables at once. These included timing of insecticides, dormancy period of different varieties, effect of air and soil temperatures on blossom duration, presence and activity of insect pollinators, percentage of fruit set before killing unwanted pollen, and availability of equipment for timely spraying of all the orchards. I was able to design a closely controlled model which I personally monitored throughout the following winter and early spring. This included keeping daily and cumulative records of temperatures in individual orchards, ensuring that insecticidal sprays were applied early in the season, forecasting type of bloom based on varietal dormancy requirements and orchard temperature records, measuring flower-visiting activity of bees at full bloom, moving bee hives into orchards with low visiting counts, allowing sufficient time for insect pollination, and giving individual "go ahead" signals to initiate spray thinning operations.

My model worked successfully. The amount of fruit set was satisfactory and the Company saved over $160,000 in hand thinning costs. The fruit at harvest was abundant, of good size and quality. J.S. Di Giorgio was pleased with the results. Having been a Major in the Marines, he considered spray thinning a military operation that needed to be well planned, well organized and well conducted. I had been successful in doing this. Once the "plum campaign" was over, I was able to enjoy a good night's sleep and devote more attention to other important matters.

The period from 1950 to 1960 was characterized by relative freedom in the development and marketing of new and increasingly more toxic pesticides. One of the emerging problems in those years was the over-use (and abuse) of these chemicals, with consequent increases in pest resistance to pesticides, escalated costs for crop protection, and augmented environmental pollution. Pesticides were also a problem in the Di Giorgio operations, particularly in cotton, grapes and pears. It was evident that something had to be done to exit from the never-ending spiral of more pesticide use, more pest outbreaks, and greater crop protection costs.

There was a young entomologist at Sierra Vista Ranch who had replaced Dr. Osner, and who shared this same concern. He was Donald L. Flaherty. After many discussions with Don, we decided to call a meeting of University research and extension staff, to start a joint project on Integrated Pest Management of grapes. There was only one successful example of integrated control in California and this was on yellow aphids in alfalfa. But there was no other example of an industry-promoted, coordinated research program on a perennial fruit crop such as grapes. The word IPM, which after a few years was to become popular at national and international levels, was essentially born in a small, poorly lit motel room where Don and I had convened a few right-minded scientists. With them, we decided to tackle one of the most complex problems affecting crop production.

I became part of a team conducting migration studies of the grape leafhopper, one of the pests considered to be at the core of our problem. If we could reduce or avoid the use of pesticides on leafhoppers, we would reduce or eliminate chemicals on other pests. We had observed that, in the spring, leafhopper outbreaks started at the edge of vineyards, but we did not know where these insects were coming from or how far they could fly into a vineyard. To find this out, we captured adult leafhoppers, and, after treating them with UV fluorescent dyes, we would release them in the open. After recapturing them at various distances inside the vineyards, we could measure how far they had traveled.

I suffered from excessive UV light exposure to my eyes, having spent too much time at the dissecting microscope. I was counting dyed insects in total darkness using a UV light source. This type of burn is frequent to welders or mountain climbers. It was a painful experience requiring medical intervention. After a sleepless night, Nicla took me to an ophthalmologist in Bakersfield, where the necessary ointments were applied to my eyes. I was then left in the dark for three days under a thick, dark bandage. Fortunately, no permanent damage occurred to my eyesight and shortly afterwards I was able to go back to work. However, from then on I promised to myself to leave to entomologists the chasing of their bugs.

A few weeks later, Nicla happened to witness a car accident which caused the death of a lady passenger and serious injury to the male driver. She saw a big truck run a stop sign and an oncoming car smash against its tail end. Both cars' passengers were thrown through the windshield. At the sight of this bloody scene Nicla went into shock, no longer able to sleep at night nor to eat. I promptly took Nicla to San Francisco for a medical check-up with Professor Ancona, a leading physician and a friend of the family. He told us that Nicla had had a nervous breakdown, likely due to excess fatigue. The car accident had only triggered what was already underway.

In fact, Nicla 's life had been particularly under stress due to a combination of factors. These included my long periods of absence and the increased responsibility of dealing by herself with three young children, a house, a garden, and many new clients in Bakersfield. She was constantly on the road to visit these clients for fittings, or to drive Victoria to ballet lessons. Isolation did the rest. Nicla remained alone for days and weeks, often without news of my whereabouts. Professor Ancona's diagnosis was correct. So was his prescription: move away from Winery Lane to a completely different environment, or drop all the sewing business, hire some help for the house and rest every day for two hours after lunch.

Only time and constant attention helped overcome this situation. Finally, in a small San Francisco restaurant, Nicla accepted some food which I provided to her, a little spoonful at a time. She slowly came out of her depression and returned to normality. This event signaled to us the need to change jobs and living conditions.

As indicated, my work at the Di Giorgio Research Department required a lot of travel and many days spent away from home. My situation worsened when J.S. asked me to take active part in battling a new disease problem called "pear decline." This disease, after causing the loss of thousands of pear trees in Oregon and Washington, arrived in the Company orchards in Marysville. By 1960, over one million trees were dead throughout the state. The cause of pear decline was yet unknown.

After assessing the situation at D'Antoni orchards in Marysville, I stopped in Davis to visit my old friend Tom Shalla at the Department of Plant Pathology. Tom, an outstanding virologist, was conducting very basic studies on virus movement from cell to cell. He was also responsible for research on diseases of pome fruits. He listened very patiently to what I had to say about pear decline and its likely viral nature. I then mentioned the Industry's interest in conducting joint investigations with the University, and the possibility of securing all the necessary financial support.

Tom was essentially a laboratory man. It was evident that he did not want to be taken away from his well-shielded and secure environment. Just beginning his academic career, Tom needed highly controlled environments to produce scientific papers of recognized value. He knew that none of these papers could result from work conducted in commercial orchards or on problems still obscure after many years of investigation. The only concession Tom was willing to make was to join me on a tour of Washington and Oregon to assess the status of pear decline research in both states.

This trip was organized during the summer of 1960. At the end of the tour, Tom was convinced of the need to conduct a series of graft transmission experiments in Marysville and on University grounds. On our return to Davis, we were surprised to find that the matter of pear decline had become a public issue, and the Governor had instructed the University to organize a state-wide committee to deal with this problem.

Tom found himself elected Chairman of a huge committee requiring the entire Regents Room in Berkeley to accommodate its many members. In spite of this, Tom and I proceeded with our planned experiments. These necessitated massive inoculations of apparently healthy mature trees with buds, root pieces and bark patches taken from different disease sources. An equal number of comparable, but untreated trees, served as control. This trial was conducted in the D'Antoni orchard in Marysville.

In a second trial, the test plants were two-year-old Bartlett trees on an Oriental rootstock growing in a University plot near Davis. More than 100 trees were inoculated in the same manner.

Both trials required plenty of manual work on our part, as we did not want to delegate any part of it to others, mainly to avoid mistakes. For the following two years we kept both plots under close observation. The results we obtained left no doubts: we had proved that pear decline was due to a graft-transmissible agent. Tom and I were the first to publish these results. Not too bad for two young plant pathologists just out of school!

During the spring of 1961, I made another important discovery. I recognized the similarity of pear decline to a disease which had occurred in Italy in 1949. The latter, called "moria," had been described by Professor Baldacci of the University of Milan, the same man who visited us at Di Giorgio Farms. I brought this finding to the University's attention as well as that of the Marketing Program for Canning Bartlett Pears. Funds were immediately made available to send Tom and me to Italy to determine if the two disorders were the same. If so, we were to find out what had been done in Italy to control the disease. This investigation was a shot in the dark, but, in the long run, it could save a lot of time and money.

We quickly made all the necessary arrangements. Equipped with a large, portable trunk containing all sort of vials and reagents to collect and preserve samples, we flew to Milan where we met Baldacci and proceeded with him to the Adige Valley in the Trentino region.

It was late in the evening when we stopped in an orchard with a few pear trees showing symptoms of decline. We immediately took a bark sample from the bud union of one of these trees. There was no question: a brown line appeared unmistakably clear on the inner face of the sample. This was a reliable symptom of pear decline in California (and one that had not been described in the Italian publication). An additional sample was taken from another declining tree, and again a brown line was present. It was getting dark in the orchard, but Tom and I could not resist taking a third sample. This time from an apparently healthy tree. No brown line was visible. There was no doubt: we were on the right track! The next day many more samples were collected, and the pattern remained unchanged: pear decline and moria were two names to describe the same disease in two different and far away parts of the world.

After a short detour through Austria, mainly to establish the source of pear seeds used by Italian nurseries to graft commercial pear varieties, Tom and I took different routes. He flew back to California with our valuable box full of samples. I went to Rome to pay a short visit to my mother and the rest of the family.

On this occasion I also visited FAO (the Food and Agriculture Organization of the United Nations), which was also located in Rome. The person I met was the Chief of the Crop Protection Branch, who appeared interested in my trip to Italy, since he was aware of the importance of pear decline on the west coast of North America. An article on the spread of pear decline in British Columbia, Washington, Oregon, and California had recently appeared in the FAO Plant Protection Bulletin, and the Chief was the Bulletin's editor. After a short interview with him, I left FAO and Italy to return to Di Giorgio Farms. Pear decline had taken enough time away from my work and my family.

Victoria, Marina and little Cynthia were all well and growing like weeds in the Di Giorgio Farms environment. They greatly enjoyed their many friends on "Winery Lane" and were busy in hundreds of games and activities. Victoria was taking ballet lessons in Bakersfield, and attending classes at the Rockpile Elementary School near Arvin (at a location vividly named Weed Patch). The teaching level was not excessively high, but there were no educational alternatives. Victoria also received piano lessons from a nextdoor neighbor. This was in the hope of discovering her hidden musical talent.

Marina, not yet of school age, had plenty of free time to lead a gang of young boys in a variety of games. In one of these, she showed them how easy it was to do somersaults on our neighbor's lawn. Performing her demonstration, she broke an arm. It was at dinnertime on Easter that this happened. We rushed her to the hospital in Bakersfield, where an orthopedist had to be called in for the emergency. No nurses were available to assist this doctor, so Nicla and I helped him set Marina's bones and apply a heavy cast to her arm. No one suspected that this same cast was soon to become Marina's most respected and convincing club.

Cynthia was probably the person who suffered most from the appearance of this new weapon. To her this was a definite change in the balance of power. She had only one alternative: her sharp teeth, including those she had been provided with at birth. As with any other weapon used around the world, Cynthia's teeth were, of course, for..."defense only."

Time was passing very quickly with a growing family, visiting friends and relatives, and many other activities. To interrupt our routine, a letter arrived from FAO in Rome with the announcement of a vacant position in the Crop

Protection Branch. They were looking for a Tropical Plant Pathologist with at least seven years of professional experience and knowledge of French and Spanish. Some forms were enclosed with the announcement, but not a single personal word accompanied these documents. After discussing this matter with Nicla, I decided to submit an application.

Several months went by and not a word was received from FAO. We had already lost hope that anything would happen, when in early August, 1961, we received a letter from Dr. Eckert in Davis. He had been approached by FAO to provide references on "my character only." Shortly after, J.S. Di Giorgio called me into his office to find out why I was looking for another job, and if there were something wrong with my present position. He had received the same request from FAO. I then explained the difficulties I had with some of the ranch managers, my concern about my future, my constant travel and its interference with research, Nicla's isolation problem, and the uncertain education of my children in Arvin.

J.S. listened to all I had to say, and then, almost in a fatherly way, he asked me if I would consider taking over the Farms as superintendent, or if I would prefer an expansion of the Research Department. "And if your wife is not pleased with the present house," he added, "tell her that we are prepared to rent you a house in Bakersfield." His words were kind and his offers generous. Evidently, he appreciated my work and did not wish to let me go. At the end, however, I felt he understood my position, and only with great reluctance tried to modify my decision. Once again, J.S.proved to be a man capable of putting himself in my place, and of thinking deeply and comprehensively.

At last we learned from some of our neighbors that FBI agents were making inquiries about us, our life style, political ideas, and even drinking habits. One of these neighbors happened to be the chief wine maker of the nearby ten million gallon winery. This, apparently, had no adverse effect on the FBI's report. The formal offer of appointment arrived from Rome after a few months, and I lost no time in returning my acceptance.

During this last period of residence at Di Giorgio I made another significant discovery. I was able to transmit the agent causing leafroll disease of grapevines. For this transmission I used mealybugs raised on potato sprouts in the greenhouse. These insects were subsequently fed on either diseased or healthy vines growing in clay pots. After this feeding, they were transferred into small cages applied to the leaves of highly susceptible "indicator plants."

Not long afterwards, some of the "indicators" which had received insects previously fed on diseased plants showed curling and reddening of the leaves. No such symptoms appeared on the controls. I was very excited by these findings, but I had no time to repeat the experiment. I was getting ready to leave for Italy. The best I could do was to turn all my experimental data and slides over to Dr. Hewitt with the request that he run another test. Unfortunately, Dr. Hewitt was also leaving Davis to become director of the University of California Kearny field station.

Twenty-two years later, research workers in Sicily published their successful transmission of leafroll by mealybugs. Dr. Hewitt pulled from his files the documentation I had provided, and sent it to Professor Martelli in Bari, who, in turn, reported my old findings at an international meeting. But this was the only credit I was entitled to receive. I was wrong in not publishing my original results, and I was punished accordingly. After all, science has certain rules that must be observed.

Once I informed J.S. Di Giorgio that I had accepted the FAO's offer, he agreed to pay me a substantial bonus, including my profit sharing entitlement from having been with the Company for ten years. Before informing Nicla about this unexpected income, I purchased a large, green plastic garbage can in an Arvin hardware store. When I entered the house, Nicla was surprised about my unusual purchase. "What is this for?" she asked. "Well, I thought that garbage cans in Rome are usually small. This one, instead, might be more useful to us," I replied. "But please, open the can and look inside," I insisted. She removed the cover and picked up the envelope laying at the bottom. It contained the Company's check for five thousand dollars. Her response was surprise and happiness mixed together. We spent the evening dancing around the large, green plastic garbage can in the middle of our living room.

My decision to leave the Company proved to be the correct one. Only two years later, Di Giorgio Farms were sold on the open market and the Corporation liquidated all other assets in agriculture. It was the end of the fruit company. It was also the end of the dream of an outstanding immigrant from Sicily.

PART THREE

International Life

10
An International Experience

*We shall be judged more by what we
do at home than what we preach
abroad.*

—John F. Kennedy

In early November, 1962, a prepaid first class air
ticket was received from FAO for our entire
family's trip from Bakersfield to Rome. An
international packing and shipping company took care of
moving all our belongings at FAO's expense. The old
refrigerator, Victoria's piano, and a few household items
which we did not want to bring with us, were sold locally,
while a large deep freezer and a refrigerator were bought to
be shipped to Rome. The last night in California was spent
in the home of Dr. Ramirez, who drove us to the Bakersfield
airport on the following day. There was plenty of excitement

in our family, mixed with a feeling of sadness at leaving behind the Company and our many friends.

The flight to Los Angeles took about half an hour. The children were excited about being on the plane, but soon they were disappointed by the shortness of the flight. Upon landing in Los Angeles, Victoria asked: "Is this all?" She was reassured that a much longer flight was needed to reach our final destination. We were able to overnight in a small motel by the airport. It was still warm in Los Angeles and the girls took a long swim in the motel's pool before a good night's sleep.

The next morning, we boarded a Scandinavian jumbo jet bound for Copenhagen and Rome. The plane was very large and we found the First Class section extremely comfortable. After reaching the required altitude, cocktails and hors d'oeuvres were served to the passengers. The head chef, wearing the classic checkered pants and tall, white cap, came to the cabin to personally serve a beautifully decorated silver plate of entrées. He wanted to be nice to the girls and invited them to select whatever they liked. Cynthia, after much studying and indecision, took one of the lemon pieces garnishing the rim of the plate, saying, "I'll take this if you don't mind." The chef was evidently embarrassed, but Cynthia's decision left no room for alternatives.

The flight continued uneventfully until the plane landed in Iceland for refueling. Passengers were invited to disembark, and for the first time in their lives, our children walked on freshly fallen snow. For girls raised in warm California weather, close to vineyards and around swimming pools, this was an unbelievable experience.

After a short stopover in Copenhagen, we boarded a smaller plane. This time our destination was Rome. It was an appropriate time for Nicla and me to look at each other and to talk about achievements and recent developments. We recognized that we were a special type of emigrant who had made many sacrifices. We had always worked very hard at any job we were able to find, and we had always kept a low profile. We were now flying back to our native country as First Class passengers and well paid international civil servants. Were we "lucky," or did we deserve this type of reward?

The arrival at the Ciampino airport was again full of noise and excitement. The entire family and many friends were there to see our girls and give us a warm welcome. This time it was not for a short visit: our return to Rome was for a long stay. No one expected that this was to last for nearly a quarter of a century.

I reported to my new job the day after our arrival. It was a typical rainy November day in Rome when I entered "Building B" of FAO where the Crop Protection Branch was located. All offices of the Plant Production and Protection Division, one of the most important of the Organization, were on the seventh floor.

Long strings of corridors had hundreds of small niches opening on both sides. Most of these offices had closed doors. Occasionally, a few doors were left open and one could see groups of secretaries busy around their typewriters, or a single "professional" engaged in writing or in serious "meditation." People appeared somewhat stiff behind the desks in the small niches. For a moment I wondered if these men and women were still physiologically and functionally alive.

The overall atmosphere was one of stagnation and close confinement. By comparison, my mind went back to California's wide open farms, the long walks in the hot Delano vineyards, and the chilly mornings spent grafting pear trees in Marysville. Was I going to adjust to this new, austere, and constrained environment? Only time would tell.

My first concern was reporting to my Branch Chief to see what plans he had for me and my work. This was not as easy as I thought. The Chief was "busy" and could not see anyone for some time. It was up to his secretary to show me around and find me an office. This secretary was a very cordial person. She was from Switzerland but, having married an Italian, she was perfectly at ease with Roman life and habits. To my great surprise, I discovered that she had seen me before. The previous evening one of the local TV channels had shown a documentary on California agriculture. This had been filmed a few months earlier at Di Giorgio Farms and Marysville by Antonio Cifariello, an Italian movie actor and director. In this documentary I had been interviewed about pear decline and other matters. This unexpected popularity in Rome helped me to become more easily acquainted with several other people at FAO, including Luciana Balvetti, the secretary who had been assigned to my office.

Luciana was an extremely shy person and, as a result, only a few people were able to fully appreciate her very special human qualities and wonderful resources. She was probably the greatest asset I ever had in my new position in Rome.

After a few days, I was able to arrange an interview with my new boss. He was a Chinese national with a Ph.D. degree in Plant Pathology from the University of Minnesota. He had joined FAO in the early days, when the Organization was in Washington, D.C. A tall, lean man, he possessed the expressionless face of a Nevada gambler. Although he was already in his early fifties, his hair was still jet black and shiny, making it difficult to guess his age. Also glossy was the bottom of his trousers and the back of the dark suit coat that he wore summer or winter, year after year. This glossiness was probably an external sign of wear from the extended rubbing of his clothes on FAO's chairs for many years. At first sight, my new boss appeared to be a very unusual person: extremely intelligent, with unique skills that allowed him to function effectively within the realm of a large international bureaucracy. He was difficult to understand in a conversation because he was nearly voiceless, but his flawless command of written English largely compensated for his aphonia.

The first interview was incredibly short. As I entered his office the Chief was concentrating on reading the Wall Street Journal. (Later I discovered that he actively followed the New York stock market, and that he dedicated much of his office time to this important task.) Setting the newspaper aside, almost annoyed for the interruption I caused, he told me that my position was entirely new, and that I had to create my own program of work, for which he was unable to provide any direction. The best he could offer was his authorization for my travel to Egypt and the Far East, where I could best "become acquainted with plant pathological problems at national level, and stimulate new projects for FAO's assistance."

A better briefing on Branch activities and personality-related problems was given to me by a fellow "officer," Roberto Egli, with whom I shared an office. Apparently, Roberto had plenty of free time at his disposal. He was partially responsible for the editing of the "FAO Plant Protection Bulletin." The actual editor was still the Chief, who allowed Roberto to carry out only the menial tasks of this job. Repeatedly the Chief was heard saying that he could do the entire editorial work by himself and "during his lunch hour."

Thus, a little at a time, I became acquainted with my new work environment and the people around me. It was a sharp departure from what I had had in California. The first question that came to my mind was, "Will I be able to change this environment, or will the environment change me?"

There were three priorities for settling to work for FAO: securing a place to live, finding schools for the children, and buying a car.

For the first few months Nicla and I found hospitality at her parent's apartment in Via Ovidio. After many years of separation, father Vittorio and mother Gina were most happy to host their daughter's family and to enjoy their grandchildren at close range. There was only one problem. These children were American. They spoke a different language, they had their meals at different hours, and they were not used to living in a confined apartment. In fact, the girls kept looking for areas in the neighborhood where they could find some grass on which to play and run, just like in California. It was amazing to see how the grandparents were able to overcome these problems, and how grandchildren could easily adapt to new conditions.

In only a week, a suitable school was found for Victoria. This was at St. Francis, a Catholic elementary school run by American nuns. St. Francis was located on the Via Cassia, one of the consular roads built by the Romans and still in good usage. The buildings were modern and well kept. The grounds were planted with lawns and surrounded by beautiful pine trees. It was definitely an improvement over the "Rockpile" school in Arvin. A small school bus took care of the daily transportation to and from school. More difficult was to find a kindergarten for Marina, but after one month she was accepted at the American School of Rome. Cynthia was still too young for schooling and remained home in the grandparents' apartment.

The problem of transportation was also easily resolved. Through the FAO automobile service, it was possible to acquire tax-free a Ford Taunus made in Germany, which proved to be an excellent car. Gasoline coupons were part of the FAO commissary entitlement, so our transportation costs were altogether irrelevant in a city in which gasoline prices were four times as high as in California.

Nicla and I began looking for an apartment shortly after our arrival. Having considered the unbearable Roman traffic, we decided that the location of this apartment must be halfway between Via Cassia and FAO. This would cut in half the driving time to work or school.

Finding an apartment was not easy also because extra space was needed in the kitchen to accommodate our bulky freezer and refrigerator. A large number of apartments were visited, but nothing came close to our needs. One Sunday, we took a walk from the Gianicolo hill to Viale Piccolomini. This hillside boulevard had been designed to frame the spectacular view of St.Peter's dome in the distance. Seen from far away, this structure appeared abnormally large. But, as one approached the end of the boulevard, the dome looked much smaller when the view of the city below enlarged.

At the corner of Viale Piccolomini and Via San Lucio, we saw a nice looking building with five apartments. One of these was still for sale. The building had an unusual trapezoidal shape. Each apartment occupied an entire floor and was surrounded on three sides by a long, narrow terrace. The terraces sported distinctive iron railings painted white in striking contrast to the tan of the building. The windows were large, and each room opened onto the terrace, like cabins on a boat deck. The building's design was unconventional. We later discovered that it had been designed by a renowned architect from Brazil, Julio Lafuente, and that it had been publicized in L'architecture d'aujourd'hui—Habitat, a well known architectural journal.

We promptly asked the portiere (doorman) to show us the apartment. Inspecting the interior, we were immediately impressed by the spectacular view of Rome, St. Peter's dome and the Gianicolo hills on the horizon. The breakfast room near the kitchen had plenty of space for our refrigeration equipment, and the pink marble floors in the corridor and in the large living/dining room added increased beauty to the well designed floor plan. We liked the apartment and wanted to buy it.

The only problem was its cost, which appeared quite high: close to 32 million lira ($46,000). A price much above our resources, considering that in Italy, most of the money must be paid up front and in cash at the signing of the contract.

This problem was discussed with mother Gina. She listened, smiled and promised to talk it over with father Vittorio. Maybe a solution could be found. After a few days she was glad to announce that they could provide us with a loan of 14 million lira (nearly $19,000). The only requirement was that we pay them the same interest paid by their bank. This was a welcome arrangement, and we proceeded with the purchase.

By mid-January, we were able to move into our new living quarters, in time for the arrival of our belongings from California. We were extremely happy with the purchase of our first piece of real estate. However, the first nights at San Lucio were sleepless for me. "Am I going to be able to pay for all this?" I kept asking myself. Only time (and inflation!) returned my sleep to normalcy and answered this recurrent question.

Our life in Italy was essentially divided into three modes: life in the city, life on the coast, and life in FAO. Each of these modes required special attention, time and a good dose of energy.

LIFE IN THE CITY

The apartment at San Lucio soon became the center of family gatherings for festivities and other occasions. It was also the place where many FAO experts and international visitors were invited when passing through Rome. On numerous occasions, and usually on very short notice, Nicla organized superb cocktail parties or unforgettable dinners. We soon learned that diplomatic life was essentially made up of these types of social events. And Nicla's elegance, class, good taste, and wonderful food was by far superior to any caterer or restaurant in the city. Many of my successes in FAO were unquestionably due to this kind of hospitality.

Life for the children had greatly improved with the purchase of the apartment. There was ample space for everyone. Victoria had her own room, while Marina and Cynthia shared another bedroom. The long, narrow terrace offered a chance to play outdoors and even do some skating. Within a few years, all three daughters were going to St. Francis School. Later on, they moved to Marymount International School. Their teachers were all outstanding. By fostering close communication with them, it was possible to establish a solid family-school relationship, through which the girls were able to grow and become well balanced individuals. In record time they learned to speak fluent Italian. This made their grandparents most happy, as they could now communicate freely with them.

The rich cultural surroundings of Rome, and the many school trips to other Italian cities and abroad, also helped develop our daughters' appreciation for architecture, music and history. All together, our stay in Rome contributed to a very positive educational experience.

Our apartment at the second floor of Via San Lucio.

But life in the Italian capital was not always easy. There were times when frustration and anger made the city unbearable. Roman traffic is a good example. It was chaotic, noisy, bringing out some of the worst features of the local people. With narrow streets, excessive cars, wide public buses, cumbersome trucks, noisy motorcycles, incompetent traffic police, impatient drivers, and no parking places, the public responded by being pushy and inconsiderate. The word "traffic" implies some kind of movement. Instead the Roman traffic often resulted in total paralysis. I was frequently caught in this situation when I returned home from work or when I tried to drive during rush hour to Via

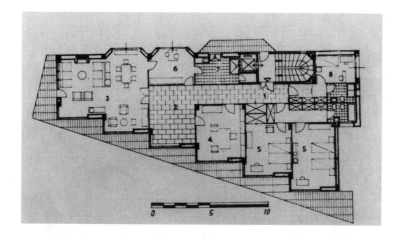

The floor plan of the same apartment.

Ovidio, where Nicla's parents lived. Occasionally, I was forced to leave my car in a side alley or in somebody's courtyard, and walk home. The car was picked up later at night, when Roman drivers were finally out of the streets.

At other times, I had the courage to step out of my own vehicle to help entangled automobiles disengage from what looked like a perfectly static parking situation. Without my assistance, the impatient Roman motorists would have remained sitting ducks in their cars for many more hours.

In situations of this kind, the chance of collision was always high. Accidents could be seen on any street and at all hours of the day or the night. Most cars had numerous scars from this never-ending battle. Body shops made a fortune out of the whole mess, and insurance companies tried to find clever ways to avoid paying compensation.

Nicla was caught in such a situation. One day, while driving to my office, she barely touched another car next to her. She did not realize what had happened and calmly proceeded to FAO. But soon she discovered that she was being followed by the "damaged" party honking and screaming behind her. Finally she was stopped by two furious men who demanded her name and address. The damage was barely visible, but their anger was very conspicuous, like in Verdi's final act of " La forza del destino."

After a few days we received a claim for a substantial sum of money. I arranged with my lawyer and friend Gino Crisanti to meet these two men in his office. The meeting was short and to the point.

I began by explaining that the "accident" was not due to Nicla's driving. Rather, it was the fault of one of the two men who, with the intent of passing a bus, had suddenly moved into Nicla's lane. Then I added that I was not prepared to pay a dime for a scratch barely visible on their car. In conclusion, and to demonstrate that it was not a matter of money but of principle, I further suggested that I would be prepared to pay the requested claim in full, but not to the two men. My "donation" would be given to the earthquake victims in Sicily, in the names of both parties. The proposal was accepted and the problem was resolved.

Another unbearable situation in Rome existed in the local hospitals. During our many years in Rome, Nicla and I acquired a broad experience of these hospitals, having to provide assistance to many relatives and friends. Public hospitals were dirty, crowded, and often without a minimum of essential equipment or even of disposable materials. Giving assistance to sick people under these conditions was a nightmare. The only alternative was to avoid public hospitals altogether and use, instead, private "clinics." These were shiny, exceptionally well served, and extremely expensive.

A typical feature of modern Roman life was that seldom there was a "normal" day, where normality means a day without unexpected events. Strikes and political rallies were frequently organized without warning. Their specific objective was, in fact, that of disrupting "normal" city living. In this way, students and teachers, garbage collectors and bank employees, public transportation personnel and firemen, all went on strike to claim some union request or to condemn some political event. The worst period was between the years 1969 and 1987, when new-Fascist and Red Brigade terrorists killed more than 400 people and injured several thousand citizens. Among the dead was Italy's former Premier Aldo Moro and his police escort. In the weeks immediately following his kidnapping, we were frequently stopped by the police because we were driving a Mercedes. Its large trunk was considered "highly suspicious," as it could easily contain dead human bodies.

In many ways, our life in Rome was "easier" than that of local people because of our diplomatic status and FAO's facilities for travel, banking, post office, commissary, insurance, and automobile registration services. In other words, as "Americans" and as "foreign diplomats" we could avoid the rites of the Roman fila (queue), in which enormous amounts of time were wasted paying utility bills and taxes, buying railroad or airplane tickets, or getting any sort of "certificate."

Roman bureaucracy is probably one of the slowest and most useless in the world. Paul Hofmann, in his book That Fine Italian Hand, properly defined this bureaucracy as " baroque as a dilapidated Neapolitan palazzo." And we could not agree more, having only experienced minor encounters with it.

One of these experiences was the result of a bank request for a certificate showing that I was no longer an Italian citizen. Only as an American I could legally maintain a dollar account in Italy. To secure this certificate I paid a visit to the City Hall Recorder, where I was surprised to discover that I was still an Italian citizen with legal residency in Rome. According to their books, Nicla had disappeared from Rome in 1952 and there was no further record of her, nor of any children.

I tried to explain that when Nicla and I left together for the United States, both of us signed separate documents for the Recorder relinquishing our residencies. Apparently, only Nicla's declaration had been duly recorded. I insisted that I was an American citizen, I showed my U.S. Passport, and then I inquired if the matter could not be corrected by signing a new declaration. I could officially do this in their presence. The public servant, sitting behind a worn out desk and surrounded by a carousel of rubber stamps of all shapes and sizes, looked at me and smiled in a cold and distant way. "My dear sir," he said, "You are now working in Rome. The Italian law says that upon returning and working in Italy, after three months you are automatically reinstated as resident." I could not believe what I had just heard. To fully convince me, the public servant pulled out a discolored booklet from an enormous pile of papers. This was the text of a law passed under King Umberto the First at the beginning of 1900. "After all," continued the patient man, "I really cannot understand why this residency should upset you so much when thousands of people would like to have it in your place!"

As I was ready to leave the office, the man smiled again and called me aside. Then, in a soft whisper, he said, "Sir, if you really want to have your residency canceled, go to the Italian consulate when you are in San Francisco and let them officially communicate to us that you are a California resident. But, please, when you return to Rome, don't ever let us know that you are here and working." It was clear that the Italian bureaucratic machinery was old and malfunctioning and that the "dilapidated Neapolitan palazzo" had lost more of its worn out stucco, but it was also fortunate that Italian bureaucrats knew too well how to navigate in difficult waters. After all, Italy is the country of Amerigo Vespucci, Christopher Columbus, Giovanni da Verrazzano, and many other skilled navigators who crossed the oceans at will.

To really learn about modern Roman life, one must be part a Roman condominium. In the beginning, only five families lived in the apartment house in Via San Lucio. On the ground floor was a young and ebullient attorney with his wife; on the second floor lived our family; on the third floor were two bachelor brothers in their sixties, their waiter, and a cook; occupying the fourth floor was the former mayor of Rome, his wife, a senator-to-be son, and a couple of Ethiopian servants. On the top floor lived a well-to-do spinster from Apulia in the South. It was a highly diversified group of individuals. Common to all was the strong desire to outdo others in maintaining a first class, elegant dwelling. The "Americans" were accepted in this environment only after the former mayor discovered that Nicla was one of the daughters of Professor Ronchi, a former member of the Italian government and a highly respectable person.

We were the only family with young children, but, fortunately for us, this was regarded by everyone as positive. When the time came for the first condominium meeting, we had not yet moved into our apartment. The assembly took place at the two bachelors' apartment, where the business meeting turned out to be a most elegant gala dinner. For many years we had not seen such a great display of crystals, silverware, finely embroidered table linens, and a most sophisticated menu. Old paintings, rich velvet curtains and expensive antique furniture did the rest, in a most elegant choreography that only Italians could arrange and manage so perfectly. It was an opportunity for the two brothers to show off their apartment and to display their very sophisticated arrangements, including luxury bathrooms and finely-made closets full of elegant clothes.

Discussing a condominium budget after a reception of this kind was a difficult undertaking. As expected, everything on the agenda was easily approved with a minimum of discussion. After all, the old Romans had learned long ago that, following a wonderful meal, the digestive process must never be disturbed by useless business talk. One item that remained unsettled was that concerning space allocation for parking in the crowded underground garage. This, in fact, had been established on a "first come, first serve basis," the equivalent of territorial imperative in animals. We had been left a narrow slot with only a few inches on each side for backing up without denting our car against a robust concrete pillar on the left side, or the car of the young attorney on the opposite side.

The tradition of using a condominium assembly to organize showy gala events went on for several years. But, as everything else in life, it came finally to an end. The southern spinster moved away, the mayor and his wife died in quick succession, and one of the bachelors also passed away. Definitely, the original San Lucio population had greatly changed. As a result, the annual condominium meetings could only be held in an attorney's office. The "finesse" of past dinners was replaced by endless quarrels and occasional harsh words. We found ourselves the only ones still able to share old memories with the bachelor on the third floor. Indeed, there was much to be learned about Roman life by living in a Roman condominium.

LIFE ON THE COAST

As already mentioned, much of our time spent in Italy was devoted to the house, garden and natural surroundings of Terracina. Life in a city as chaotic as Rome needed a place to escape to on weekends. Work in a sedentary bureaucracy like FAO required a site where physical activity could be performed. Terracina satisfied both conditions. At first it was an adventure leaving Rome on Friday afternoon and going to this place so isolated and far away from civilization. Punctually at 5:00 pm, Nicla was outside the FAO entrance with three girls sitting in the car loaded with school books and beach gear. In no time Rome and FAO were left behind and after a one and half hour drive, our family arrived in Terracina. Since the house had no electricity, there was no refrigeration. Upon arrival, the first stop was to procure bulk ice from the fishermen's cooperative at the pier. Big, hairy, sun-tanned men, sitting lazily in front of the co-op, stared with amazement at our car loaded with foreign-looking girls, books and beach gear. Bulk ice was placed in two capable garbage cans that were assigned to this indispensable function. The next stop was at the alimentari (grocery store-deli mixture). This was mainly to purchase bread, nutella and candles. The Terracina bread, made daily in firewood operated ovens, had a unique flavor. The nutella was a hazel nut paste that spread quite well on large-sized bread slices. And the candles were for lighting the dark house that had no electricity.

In the winter, it was dark very early in the evening, and our arrival at the house on the beach in full darkness was often dramatic. It was a mixture of game and adventure. Nothing looks more dejected than a summer resort house in the middle of the winter. In one corner of the living room, a partially inflated rubber raft, abandoned from the summer before, was sadly resting on the tile floor. Signs of humidity and mold were all over the walls and furniture. Dead ants, flies and other bugs lay in abundance on the floors and window sills. Spider webs hung freely from the ceilings and danced with air drafts, their shadows greatly enlarged by the dim candle lights. Large areas of the ceiling were marked by spots of moisture where the rain had penetrated the roof.

All this did not discourage our family. Outside the house the roar of the waves and the blowing of the wind were reassuring sounds. Supper was prepared in a very short time, and the steam of strained spaghetti filled the kitchen air in a most welcome, appetizing cloud. After a good meal there was nothing left to do but go to bed. All bedding was brought from Rome because mattresses and sheets were soaked with moisture and smelled moldy. Our daughters remained clothed in their parkas as they crawled into their cold beds. They were good campers and knew how to face adverse environmental conditions. They seemed to enjoy camping in the house on the beach.

Early mornings at Terracina were very special. There was absolutely no breeze. The sea, only a few yards away, appeared as calm as a large pond. It had a silvery color until the sun rose high in the blue sky. The air was clean and crisp, with a very special smell: it carried a scent of salt and orange blossoms. Far out at sea were a few boats returning to port after a night of fishing. On the beach some men prepared to enter the cold waters to dig for clams. They were strangely dressed. On top of everything they wore black raincoats probably purchased in some navy salvage store. They had a special tool that they buried into the sand and dragged while walking backward. Often these men would sing as they worked in water up to their chest. And the sound of their voices blended nicely with that of the sea gulls circling high in the sky. It was indeed a peaceful, harmonious and

Backside of the Terracina's house.

enjoyable scene: the sea, the sand, the clam diggers, and the birds!

The sturdy house had been designed by Nicla's sister Lisa to resemble a typical farmhouse in the Roman countryside. The front section was built on the lip of a sand dune running parallel to the sea. The back of the building faced inland and overlooked the mountains surrounding the Fondi Valley. These mountains protected the area from cold northerly winds and provided abundant underground water. The valley floor had been at one time covered by marshes and small lakes, where water buffalos were raised in large numbers and malaria prevented human settlement.

Following Mussolini's reclamation of the Pontine marshes not far to the north, the flooded Fondi Valley was also reclaimed. As a result, agriculture started to flourish, and citrus, deciduous trees, early vegetables, and vineyards were planted throughout. The vineyards were mainly confined to the sandy seaside soils up on the dunes facing the sea. The Ronchi's house was mostly enclosed by these vineyards. It was a strange feeling for Nicla and myself to be again surrounded by grapevines like those we had left behind in California. Where vineyards could not be planted, the wild Mediterranean vegetation was left untouched. These unique plants could withstand long summer droughts and fierce salty winds from the sea, and offered aesthetic potential for landscaping.

There were no other houses in the surroundings. A campground, managed by a German couple, was not too far away. Its clientele consisted of German tourists, who, for their stay on the white sandy beach, were asked to pay in German marks only. The beach itself, wide and unspoiled, appeared dank and desolate during the winter.

During the summer, the daily northwesterly winds picked up late in the morning and increased in force by early afternoon. The sand was then blown in an easterly direction, forming all sorts of designs on the beach. These winds also caused serious erosion of the dune and of the area in front of the building.

The house had been essentially designed to meet the summer requirements of a family of a certain size and composition. It was also built with budgetary constraints. Once finished, the house was left to itself, with no or very little upkeep. Occasionally it was not used by anybody during the summer, so that it remained tightly closed for an entire year. When it was opened again, the combined damage of winter moisture, summer heat and a year's neglect was most apparent.

As indicated, electricity was not available and no one really cared about it. After all, summer nights were short in Terracina and the beauty of the stars in the clear, dark sky was most enjoyable in the absence of artificial light. The only problem was the domestic water supply. There was no aqueduct in the area and all the water for cooking or hygienic purposes had to be lifted from underground into a storage tank located in the highest spot under the roof. A hand-operated water pump, installed outdoors, served this purpose. Turns were taken by adult residents to move its handle back and forth until an overflow started dripping on someone's head. It was a primitive system, but it worked. In the summer, after all, who really cared about time spent pumping water? In fact, this was considered a sort of relaxing exercise if done during the day, when accompanied by radio music or by a good mystery book. Of course, the situation was different if water in the storage tank ran out during a cold winter night or when it was stormy outside.

To resolve this problem, I approached the local power company. At first, I was requested to pay a large amount of money for extending the power line from a substation some miles away. When I argued that this was their cost for developing the area, another issue was raised. The power company did not know the names and addresses of the owners of the lots that had to be crossed by the power line. I patiently collected these names and addresses and returned my list to the company. At this point there were no other arguments. "Where would you want the line to run? You show us where," said the exhausted company representative. In this way, with great patience and perseverance, electricity finally reached the dark and lonely house on the beach. With electricity, progress also arrived in the form of much increased comfort.

Many things changed, both in the house and in the garden. An electric pump took the place of the old hand pump and an ample water supply became available. Water heaters were also installed to make life a little more pleasant when showering. And a number of electric heating pads were purchased to help remove humidity from the damp mattresses on cold winter nights. Most important of all, a refrigeration unit was added to the house to keep food from spoiling and to cool drinks.

Two additional wells were drilled for use in the thirsty landscape. Mother Gina had been the only one in the family who had attempted to plant a few trees and shrubs. But most of her effort had been unsuccessful. The long summer drought and the rapidly drying sandy soil did not permit any type of gardening without frequent irrigations. A sprinkling system was installed to water the areas of primary importance. It was necessary first to stabilize the existing sand dune against wind erosion. This was achieved with the planting of a lawn and the laying of concrete stepping stones on the sandy ground to give easier access to the beach and to create a sitting area in front of the house. Here the single ilex tree standing in the center of the dune, greatly benefitted from the irrigation water and grew to form a magnificent natural umbrella. Through its dark green foliage it was possible to admire all of the splendor of the blue sea below.

Gardening two days a week and worrying the other five became our normal way of life, especially during the spring and early summer months. Deeply engaged in these activities, Nicla and I did not notice the years passing by so quickly. Twenty-three years of hard work were directed to a single continuous project, at the end of which a most rewarding garden of colors was created.

There are three major things worth remembering about Terracina summers: swimming in the early mornings, sailing in the afternoons, and gathering with friends and relatives in the evenings. Before the sun rose high over the horizon, the sea shone like silver. The water was crystal clear, allowing us to see the very active animal life on the sandy bottom. Small crabs fought each other, while clams of all sizes and shapes were barely buried in the sand. Schools of small fish passed by, rapidly changing direction at sharp angles, while solitary jellyfish were seen passively bouncing around. It was fun to watch this marine life while slowly swimming in the crisp sea water. There were only a few people on the beach early in the morning. The German owner of the campground and his many dogs would take their routine walk, while the proprietor of the small coffee shop on the beach was setting up his umbrellas. Otherwise, there was only the gentle lapping of small waves lazily breaking on the shore.

By mid-morning, the sea breeze would pick up, and by noon the wind was usually strong. It was time to raise the sails and go out on the blue waters. Fom the beach it was difficult to judge the size and power of the waves. One had to be out there, a few miles from shore, to appreciate their height and strength. The beauty of it was that the waves followed the wind direction, nearly always blowing to the southeast. This added an important safety factor. If a sailboat capsized, the sailors would, sooner or later, land on the beach circling the bay.

Of our three girls, Marina was most attracted to sailing. When we found out that a used Vaurien boat was for sale in Leghorn, Marina and I went to see it. The boat was purchased, loaded on top of our car and then slowly driven back to Terracina. After the necessary repairs and repainting, "Harvey" was finally placed in the blue water. It was a good and sturdy boat, well suited to beginners and to people with strong backs. In fact, the boat was heavy when taken out of the water and then lifted to the top of the sea wall at the end of our stays in Terracina. A good system for lifting and lowering the boat to the beach was soon developed, using the best of my engineering skills.

It was great fun to go out sailing with Marina. She was especially attentive to changes of the wind. She was also good at making the boat acquire speed by planing on the crest of waves. Sailing and planing with "Harvey" were the source of many rapturous, unforgettable moments.

After a few years, another boat was added to our fleet. This time, a used Minisail was purchased "sight unseen" in the city of London. After reading an ad in an English yachting magazine, I had the courage to ask one of my British colleagues in FAO, who was driving his car to England, if he could bring the Minisail back to Rome. Ed Turtle was willing to do this for us. He was a very patient and cooperative man. After a month or so, early one Saturday morning, Ed phoned to announce that the boat had arrived in Rome after a long journey through France and northern Italy. The whole family went to Ed's residence to meet the Minisail and transfer it to the top of our car. In appreciation for Ed's effort, two things were offered to him and his wife: a free ride on the boat and a weekend as our guests at Terracina. Only the latter was accepted by both.

With the Minisail, Marina acquired more sailing freedom. She could go out to sea alone, since she could handle the single sail. She could do without me, even in strong winds, because a sliding seat was added to the boat to permit her to counterbalance their force. It was always a sight to follow her maneuvering at sea. Nonno Vittorio, being particularly apprehensive, would always watch her from the beach, using his powerful binoculars.

One windy afternoon Marina skimmed along next to a fishing boat with such speed and dexterity that the bewildered fisherman dropped all his nets in the water, surprised to see a young and beautiful girl sailing so skillfully near his heavily bouncing vessel. Evidently, he had never made such an encounter in his entire life at sea.

Many more stories could be told about the Minisail. No one could have foreseen that this little boat would be shipped to California when Marina went to college. Then the boat faithfully followed her by land to San Diego, Birmingham (Alabama), Madison (Wisconsin) and then back to Livermore in Northern California. It might be difficult to find another Minisail in the United States, and probably in the world, that has accumulated such road mileage.

A third member of our fleet only lasted half a summer. Its story, however, is worth remembering, because it vividly describes the contemptuous characters of some Italians.

After a strong winter storm, Nicla and I found on the beach one-half of a dual-hull row boat. This section was buried under several feet of sand. At first we did not pay much attention to this relic. Then, after several months, we discovered the other piece of the hull behind the sand dune on our neighbor's property. We inquired with the nearby residence's watchman and we were informed that he had retrieved this second piece from the beach. Having no use for this relic, he was glad to let me have it. I went back to the beach and started digging up the other half. This looked severely damaged but, in my opinion, not beyond repair. With Nicla's help, the second piece was taken from the beach to the boat shed at the top of our sea wall.

I spent numerous weekends fixing the damaged hulls with fiberglass and doing extensive sanding. A welding shop in town was able to rebuild the entire iron framework connecting the two sections, and two new oars were purchased from a local shop. The salvaged boat was then assembled, painted bright red and launched at sea.

Several months later, a woman from a nearby residential compound came to our house claiming to have recognized "her" boat. Under the red paint she had seen the original yellow color of the boat that "had disappeared from her house." I explained what had happened and immediately reassured the lady that I had no intention of keeping the boat. All I wanted was a refund for my expenses and labor (about

$200 in total). She looked at me and told me angrily that she had no intention of giving me a dime. "If you do not give me back my boat, I will go to the police," she added. But I was firm in my decision. "Sorry, lady, no refund, no boat!" I insisted.

A few days later, the same woman was sitting in the boat on the beach. She was determined not to move from "her property." I patiently invited her to move, but without success. So, with the help of a few friends, I lifted the boat (with the lady in it) and placed it in the water. "For the last time, lady," I said with a voice that left no doubt, "either you get off the boat now or I will take you out to sea. I hope you know how to swim, because I cannot guarantee your safe return on the boat!" She looked at me, and mumbling words not worth repeating, the unyielding lady left the boat and I went out to sea.

Two days later, three carabinieri (military police) showed up at our house. I explained in detail what had happened and also indicated that I was willing to return the boat once I was compensated for my labor and expenses. The carabinieri understood the situation and left, apologizing. After two more weeks, I was called by the police in town. This time I had been formally accused of the boat's theft. I went to the police, and again explained what had happened. I told them about my request for compensation, and warned them that, since I was protected by diplomatic immunity, I would report the whole affair, including the call by the police, to the Ministry of Foreign Affairs. The citation was immediately dropped, and I never returned the boat to the stubborn lady. Instead, I donated this boat, which was really never mine, to a third party: the man running the coffee shop on the beach, who could make some money by renting it out by the hour. But only on one condition: never to rent it to the obstinate lady.

When the wind would suddenly die down in the bay and the sun, having turned red, dropped into the sea, there were two things that could still be done to enjoy the ensuing evening: either go back in the water and take another long swim, or celebrate a "happy hour" with friends and relatives.

After electricity had been connected to the Ronchi house, the surrounding area started booming with new construction. Many new houses were built along the shore line or inland. The area lost its old charm, but we gained new friends from the neighboring houses. Marcella and Giorgio Sassi were the first to buy one of the houses built in a condominium complex on the other side of the highway. They were both retired and without children. They particularly admired our three foreign-looking girls playing on the beach or sailing at sea. Pretty soon they realized that these were "the Americans" from the big house on the beach, and we became good friends.

Marcella loved to travel abroad, for the most part to be able to tell others all she could about her experiences. When she discovered that I had been all over the world many times over, there was no better company nor better subject of conversation at our happy hours. This, of course, always called for good, cold, and tall drinks.

Gaetano and Tina Ciauri were also good neighbors. Every year they spent their vacation in a nearby motel on the beach. Gaetano was a medical doctor with responsibilities in the administration of one of the largest hospitals in Rome. When he came to Terracina he liked to forget all about hospitals, medicine or sick people. However, he was frequently called for most of the illnesses occurring in the Ronchi family: either the drinking water was contaminated, or the girls had eaten too much fresh fruit, or there was a bee sting that had to be taken care of, and so on. Gaetano was the only doctor in the area and he was always willing to

Nicla and Marina in the outdoor eating area at Terracina.

come to the house for a good Campari drink, a few broiled chicken wings, or just to exchange some good Roman jokes.

During the summer months, probably our favorite time was spent in the open-air dining area that we created under a nest of tall pine trees. This was located right outside the small kitchen where most of the food was cooked. Delicious dishes were prepared inside and quickly transferred to the dining table through the kitchen window, like a fast-food restaurant. But this food was an entirely different reality: abundant assortments of fried fish with polenta and green salad, red-colored spaghetti with tasty clams, spiced sea food with purple squids and black olives, and a nice combination of freshly cut ripe tomatoes, green basil and mozzarella cheese. All food with contrasting and cheerful colors, artistically placed together by Nicla, as if they were part of a most colorful palette still full of light at the onset of dusk. This food was appreciated by the entire family and the many friends who were often invited to taste and enjoy "Nicky's Fine Italian Cuisine." Was this a sign of things to come?

After dinner, everyone moved to the lawn chairs on the patio in front of the house. From there the stars, the sea and the moon could be seen at their best. The cool nights favored story telling or outright shows organized by our girls and their cousins during the preceding afternoons. It was great fun to watch them. Nonno Vittorio loved this time of the day. This was when he could recall episodes from World War I, recounting the many details as if they had happened the day before. Everyone listened in rapt silence. In the darkness of the splendid night, a few would easily close their eyes, cradled by the sound of the nearby sea. After all, Terracina's superb summer nights were made for dreaming.

11

An International Career

*While one person hesitates because
he feels inferior, the other is busy
making mistakes and becoming
superior.*

—Henry C. Link

The Food and Agriculture Organization (FAO) is one of many technical organizations of the United Nations, with worldwide responsibility in agriculture and human nutrition. FAO was founded at an international conference held in Quebec, Canada, in 1945. This was when World War II had just ended and there was great need to promote agricultural production, especially in Europe and Asia. The preamble of FAO's constitution spelled out the objectives of the new organization. These were: "...to raise levels of nutrition and standards of living throughout the world; to improve the efficiency and distribution of food and agricultural products; to improve the living conditions of rural populations, and thus to contribute toward an expanding world economy." Clearly, these objectives of great humanitarian value were especially needed when the world was facing near-starvation as a result of a very destructive war.

It appears doubtful that the few men who convened in Quebec for this noble purpose had any idea of how such ambitious objectives could ever be reached. Certainly they did not understand the magnitude of economic means required to even come close to these goals. The fact remains that, for the first time in history, a few men from different countries and backgrounds joined together to face one of man's oldest problems: starvation and undernourishment. Among these men was Nicla's father, Vittorio, who was a member of the Italian delegation.

Vittorio Ronchi was one of the conference's best-qualified participants, since he could truly appreciate the reasons for which the new organization was being established. He had just experienced the destructive war in Italy. He also knew what it took to feed millions of men, women and children in war and post-war times. Vittorio wished that the new organization would reside in Washington, DC to better benefit from American assistance, and from the know-how of both the American land grant colleges and the United States Department of Agriculture. If this was not possible, he felt that a humanitarian organization such as FAO should be in Rome, the center of Christianity and western civilization. Here, an International Institute of Agriculture had been already established by the American philanthropist David Lubin, a merchant from Sacramento, California.

FAO is an autonomous intergovernmental agency of the United Nations with a membership of more than 150 nations. Each country has one vote and participates in the organization's financing with an annual contribution based on its gross national product. For nearly twenty years the United States paid thirty-three percent of the operating costs. Every two years delegates from member states convene at the FAO Conference to approve its work program and budget. During the course of the ensuing two years, an elected Council advises the Director General on the activities approved by the Conference.

As you would expect, an organization of this kind is continually subject to great political forces. On one side there are the developing countries, always ready to ask for increased expenditures and more programs, and on the other side there is only a handful of major contributors trying to maintain their contributions at an acceptable level.

During FAO's early period the Directors General were either from the United States or the United Kingdom, and this was clearly done with the intent of maintaining an equilibrium between these contrasting positions. But in due course the majority of members belonging to developing countries overturned this situation. They organized themselves into a so-called "Club of 77" and, by holding a majority vote within the FAO Conference, they were able to more forcibly dictate their own requests and to elect a Director General from their own ranks. In turn, they secured for themselves high level, highly paid positions within the Organization. It was definitely a departure from the philanthropic spirit that prevailed in FAO's early days, when many scientists, technicians, and otherwise well-motivated men and women joined the organization to contribute to its noble objectives. This change of direction is something that

FAO's founders, in all their great wisdom, were not able to foresee.

The Organization's activities are essentially grouped into two areas: the Regular Programme and the Field Programme. The former includes collection and distribution of statistics on world agriculture, organization of specialized meetings on subjects of international interest, administration of international conventions, publication of specialized journals or books of interest to member countries, and so on. The Field Programme is essentially directed at solving local and/ or national problems. These may include surveys of land use, building of dams and irrigation systems, better utilization of water and forest resources, or control of animal and plant diseases. This type of assistance is provided in the form of field projects, the majority of which are financed with outside resources. The United Nations Development Programme (UNDP) is the major contributor to these field activities. Other donors, however, also find the convenience of utilizing FAO infrastructures to implement their own bilateral projects. In this way, FAO is always in a state of continuous change, moving in many different directions at once, but never with a well defined and properly financed program of its own.

The FAO organizational structure and modus operandi can best be understood if one visualizes the existence of a large, solid, well insulated box, perfectly sealed and protected with white travertine from the adversities and uncertainties of the real world outside. This large box contains four well defined horizontal layers, each thicker than the one above it.

In the top layer is the Director General himself, surrounded by his Deputy, a small army of advisers, the Chief of Protocol, secretaries, bodyguards, and so on. At this layer a massive discretionary power is exercised over development programs and the lives of millions of people. From this well protected "eagle's nest" operates one of the "Lords of Poverty," as Graham Hancock, the British writer and international consultant, defines them.

At the second layer, immediately below, are the top officials of the Organization: the Assistant Directors General, the heads of Departments and Divisions. All of these "generals," at D-1 to D-3 levels, are personally appointed by the DG himself. In doing so, he nearly always must yield to political pressures exercised by the representatives of member states, comfortably located in Rome, often with ambassadorial titles. Frequently, these same representatives find their way to become "generals" in FAO's bureaucratic Armada. Understandably, this second level operates in a cloud of its own, greatly influenced by the whims of international politics and the mood of the DG himself.

The third layer consists of an apparently robust body made up of the so-called "professionals." These come in a descending order of ranks, from P-5 at the top to P-1 at the bottom. Over the years, the lower grades have had a tendency to disappear while the upper ones (P-4 and P-5) have increased in number. (My position, when I joined FAO, was P-4 step 1).

In many aspects, "professionals" are those who make the organization click. In the Technical Department, for example, these are the specialists in different disciplines, from agronomy to plant pathology, veterinary, and engineering, who can provide useful inputs within their field of specialization. The remaining personnel, however, are mostly generalists of different kinds, and varieties, with varying levels of education and experience.

When I joined the organization, there was a large representation of staff from the former colonial services of Great Britain, France, Belgium, and Holland. In many ways, these were the real experts in tropical agriculture. A smaller group consisted of displaced people who, for one reason or another, had been cut off from their country of origin and had no other place to go. A third group was that of idealists who still cherished the noble purposes of FAO. Finally, a fourth group, probably the largest one, was composed of people who could see in FAO the possibility for salaries many times higher than those obtainable elsewhere. These were the "officers," often without specialized skills or qualifications, ready to "push papers" and accept any job and responsibility, as long as their paycheck would arrive at the end of the month. Most of these people had no motivation other than money. Their input was questionable and, occasionally, entirely negative. In general, it was difficult for these different kinds of "professionals" to link together and form a harmonious group.

The bottom layer of FAO's work force was formed by "general service" personnel. Within this group were the secretaries, the guards, the workmen in the print shop, and so on. Without these people, FAO could not function. They were the real workers who type, translate, print, drive, repair, and deliver. They also ranged in a progressive order of grades from G-1 at the bottom to G-6 at the top. Moving from one grade to another was usually difficult, moving from one layer to the one above was nearly impossible.

The majority of "general service" personnel was made up of Italians who, especially in the early days, were paid at a top salary scale, compared to outside possibilities. Many of the multilingual secretaries were from England or France. Most of them were married to Italians and they could "think" and talk fluent Italian. This, in fact, was the "unofficial" language of the Organization, certainly the most useful if one wished to have a better prepared sandwich at the FAO cafeteria, or a priority document from the print shop.

Within this robust and protected box, populated by so many different people, the staff was called to operate eight hours a day and five days a week. The system was extremely rigid and people did not easily cooperate with one another, especially at the higher levels. Since promotions were difficult to come by, there was a constant drive throughout the Organization to expand or to re-organize into larger units, often performing the same functions but under different names. This ultimately justified the upgrading of certain positions. Quite frequently, entire new Services or Divisions were created only to promote someone at the top. And with each re-organization came a change in office location. After three consecutive re-organizations one might find oneself back in the same office from which he or she had first departed.

The rigid system resulted in an unusual working environment. As indicated, cooperation was frequently nonexisting. Each person carried out his or her own work in isolation, well within the boundary of the assigned office space and with the full protection of a closed office door. If one tried to open that door and cross the boundary, he or she could be met with downright hostility. Under these conditions, the art of stonewalling was frequently exercised to intentionally block, stall or resist somebody's else initiatives. This was especially common when authoritarian bosses wanted to demonstrate their dissatisfaction with one of their staff. The system's rigidity did not permit firing someone who was not performing well. Stonewalling was the only alternative to "invite" someone to leave. It frequently happened that the person in question would find another job in a different unit, often with the assistance and warmest recommendation of the old boss.

When I joined the Organization there were about six thousand people working in the FAO headquarters in Rome.

This number might seem large, but it was less than one-fourth the staff of the United States Department of Agriculture in Washington, DC.

There was a joke in Rome about people working at FAO. According to this, a German tourist, who eagerly collected statistical data about the Eternal City, was taken around by a taxi driver, who proudly showed him the sites and monuments. The German tourist first asked how old and how wide was the Coliseum, then he wanted to know how long the Appian Way was. He kept good notes of what the driver was telling him. When the two drove by the FAO building, the German tourist inquired again, "How many people work here?" The taxi driver promptly responded, "Five per cent!" He knew it: his daughter worked for FAO.

Unfortunately, this was the way many people judged FAO's working capability. Furthermore, if one took a quick look at the many FAO coffee shops, the bank, the book stores, the cafeterias, the commissary, and the travel agencies full of employees at all hours of the working day, one must agree that the taxi driver's estimate was rather high. Nevertheless, some things were run more efficiently at FAO than anywhere else. English is FAO's most commonly spoken language, while French, Spanish, Arabic, and Chinese are also used in conferences and official documents. During international meetings, including the biennial Conference, delegates discussed matters until late into the night and to the very last day of their stay. Verbatim records of these discussions were taken. Each morning, when the delegates reconvened, they found a printed report fully covering their discussions, written in well edited English, French, Arabic, and Chinese. Someone in FAO deserved credit for the quality and speed of that work.

As already mentioned, my first impression of FAO was completely negative. I did not like the atmosphere in my

Branch or the rest of the Organization. I did not like my new boss, nor the majority of my new colleagues. I had no defined work program and no one cared to provide me with advice. Work isolation and closed door policies were not made for me. I was not a bureaucrat, nor did I want to become one. I had no intention of wasting my life drinking coffee in the cafeteria or chatting nonsense in the FAO corridors. I wanted to engage in something productive and rewarding as I had done in the years of work in Davis and for Di Giorgio. "A way out must be found," I kept repeating to myself. "I must either change this environment or find a way to beat this system."

These were the days when Nicla successfully intervened to solve my problem. She harmoniously combined fine perception, tact and political gusto. She understood my situation and was willing to help. To change things around, there appeared to be nothing better than to remove all the Branch staff (including secretaries) from the FAO building and invite everyone to our home to enjoy delicious Italian food and plenty of good Italian wine. Nicla's initiative worked like a charm. Soon these people, who had been working in isolation for many years, started talking with one another, appreciating each others' problems. Their dialogue continued within the work environment, where office doors started opening up. A beam of light and a gulp of fresh air began changing the inhospitable atmosphere. It also seemed as though the territorialism which had previously existed was gradually melting away, leaving room for a more humane perception of collaboration and trust.

Nicla's approach to soften rigid rivalries and distrust was frequently used in subsequent years to resolve controversial or antagonistic situations. It is now impossible to recall how many dinner parties Nicla organized during the twenty-three years of our stay with FAO. It is no wonder that she was

Nicla at one of the many cocktail parties of FAO.

acclaimed by visiting FAO experts as the "best chef in Rome." After all, effective international diplomacy is also made of good lasagne and tasty red Chianti!

It was clear from the onset that I had no role to play under the Regular Programme. I had to go "outside" and promote field projects. This was, in fact, the meaning of the first interview with my boss, who was only able to offer me an airline ticket and advice to visit several countries for this purpose. This hunting for projects was well known to most FAO country representatives in member states. They would abruptly ask me upon arrival, "What do you have to sell? Which kind of projects are you trying to sniff out?" There was no question that a certain amount of salesmanship was needed to convince local officials of the need for this or that activity. But I had an advantage: plant disease problems are self evident, especially when they occur in epidemic forms. In addition, I combined a good scientific background with a practical approach to problem solving. Within six years, the number of projects under my supervision increased threefold.

I liked being involved in field activities. I was able to design and develop sound projects, and I enjoyed my personal contacts with FAO field experts. I scrutinized, recruited, briefed, and supervised plant pathologists from many countries and different backgrounds. Several were Americans, because I knew most of them personally and because occasionally host countries did not wish to accept former colonialists. In French speaking countries, for example, it was easier for me to send Italians or Swiss experts. Generally, their success depended on how well they could understand local conditions and get along with local people. Two examples may illustrate this point.

Bruno Fassi, an Italian phytopathologist with long experience in the former Belgian Congo (where he had married a native woman), was sent to Guinea, on the west coast of Africa. This was to assist the local government in controlling a newly introduced coffee disease. He spoke fluent French and, most important, he fully understood the African mentality. He knew how things were to be done under African conditions. Using his technical and sociological knowledge, Bruno was able to launch a nationwide campaign to replant more than one hundred million resistant coffee plants. This was extremely successful, and the value of his work was a net gain to the country of several million dollars.

R.S. Vasudeva was a famous plant pathologist in India. He had been working for FAO in Togo before I joined the Organization. At that time the Director General was also from India, and I had no alternative than to agree to his "friendly advice" to send Vasudeva to Cuba. Vasudeva did not speak Spanish and he could only communicate through an English-speaking Cuban counterpart. Furthermore, he was an authoritarian who knew very little about Cuban culture or their newly adopted ideology. Not long after his arrival on the island, he was arrested under suspicion of being a CIA agent with plans to sabotage the country's economy. What had really happened was that some staff member in the plant pathology laboratory, not liking Vasudeva's authoritarian approach, reported him to Castro's police for having introduced fungus cultures from India "with the intention of destroying the local sugarcane crop." When I was informed about these accusations, I immediately secured a copy of the list of fungi introduced by Vasudeva. After a thorough review, I did not find any pathogens of sugarcane, nor of any other crop, but only cultures of common soil inhabitants. Furthermore, Vasudeva's fungus cultures had never left the inside of the laboratory refrigerator, where they had been safely kept "to start a culture collection." Evidently, the FAO expert lacked in energy and wisdom: he could have done the isolation himself or secured an entry permit from local authorities.

Through the personal intervention of the Secretary General of the United Nations, Fidel Castro was finally convinced that no harm had been done. After some time, Vasudeva was released from prison and quickly moved out of Cuba and FAO. No fruitful development was ever derived from his project.

Within these extremes, several other challenging situations characterized the projects I supervised during my early years at FAO. This period required a lot of travel and plenty of skill in matching individual experts to particular situations. But no one at FAO headquarters appeared to give any recognition to the progress made by my program. The only recognition came from the experts themselves. On the occasion of the first congress of International Plant Pathology in London in 1968, Dr. Walter Carter, an entomologist working in Jamaica on lethal yellowing disease of coconut, openly recognized the value of my scientific and human support. His words of appreciation were followed by a standing ovation. Twenty years later, this recognition was further confirmed by the American Phytopathological Society when I was granted an award for "outstanding services as international plant pathologist."

Two situations developed in the early seventies which greatly influenced my work at FAO. The first predicament resulted from one of the many "re-organizations" which ended in the creation of a new Division responsible for all field activities. This had the effect of severing me from my experts and projects. The second situation, due to the same "re-organization," affected me in a personal way. Our Branch was upgraded to "Service," and my boss promoted to D-1 level. This meant that his P-5 post was vacant and that I could have my chance for a promotion. Instead, to my disappointment, this was given to another officer with less seniority and no experience in agriculture. He was a former medical entomologist in the US Army with "international" expertise limited to killing mosquitos, house flies and body lice during war campaigns in Morocco, Algeria and Sicily.

What upset me most was that this promotion had been irregularly enacted. According to a new directive from the DG himself, all promotions "were to be approved only after scrutiny and endorsement by a newly established Selection Committee." This procedure was to be effective on a certain date. I accidentally discovered that my colleague's promotion had been granted after that date and without submission to the Selection Committee. A long and tedious exchange of memoranda took place between me and FAO's administration. The latter was trying to cover up for the illegal blunder. Their position was that the DG did not need previous approval by the Selection Committee for his decisions, and that, in this particular case, his mind had been made up "much before the set deadline."

One day, a person walked into my office to offer legal advice. He was a young lawyer from Malaysia who was also a member of the FAO Staff Association. I felt that his unexpected assistance was worthy of consideration, in view of my complete ignorance of legal matters. Following his advice, I started a long and lonely journey to lodge an appeal with the International Administrative Tribunal of ILO (International Labor Organization). A lonely journey because I was left all to myself, as no one in FAO wished to become involved. Only Luciana, my good and trusty secretary, was supportive of the action I had taken. She had to suffer part of the consequences for having to type in secrecy all the necessary legal documentation for the appeal and for responding to ILO's Tribunal letters. Meanwhile, my boss, who was really responsible for the entire Procrustean

Fishing village in the Keta peninsula of Ghana.

Same village devastated by coconut lethal yellowing.

situation, protected himself by ignoring my actions, closing himself tightly in his office.

After nearly three years, I was informed that my case had been rejected and that there was no appeal against this decision. I was never able to find out if the young attorney from Malaysia had given me the proper legal advice, or if he had been asked by the Administration to drive me into a blind alley and leave me there alone.

Having lost my connections with field projects and with my direct supervisor, I seriously considered developing my own programs. In doing so, I wanted to select areas which were useful, but not competitive with those already covered by other international groups. One such area was the coordination of research on coconut diseases of unknown etiology. For several years I had observed the development of many of these diseases in the Philippines, Jamaica and West Africa, and I had also organized their first worldwide survey. This had been accomplished in collaboration with Karl Maramorosch, his camera and his untiring desire to travel. Karl was an outstanding entomologist with a world-renowned reputation in insect-transmitted viruses. A slender fellow with a very short butch haircut, Karl's smiling tan face contrasted strongly with his light blue eyes. He had worked for FAO on the cadang-cadang problem of coconuts in the Philippines.

Karl was a man who could always find a way out of difficult situations. To his great advantage, he knew how to make new friends, either by playing his accordion or by performing clever tricks with his hands. Once when we were together in West Africa, we were denied entry into Togo by the local border police. This was because of strained relations between that country and Ghana. Karl promptly pulled out of his pocket a certificate given to him by the New York Academy of Sciences, which bore an impressive, large, shiny

Planning a worldwide survey of coconut diseases with Dr. Karl
Maramorosch.

Karl taking a picture of a diseased coconut inflorescence.

golden seal at the bottom. It was evident that the border policeman could not read the writing on the document. It also seemed clear that he was highly impressed by that seal. In no time we were allowed to cross the border. It was not by chance that Karl and I remained good friends for many years. After two months of uninterrupted travel, he was able to produce a beautifully illustrated report, which became one of the most requested publications of FAO.

In the late sixties I visited the US Navy submarine base in Key West, Florida, to become acquainted with some experimental work being done on coconut diseases under strict quarantine. On this occasion, I invited Florida plant pathologists to join forces with FAO on lethal yellowing research in Jamaica. The disease was killing millions of palms on that island, and it was a serious threat to other countries in the Caribbean area. The response to this offer was extremely cool, if not altogether indifferent. The Jamaican problem was of no concern to Florida, nor to US agriculture.

By 1972 an unidentified "blight disease" became established on the Florida mainland. Not only were coconuts affected, but also several other ornamental species of palms. Local authorities and private organizations were greatly concerned, because they knew that Florida without palms was no longer Florida, and that the tourist trade would suffer serious losses. Something had to be done to remedy this situation. The Palm Society of America organized a Symposium at the Fairchild Tropical Garden in Miami in the hope of receiving some useful advice. I was also invited to attend with all the experts working in Jamaica on lethal yellowing. The Florida invitation was brief and clear: "all expenses will be paid by the Society."

For the first time it was possible for an international multidisciplinary group to examine various aspects of the disease and compare notes. At the end of the symposium, I

Effect of lethal yellowing on coconut palms in Jamaica.

Nylon cages used in insect transmission experiments.

Dying of coconut and other palms in the streets of Miami, Fl (1972).

proposed the formation of a permanent international team to coordinate research activities. In this way, ICLY (International Council on Lethal Yellowing) was born and I became its permanent secretary. Late that year, mycoplasma bodies (e.g. pathogenic organisms intermediate in size between bacteria and viruses) were found simultaneously in diseased coconut tissues in Germany, England and the United States. Karl Maramarosch had struck again: he was a member of one of the teams that had made this important discovery. The vector and control of the disease were discovered by other ICLY scientists shortly afterwards.

In the Philippines, the causal agent of the cadang-cadang disease remained unknown after more than twenty years of investigations. An estimated 30 million palms had succumbed to the malady, and during all those years FAO had spent

Cadang-cadang disease of cocunuts in the Philippines.

substantial amounts of money to provide assistance on this problem. An endless sequence of FAO experts had served short assignments at the isolated and poorly equipped Guinobatan experiment station. Working under very primitive conditions, each of these experts was only able to prove his predecessors wrong. Finally, the essential clue was found when I entered into formal agreement for a long-term collaboration with the Waite Agricultural Research Institute in Australia. In 1982, John W. Randles, a staff member there, working with two FAO experts, discovered the viroid nature of this disease. Along with lethal yellowing in Florida, the Caribbean and West Africa, this was an additional feather in my cap.

Another initiative which received my attention, and later turned out to gain worldwide recognition, was the FAO

International Collaborative Programme on Crop Loss Appraisal. Reliable information on losses caused by pests and diseases in agriculture was of importance to the pesticide industry, to regulatory agencies, to administrators of research and assistance programs, and to the farmers themselves. This type of information was not generally available. The program I developed revolved around three main areas: the production and distribution of a Crop Loss Manual (giving examples of how to establish quantitative relationships between pest intensities and yield losses), the organization of training workshops and consultations, and the assistance to national projects. The Crop Loss initiative proved successful in generating information which was needed in Integrated Pest Management (IPM) and in plant breeding for disease resistance.

A parallel activity I also initiated was called the "FAO International Programme on Horizontal Resistance" (IPHR). This was essentially an offshoot of a FAO project in Kenya under the leadership of Raoul A. Robinson, one of my experts working on the development of potatoes resistant to two locally important diseases: blight and bacterial wilt.

Raoul was born and raised on Jersey, a 45-square mile island in the British Channel which was occupied by the Germans from the beginning of World War II until after their unconditional surrender. During this period, Raoul experienced starvation on his native island, which remained totally isolated from the outside world, incapable of feeding its 65,000 inhabitants and the 12,000 German troops stationed there. Most of Raoul's professional career was later spent in East Africa working as a plant pathologist with the British Colonial Service and, subsequently, with the Kenyan government. He had never forgotten having been hungry during his youth, and he was deeply motivated to do something "worthwhile" for mankind. It was inevitable that

Raoul and I would appreciate each other's values and become good friends.

I went to Kenya to become acquainted with his approach in breeding for durable ("horizontal") resistance. He had some 300,000 potato seedlings being screened each year in a process of recurrent mass selection which allowed him to identify individuals with increasing levels of resistance to blight and bacterial wilt. His approach was totally different from that of potato breeders in America or Europe, who were strictly following the Mendelian laws of heredity. Raoul's approach was population breeding at its best, based on the Darwinian concept of the survival of the fittest. I was impressed by his ecological approach to control crop parasites. This, in turn, influenced my way of thinking in future years of work in FAO and afterwards.

In 1971, I invited Raoul to Vienna to attend a meeting on Mutation Breeding for Disease Resistance, jointly organized by FAO and the International Atomic Energy Agency (IAEA). Most of those in attendance were Mendelian plant breeders, including my Division Director, José Vallega from Argentina. I first introduced the Kenyan project as a type of "futuristic, pioneering plant breeding" which would make available nearly 300,000 hectares of potentially high yielding potato land to peasant farmers without the use of pesticides or expensive seed certification schemes. Raoul followed my introduction describing his methodology and results. There were many discussions and plenty of criticism. We suddenly realized that we were totally out of place: the scientists convened in Vienna were only interested in radiation effects in modifying genes, which were then to be used for Mendelian breeding. We did not expect that the Vienna meeting was the beginning of a long and unresolved conflict between crop scientists believing in two kinds of genetics (Mendelians against biometricians) and two types of genetic resistance ("vertical" against "horizontal").

Raoul became the first casualty of this conflict. While his programme was well under way in Nairobi, the British ODA (Overseas Development Agency) offered to the Kenyan Ministry of Agriculture the services of a famous potato breeder from Scotland. He would, no doubt, boost Raoul's programme. Instead, this renowned scientist immediately expressed the view that there was no such a thing as "horizontal resistance" and that Raoul's work was nothing but "a waste of time." The perplexed minister of Agriculture came to my office in Rome to report his problem. He admitted that the man from Scotland knew about potatoes, but that Raoul, on the other end, knew Africa. "What shall I do? These two scientists share the same office but they do not talk to each other," the Minister added. For him this was a real "hot potato" issue: I was asked to intervene and remove this potato from his fire. To this end, I politely offered to take Raoul out of Kenya. I already had another important assignment for him.

Many years later, when I visited Kenya again, I discovered that nothing had come out of the work of the famous potato breeder from Scotland. On the other hand, two of Raoul's potato varieties, called Akiba and Baraka, were grown on sixty percent of a greatly expanded potato acreage without the use of pesticides or certification.

To my mind it was FAO's responsibility to enter the ongoing conflict among plant breeders and prove or disprove the validity of the "horizontal" resistance concept in breeding crops for low-input farming. Therefore I contacted a number of highly qualified scientists in the United States and Europe to whom I asked the question: should FAO start a program on "horizontal" resistance in major crops of Africa and Latin America? The response was most encouragingly positive.

The first opportunity to start the International Programme on Horizontal Resistance (IPHR) was provided by a request from Ethiopia to assist with the control of a newly introduced coffee berry disease (CBD). The disease was destroying 40 percent of coffee yields, which produced 60 percent of Ethiopia's foreign earnings. I asked Raoul if he wanted to tackle this problem. He was uncertain at first, then he accepted the assignment, seeing in it an opportunity to test his own theories on a perennial crop grown under primitive conditions. The CBD project, initiated in 1973 was successfully completed seven years later by Nick Van der Graaff, Raoul's former associate expert. As a result, good yielding coffee plants, with "horizontal" resistance to CBD and other local parasites, were released to Ethiopian farmers. No pesticides were needed to produce a good crop from these selected varieties. Raoul Robinson succeeded in demonstrating the validity of his ideas and his approach. Nick Van der Graaff was given a permanent position at FAO Headquarters, and he was later granted a Ph.D. from Wageningen. A success for all concerned!

At the end of his assignment in Ethiopia, Robinson was asked to visit several countries in Africa, Asia and Latin America. This was to convince local scientists and their governments to participate in the IPHR. Countries were invited to select a crop of their choice and they were to receive a FAO associate expert to do the necessary work under Robinson's supervision. Tunisia, Morocco, Brazil, and Zambia became part of the IPHR. The governments of the Netherlands and Belgium provided the manpower. By 1977, when a meeting of all participants was organized in Nigeria, as many as ten experts were involved in the program, and crops included wheat, tomatoes, chickpeas, and coffee. Life for most of these experts was not easy. Their living and working conditions were usually primitive. Their projects, being a total departure from conventional plant breeding, were subject to hostility or criticism from older plant breeders. And there were also failures in facilities and logistics support. But these dedicated young men fully understood the value of the work they were doing. And most of them succeeded. As a result, five out of the nine associate experts were granted a Ph.D. in Holland or the USA. The participant countries were left with improved genetic material of coffee, wheat and chickpeas.

During this period, some important changes were also taking place in the newly established Plant Protection Service. The Service Chief finally retired and no one in FAO ever missed his presence. Shortly after his departure, a new Chief was appointed. This was Bill Furtick, an Agronomist from Oregon with extensive experience in weed control. Actually, Bill was already with FAO, as manager of a plant protection project in Taiwan. His personality was totally different from that of his predecessor: he was open, jovial, full of energy, and always willing to help. Just about at the same time, Felix Albani from Argentina, became the new Division director. The atmosphere in FAO was clearly changing, and things started improving for me. I was granted a one-year sabbatical leave at the University of California in Davis. In exchange Bill Moller, one of the Extension Specialists from UCD, was to take my place in FAO. On a hot August day in 1975 our family left Rome to return to America. Victoria remained in Italy because she wanted to study at the University of Pisa.

Our return to Davis, after so long abroad, brought back many memories and the opportunity to enjoy our old friends. Sadly, Dr. and Mrs. Eckert had passed away, leaving a great emptiness in our hearts. Their daughter Jean was living alone in the family house. She was very useful in solving our logistics problems. Nicla and I wanted to "travel light" and for this reason we had left Rome with only a few suitcases containing a minimum of personal effects. Jean retrieved from her storage the pots, pans, sheets, glassware, and flatware we needed to manage our life in a rented apartment in "Stonegate," a residential complex on the west side of town. For transportation we were given "on loan" a car belonging to our good friend Dr. Ramirez of Bakersfield. This was an old, dilapitaded Buick which required continuous mechanical attention and costly repairs.

Marina started her undergraduate work in Biology at UCD, while Cynthia was enrolled in the local high school. Three bicycles were purchased to maintain mobility while the car was stuck in some repair shop. Financial problems appeared on the horizon when I went to pay Marina's registration fees. The University considered me an "out of state" resident, therefore I had to pay much higher fees. My argument, instead, was that I had residency in California, but that I was temporarily on a foreign assignment with the United Nations. I reasoned that if they did not recognize this situation, then I was a "man without a country!" Of course, the University had its own criteria for establishing residency, and these, clearly, were not being met. The debate went on and on. Remembering that I had successfully faced the old Roman bureaucracy, I thought I could also cope with that of California, since it was much younger and definitely less encrusted. Yet, it was still a bureaucracy. Finally, the supervisor of the registrar's office was called in. By pure coincidence he was a former next door neighbor when I was a student in Davis. Immediately he recognized me both as a friend and as a California resident. This showed me how important it is in life to have good neighbors and trusty friends.

The objectives of my sabbatical leave in Davis were to attend courses of special interest, do research on methodologies for disease/loss appraisal, and assist Dr.

Hewitt in editing a book for the International Board for Plant Genetic Resources (IBPGR). The subject of this book was the safe international movement of plant propagation material. As we know, the transfer of plant materials on a global scale involves risks of accidental transfer of pests and pathogens. IBPGR was aware of these risks and wanted FAO to come forward with up-to-date information on the subject and with specific recommendations.

In December, 1975, I convened a meeting of a special task force at the Department of Plant Pathology. This was to review several manuscripts on the subject, crop by crop, and to make specific recommendations. Among the members of this task force was Raoul Robinson. Raoul was a chain smoker, and he could not think unless he had a lit cigarette in his mouth. In the same meeting room was Bill Hewitt, who, being asthmatic, could not stand cigarette smoke. I was facing an apparently unsolvable problem: how to keep the meeting moving in a small room and for three consecutive days. But both Hewitt and Robinson were very conceding. Soon Raoul offered to walk out of the room to light a cigarette, while Bill encouraged Raoul to stay and smoke because he had other business to attend to elsewhere in the building. This meeting was memorable from a human point of view. Once again I discovered how easily people could fluctuate between the good and the bad, the virtue and the vice, the strength and the weakness, the bestial and the divine. What was needed to shift the complex human nature was only reciprocal understanding and great respect. Bill and Raoul had both. And in large quantities.

Life in a small apartment could be very dull. However, Marina and Cynthia managed to make many friends in the Stonegate complex just by sitting around the pool and talking to each other in Italian. There was a group of boys who lived together in the next door apartment. They were greatly interested in becoming friends. Among them were Dave, a student in Range Management, and Gene (Italianised to "Gino"), a student in Botany. Dave had very limited financial resources. As a result, he had no right to sleep inside the apartment he shared with the others. His territorial boundaries were confined to a little balcony where he camped out every night, summer or winter. On rainy nights, he pulled a plastic tent over himself and went peacefully to sleep dreaming about green meadows and beautiful waterfalls. Gino was better off financially and could afford the comfort of a regular bed and an enclosed room. Coming from a family of hard working farmers, Gino combined the physical strength of a heavy-weight boxing champ with an exceptionally good mind and great finesse of sentiments.

One day, Nicla decided to invite "the boys" for dinner. At the appointed hour, they knocked on the door and stood there waiting to come in. They were all dressed in their finest clothes, all freshly shaved and showered, and they displayed the best of their smiles. The only thing they lacked were shoes: they were all bare footed. This was a scene I had not witnessed since the early days of my travel to deepest Africa.

Life in a small apartment could also be crowded. So, Nicla and I took long walks in the neighborhood, looking at gardens and houses under construction. One evening we saw something that attracted our attention. At the corner of Whaler and Halifax there was a new house which we admired for its design and location. The next day we went back to see it again and then again the following day. "Why don't we buy that house?" I asked Nicla. She had exactly the same thought and, without hesitation, we went ahead with its purchase.

By the end of the month, the whole family loaded the old car with pots, pans, suitcases, sheets, glassware, and flatware and happily moved into the new house on the corner. But there were no beds, chairs, tables, shelves, fences, or even neighbors. After a few days of shopping in Davis and Sacramento, the new house was furnished and made comfortable. It was then necessary to re-load the car and return the borrowed pots, pans, sheets, glassware, and flatware to Jean Eckert. We had wanted "to travel light" on our sabbatical, but by this time we both had to concede that this was no longer possible.

Landscaping is something best done in the spring or summer. But there was not much time for us before we had to return to Rome in June. So, at an incredible speed during the winter, concrete was poured, fences went up, sprinklers were installed, trees were planted, and grass was rolled out. To assist us in this work, we received an unexpected gift from someone who wanted to remain anonymous. It consisted of a brand new wheelbarrow and a bonanza of gardening tools.

We later discovered that Bill Hewitt, my former professor, had his own special way of saying, "Welcome back to Davis."

By June the house on Whaler looked beautiful. It was ready to be left under the management of Marina and, a year later, of Cynthia as well. There was no longer need to argue with the University registrar. Residency in California was definitely established. And the old car was gladly shipped back to Bakersfield by piggy-back system. It was too much of a trip for a "costly" old Buick to make on its own wheels.

There were two new situations to be faced upon my return to FAO. Prior to leaving for Davis, I had requested a new position to retain the services of Raoul Robinson as coordinator of the program on "horizontal resistance." This request had been ignored. In its place a new post for a weed control expert had already been advertised. After all the work Raoul had done for FAO, he was left unemployed, forcing him to start a consulting business of his own. There was nothing I could do to change this situation.

The other problem was an attempt made by the Panel of Experts on Integrated Pest Management to take over all the associate experts working under the IPHR. This was with the intent of using them in some entomological projects. I arrived in time to stop this maneuver. Nonetheless, the report prepared by the Panel was totally negative against IPHR. Fortunately, the DG paid little attention to the recommendations of this body of experts.

Two other important events occurred after my return: Raoul's book "Plant Pathosystems," for which I wrote the Foreword, was published in Germany, and I received my first promotion at FAO after 14 years. I became "Senior Plant Pathologist" at the P-5 level, and to acknowledge my appreciation for a job well done, my old post was filled by Nick Van der Graaff upon completion of his Ethiopian assignment.

As "Senior," I was responsible for a newly established group dealing with plant pathology and plant quarantines. Emphasis continued to be given to the Crop Loss evaluation program, now under the responsibility of Clive James, and the IPHR, which remained under Nick's supervision. A third program was also initiated, which had to do with the safe international transfer of genetic resources. A scientist who helped in this area was Dr. Robert P. Kahn, from the Plant Importation and Technical Support Staff of the United States Department of Agriculture. Having taken part in the Davis Task Force meeting, he had good ideas on how these plant quarantines could be improved.

An unexpected change took place in the Service. Bill Furtick resigned from FAO to become Dean of Agriculture at the University of Hawaii, and a Dutch entomologist was appointed Chief. He reflected in many ways the characteristics of his remarkable country. According to Barzini Jr., the Dutch are stolid people, hard working, parsimonious, earnest, unimaginative, methodical, meticulous, slow-thinking, and self-reliant. On top of all this, the new Chief also had great ambitions for his own career and an insatiable love of travel. As a result, he was always away from his office and from the day-to-day managerial responsibilities within the Service.

When I was asked by the organizers of the third congress of the International Society of Plant Pathology to suggest names of young scientists who could bring new and fresh ideas to the meeting in Munich, I recommended C.A.J. (Tonie) Putter. Tonie was from South Africa, the first Putter having gone to the Cape in 1659. He had a unique appreciation for the well being of peasant farmers. One day he walked into my office with a copy of "Plant Pathosystems" under his arm. "There are only two people in the world for whom I would like to work. And they are both in this book," Tonie said. I was surprised at this unusual introduction. But then, after reading Tonie's thesis on the work he had just completed in Papua and New Guinea, I felt that this motivated man should be recruited by FAO to address specifically the problems of subsistence farmers. I was able in later years to have Tonie join the Plant Protection Service.

In Roman times, Ceres was the goddess of healthy and bountiful crops. In FAO's time, Ceres was the name of a program aimed at the recognition of outstanding women of the world who had contributed to high humanitarian objectives. A series of bronze, silver and gold coins were released each year with the image of one of these "Ceres" women. These coins were sold to collectors worldwide, and the income was used to finance projects in developing countries. The image of Sophia Loren was the first to appear

Dr. Tonie Putter in FAO, Rome: an epidemiologist devoted to peasant
farmers.

Ceres medal to Vittoria Ronchi-Nuti (center). Raymond Lloyd (at far
right).

in the series, followed by that of Sister Theresa. There were striking differences between these two women, but, in many ways, they were both outstanding.

One day Raymond Lloyd, the manager of the "Ceres Program," called me to assess the value of research achievements of a certain woman scientist from a European country. He also provided me with her picture. I was not impressed by either the lady's research or her image. "If you will allow me, I have someone better to suggest," I said to Ray. "All you have to do is take a train to Pisa and interview Vittoria Nuti, head of the Plant Genetics and Mutation Laboratory. Please, let me know if you find her suitable."

Ray was a unique individual dedicated to agricultural development and humanitarian initiatives. He immediately went to Pisa, made his interview and came back to Rome enthusiastic. He had found a woman scientist who combined an outstanding research career with a beautiful image, a family of five children, and a long record of humanitarian civic service. Most important, she was Italian, and FAO wanted to give a special recognition for Italy's increased financial support. Vittoria Nuti was selected to be the 1978 Ceres. There was only one point I had forgotten to clarify with Ray: that Vittoria Nuti looked very much like Nicla. In fact, Vittoria was Nicla's sister.

There must be something exhausting about being the Chief of the Plant Protection Service. After only five years in this post, the Dutch entomologist also decided to resign. He publicly announced that there was nothing that he "could usefully achieve by staying with FAO," and that he wanted to join a large chemical company as an "environmental advisor." Shortly thereafter, Dr. Bommer, the Assistant Director General and head of the Agriculture Department, called the two of us into his office. This was to announce that the Director General had decided to nominate me in the position of Service Chief. "But please," added Dr. Bommer, "do not tell anybody about this nomination until an official announcement is released." There was a moment of silence in the room. My heart was beating faster than normal, but I did not want the others to perceive it. The former Chief, instead, looked kind of pale. He was a good poker player able to cover up his feelings. We walked back to our offices without exchanging a word. My only desire was to phone Nicla. "We made it," I announced over the telephone. "After many years and many delays, I made the nomination." And Nicla, on the other end, was very happy about this last minute recognition. Another person who needed to be informed was Luciana. She had been already promoted to G-6 to become the personal secretary of the Service Chief. But she did not know that I was now to become her old new boss.

For the first time in twenty years I had the feeling of being my own master. This was a strange feeling, probably like what candidates for the presidency of the United States feel when they win the elections and start working in the Oval Office. It is totally different to criticize from the outside and to be on the inside. However, having the advantage of being the most senior in the Division, my long experience started to pay off. Under the new circumstances there was nothing better than doing what Ross Perot repeatedly proposes: "Let's take out the shovel and start cleaning the barn." And the Plant Protection "barn" by that time needed some good cleaning.

It took nearly two years to bring the Service to its full functioning capacity. I was able to recruit six new professional officers in less than six months. These included Tonie Putter and Mahmud M. Taher.

The latter was a plant pathologist from Libya who had been trained in England. He was working for his government in northern Italy as health inspector of plant material for export to his country. I selected him for the Regional Plant Protection post in the Near East. Soon after hiring him, I sent Mahmud to the University of California in Riverside for additional training in the detection of citrus viruses. Following this, he became responsible for a large program producing and distributing virus-free propagation material. For this purpose, in 1985 an International Center was established in Valenzano, near Bari, in collaboration with ICAMAS (International Centre for Advanced Mediterranean Agronomic Studies). Technicians from countries in the Mediterranean basin were to come to Valenzano for one year or more to train in the production of virus-free material. While the idea of this whole undertaking had been mine, Professors G. Martelli and V. Savino, of the University of Bari, actually created and managed this important initiative. Also Chet Roistacher from U.C. Riverside helped make sure that the Center continued on its road to success. By 1995, as many as 124 young men and women from 24 countries had been trained in Valenzano not only in plant virology, but on how to work together and how to help each other. All this in a part of the world where different cultures, religions, and political systems have only created fierce hostility and bloody confrontations. Science, technology and open minded men confirmed once more E.F. Schumacher's statement : "Nothing succeeds like success, and nothing stagnates like stagnation."

After having worked hard to "clean up the barn," I was ready to put the shovel back into storage when the Division Director retired and I was asked to serve as Acting Director. Unexpectedly, a larger "barn" opened its doors. Should the shovel be used again for some cleaning at the Division level? Will there be sufficient time? I asked these questions directly to Dr. Bommer. I wanted to know if I should start this work

Professor G. Martelli, virologist and director of ICAMAS course on
Protection of Mediterranean Fruit Crops.

Students and Staff of the 10th annual course, Valenzano, 1995.

by first conducting a survey in the Division. This was to find out from each person what was wrong in the working environment, and what he or she could suggest to improve conditions and efficiency. Dr. Bommer, pleasantly surprised with my managerial skills, immediately approved the survey.

An exercise of this kind had never been conducted in FAO. In fact there was a risk of uncovering many unpleasant situations that had been pushed and kept under the rug for many years. Instead it happened that most of the staff dissatisfaction was the result of trivial matters that could be easily resolved. The most unexpected result was the sincerity with which everyone responded. It was evident that the staff in the Division had confidence in me and was willing to cooperate. Some of the persons interviewed, however, insisted that I should destroy the information they had provided if this could be used against them by the upper management. I did not realize then that, due to the events that followed, this valuable documentation would never be used.

Dr. Bommer was responsible for recruiting a new Division Director. Suddenly, the DG told him to stop his search because he had already found the "right man for the job." While traveling to France to procure fertilizers and pesticides for the ongoing food crisis in Ethiopia, the DG had been offered an aid package by the Association of Agrochemical Industries. This package also included the name of a "good" candidate for the Director post. Shortly afterwards, I discovered that the "right man for the job" was in fact my former Service Chief. Evidently, the flying Dutchman, like a well trained carrier pigeon, had found his way back to the old nest. This time, however, his pigeon hole was carved out a little higher in the travertine dovecote façade, where the birdseed was in fact considerably more abundant.

The time had arrived to take an important decision. This was to leave FAO and return to California, where Victoria and Cynthia now lived with their respective families, while Marina was temporarily in Wisconsin. I had accumulated sufficient seniority in FAO that I could take "early retirement" without losing entitlements. I felt that at my age any productive years still left were precious for starting a new life and engaging in new initiatives. There was no reason for me to waste any more time at FAO. I had completed my career with dignity and without compromises. I had contributed to world agriculture and to the well-being of developing countries. There had been many disappointments but also some notable achievements. All this I wrote in an article for the FAO Plant Protection Bulletin essentially directed at the new generation that would follow in the Service. I also bound together all the papers I had written during 30 years of work in plant protection and left this documentation with FAO. Someone could find these writings of value. I was definitely ready to leave the Organization and, once again, my native city of Rome.

The urgent matter was to dispose of the apartment in San Lucio. This had been on the market for some time, but none of the real estate agencies responsible for its sale had succeeded in finding a buyer. I decided to solve this problem by myself. I placed an advertisement in the Messaggero newspaper on a Monday morning, and by the following afternoon I had found a person interested in the purchase. The deal was closed and on the next day I submitted my resignation to FAO.

During the following three months in Rome, many things needed to be wrapped up, including the sale of household items that were not to be taken back to California. This went more smooth than expected. Many more items were purchased to be brought back to our "girls" and their families and everything was packed in a container for shipment overseas. This container was huge and during the loading it occupied the full length of the sidewalk in front of our house. It was painted in white, red and green, the colors of the Italian flag, and had the word "ITALIA" written on it in big block capitals. Nicla and I watched the container moving away just like a big ship leaving its dock. It was our slice of Italy to be taken back to America.

The San Lucio apartment remained sadly empty. The joy and beautiful experiences of twenty-three years of international life lingered in the empty home and in our hearts. From the balcony Nicla and I gave one last look at Saint Peter's Dome and the city below. The sunset splashed a soft peach color on the surrounding buildings and later deepened the green of the pine trees on the far hills to a cobalt blue. We were both silent, standing there for the last time, trying to hide our emotions from each other. But it was time to move on. We quickly turned over the keys to the new owner waiting downstairs, and walked rapidly away from San Lucio. "Arrivederci Roma." It had been a wonderful experience!

PART FOUR

'Yankees Go Home!'

12

Return of the Immigrants

Few men of action have been able to make a graceful exit at the appropriate time.

—Malcom Muggeridge

There is nothing more fascinating than watching the ebb and flow of the sea: the water dashing from the beach to the sea, then flowing back ashore. It is a continuous, endless, amazing movement. In contrast, immigrants tend to move in one direction only, from country A to country B. Occasionally, they may go back to country A to remain and to die there. Most frequently, this return is only for a short visit and then there are no more such trips. There are also people who like to play the pendulum: they spend some time of the year in country A, and the rest in country B. These are not true immigrants, but people who think they can get the best of two worlds, which seldom is the case. After some time, especially if children of school age are involved, these people must give up the idea and make a decision on where to settle. After all, man is made to live in only one world.

There is also a very special group of "one way" immigrants that must be recognized. This includes many US senior citizens who move to countries of Latin America or elsewhere to avoid paying US income taxes, to stretch their pension's dollar value, or both. These elderly people enjoy the distance from their families and basking in the sun all year round. Some countries make a business of attracting this type of immigrant. as long as they bring with them sufficient dollars and do not engage in any type of local business. In Costa Rica, these immigrants are given a special license plate for their cars indicating their status: Retirees.

People completing their service with FAO after spending 20 or 30 years in Rome, do not know where to retire. They do not want go back to their countries of origin because they no longer have friends or relatives there. Then they decide to stay in Italy. Their sons or daughters are likely to be married to Italians and they find Italy a "heaven" without income taxes. On top of this they might have some younger friends still working with FAO who can procure them "consultancies" to add non-taxable income to their monthly pension. They stay in country B until they die: they are indeed the "one way" type of immigrants.

As for Nicla and myself, we lived in Italy for many years before getting married. We then emigrated to the United States where we stayed for a decade. Then came the opportunity to work at FAO for 23 years. At the end of this period, we had to decide where to retire. This decision was readily taken: we wanted to return to California. It was in California where we had our most valuable possessions: our three daughters and their families, our grandchildren, a house, and many old friends. Our future was still in America. Our past was left once more in Italy, where our relatives firmly belonged and where we could still treasure the richness of cultural values and unforgettable remembrances.

Part of the title of this chapter might surprise some of the readers. What do we have to do with the Yankees? It all happened in a Roman trattoria, sometime between 1969 and 1978. This was when strong anti-American feelings were common throughout Italy because of the "cold war" and the great influence of the Italian Communist party in the country's life. It was also the time when the "Red Brigades" dominated the Italian political scene. Almost everywhere on the façade of beautiful palaces, on the Roman old bridges and monuments, there were red graffiti with a brief but threatening message "YANKEES GO HOME!"

One evening, Nicla and I decided to join a group of FAO experts for supper. Our objective was to enjoy the famous Roman artichokes then in season. We were seated around a nice table in the corner of the crowded trattoria talking in English about various matters. Not far from us was a group of young men who continued to stare at us and giggle. We paid no attention as we enjoyed the artichokes and our conversation. When we left the trattoria, the same young men were waiting for us outside. All together they were repeatedly chanting "Yankees Go Home!" I paid no attention for a moment, but seeing that they were following us, I stopped in the middle of the street, turned around and in my best Roman dialect I plainly told them to go to hell.

One of the young men came close to me, punched me in the mouth and quickly ran away. The others followed him running. It was the declaration of hostilities. Nicla tried holding me back by my coat, but in vain. I slipped out of the coat and started chasing the young man who had punched me. My international friends followed me in the charge. One of them began swirling his umbrella around and cussing heavily in French. But the young cowards, scared by our unexpected reaction, disappeared rapidly into the darkness of the night. When peace was reestablished, we invited our "Yankee" friends to my home for a well deserved drink. Our "Yankee" group consisted of one Frenchman, two Swiss, one Belgian, two Italians, and a lonely friend from North Dakota. Definitely, the young men we had met in the trattoria were no Red Brigade members. Our fists and a swirling umbrella would not have been a good match for their Soviet-made Kalashnikov guns.

There are at least two definitions in the English dictionary for the word "retirement." One says, "removal or withdrawal from service, office or business." The second states, "orderly withdrawal of a force according to plan, without pressure from the enemy." Our retirement to Davis could hardly fit either of these definitions. I still maintained an "office" and Nicla started a business of her own. We both continued to be of "service" to others. What all this means is that either we are not typical retirees, or that our retirement is something else, something to be yet more properly defined by Webster. In fact, our retirement is geared on several "No's:" no fishing, no mobile home, no cruises in the Caribbean, no winter trips to Florida, no bridge, no golf, and no white hairs (at least for myself). Above all, no "pressure from the enemy!"

Our first retirement priority in Davis was to clean up and modernize our house on Whaler. This looked like a ghost house abandoned in the midst of an ocean of weeds. The last tenants must have had little appreciation for gardening. The ivy in front of the house had found its way inside the garage, the espalier-trained pear trees in front had grown over the roof top. What used to be a nice vegetable garden behind the back fence had become a mixture of savanna and subtropical forest. The house itself needed attention and repairs. Recalling our experience at the beach house in Italy, we began a new "reclamation" project. This time, however, it was for our own house, so we did not need to consult anyone on what we wanted done. Quickly, the Whaler house came back to its original beauty and comfort, although it was too small for a family that was to grow to sixteen members. Plans were made to build a new and larger house.

While still in Rome, we had purchased "sight unseen" a large lot bordering Montgomery Avenue on the south edge of Davis. We wanted this type of lot to keep one foot in the city and the other in the country. Cynthia and her former husband Russ were able to find us a property which met these requirements.

Russ, having visited us in Rome several times, knew what was needed to make us happy in our future house. He even kept track of the number of steps Nicla took from the refrigerator to the stove in the kitchen. Accordingly he designed the new house to fit our lifestyle.

Although the sight of St. Peter's Dome in Rome could not be replaced, a sod farm across Montgomery Avenue offered an open, green and peacefully rural view. To admire it, many large windows were installed on that side.

The shape of the San Lucio apartment was recreated by opening many doors to the outside garden, just as they were on our long terrace in Rome.

The house was also designed to host visitors. Anyone coming to stay with us needed to be offered comfortable quarters and total independence. And we wanted to be able to accommodate large crowds for festivities and other occasions, while maintaining separate areas that could remain closed and out of use when Nicla and I were alone. We succeeded in meeting all these demands.

"The kitchen must be far away from the dining area," requested Nicla. She knew how difficult it was in standard American houses to keep guests and visiting friends away from dirty dishes, frying pans and steaming spaghetti. This separation was fully respected.

"We like having plenty of indoor plants," insisted Nicla. And a magnificent atrium was designed in such a stylish and complex way that even the building contractor was unable to build it. Russ had to intervene himself for its construction.

There was no question: plans and design were elegant and refined. With no further hesitation, ground was broken and the new house started to grow.

Landscaping is a combination of taste, knowledge and boldness. Even before the house was completed, our garden objectives were firmly set. The first goal was to utilize every single inch of the land available. The second objective was to mask the dullness of a flat rectangular lot with something appealing and rich with small places, each to be discovered a little at the time. The third was to maintain the rural quality of the surrounding environment. All objectives were successfully met.

Annual and perennial flowering plants were sequenced in a harmonious color combination throughout the seasons. The place at the corner of Montgomery and Rosario soon became the center of attention for people driving by and joggers running their daily miles. Everyone had to slow down at this corner to admire the splash of color overflowing from our garden into the green of the surrounding landscape.

There is no doubt that flowers and their colors are also the result of applied human muscles. The physical work to keep everything growing and going, including a small greenhouse on the west side of the new building, has been sufficiently intense to save money no longer needed for fitness centers. Muscles are also essential to swim laps in the backyard pool. And muscles were again used to build a deck and barbecue center close to the rock garden. With a good combination of muscles and intellectual activities, our active retirement became more and more rewarding.

When time was finally available to allow for less physical work and more retrospective thinking and analysis, we discovered that something had been left unfinished that might still be properly rectified. In my case there were at least two problems that still required my attention. Both of these concerned science.

The first had to do with giving proper recognition to Raoul Robinson for his contribution to world agriculture and to encourage a wider distribution of his ideas. The other was to give my personal input toward the solution of a serious pest problem in California agriculture.

As mentioned before, Raoul was forced to leave FAO in 1976 because a job was no longer available for him with the Organization. This indifference toward his contributions to FAO and world agriculture has bothered me since then. After a few years of freelance consulting and an attempt to teach in an academic environment, Raoul was forced to take a near-poverty retirement in Canada. In the meantime, his classic book "Plant Pathosystems" was followed by two other publications: Host Management in Crop Pathosystems and the more popular Return to Resistance: Breeding Crops to Reduce Pesticide Dependence. More recently Raoul has been involved in a cooperative Canadian-Mexican bean breeding project designed to produce new varieties for small farmers without the need for crop protection chemicals.

Recognition for the extraordinary qualities of a man frequently comes only after he has passed away and he is no longer around to cherish other people's appreciation. In my mind, this had to be avoided in Raoul's case. For this reason I took upon myself the initiative of nominating him for the

1998 World Food Prize. This is the highest individual honor for outstanding achievements in improving the world's food supply. Raoul has done so much to this effect.

The second problem was one which the New Scientist in a 1993 article called "California's lousy vintage." This referred to the outbreak in Napa and Sonoma Valleys of an aphid-like insect that parasitized the roots of grapevines until they declined and became unproductive. The estimated cost of this epidemic was on the order of $500 million to over one billion dollars.

This insect, named phylloxera, had had a long history of vineyard devastations in Europe, South Africa and New Zealand. A severe outbreak of the same pest had already occurred in California at the turn of the last century. However, since then it was so completely and effectively controlled by the use of an American wild rootstock (on which European bearing varieties were grafted) that the problem was nearly forgotten.

A wide variety of causes had been suggested by a "Phylloxera Task Force" from the University of California, Davis. Over the years these scientists tried to explain the new outbreak as being due to the appearance of a new and more aggressive biotype of the insect, or several years of drought, and also to some newly adopted viticultural practices.

One area where their ignorance appeared to be nearly total was in the genetics of host resistance. In fact, this important phenomenon was considered to be a "black box."

By pure chance, I visited some of the declining vineyards in Napa Valley and had the opportunity to discuss the problem with Ivan Buddenhagen. I knew Ivan from my past work with FAO. I had visited him in Nigeria where he was breeding rice and maize for horizontal resistance against several pests and diseases. Ivan was a professor with the Department of Agronomy and Range Science at UCD and had his office very close to Viticulture and Entomology. Yet no one from these departments ever asked for his collaboration in interpreting the genetics of what appeared to be a breakdown of disease resistance.

We studied the problem together, collecting plenty of literature on the subject, and then we decided to apply our knowledge and experience to explain what had gone wrong in Sonoma and Napa Valleys. We also asked advice from Raoul Robinson in Canada and Dr. Hewitt in Washington state. In the end we all agreed: this was a typical case of "false erosion of horizontal resistance," an elegant way of saying that the phylloxera epidemic was due to faulty testing by UCD of a new hybrid rootstock wrongly believed to be resistant. Under these circumstances, it was easy for the scientists involved to blame nature rather than admit human carelessness.

The result of our study was a paper submitted for publication to the American Journal of Enology and Viticulture in May of 1993. It took until the middle of the following September for this very reputable journal to decide to reject our manuscript. We had struck the truth, but this was found to contain "a number of serious shortcomings."

On October 31, 1993, the San Francisco Chronicle published a long article entitled "At the Root of Napa's Dying Vines." The question was asked "Why did it take a decade for UC Davis scientists to figure out what was killing the wine grapes?" The explanations given by a well informed reporter appeared more accurate than those offered by the UCD task force. He recognized that the same task force had stymied the issue, releasing a statement in late 1993 that was a model of "evenhanded obfuscation." I contacted this reporter to congratulate him for the good coverage and offer some scientific information to further validate his findings. But the reporter was no longer interested in phylloxera. He was chasing some other matters. This is exactly what Charles Kuralt, the famous CBS reporter, writes about himself and his journalist colleagues: "The reporter is a stone skipping on a pond, taking an instant to tell one story and ricocheting to the next, covering a lot of water while only skimming the surface."

As for the "rejected" paper that Ivan and I had written, we wanted make sure that this would safely reach the protected sphere of world literature. To achieve this, and following Solzhenitzyn's example in the former Soviet Union, we had our manuscript securely and rapidly published abroad, in Phytopathologia mediterranea.

During our stay in Italy, Nicla had gained the reputation of being the "best chef" in Rome. She became an expert at organizing tasty dinners for large crowds, in selecting menus suitable for multinational groups, in serving diversified cocktail parties for all occasions. It was incredible to see how diplomatic life was so contingent upon good food and drinks. The best time to appreciate this was during the FAO Conference period, which lasted four weeks.

First came the Director General's welcoming reception, which opened the series of drinking and eating events. A large cocktail party was offered to all the delegates and their spouses. All the top brass of the Organization, their wives and most important "professionals" were also invited. The DG party's was a very crowded event with plenty of handshaking, a profusion of phony smiles, many drinks, but always with the same tasteless finger food.

During the following period, each delegation organized their own cocktail party, usually at their respective embassies. Often, three or four such events took place during the same evening. It was surprising to see how people could swiftly move from one embassy to another through the heavy

Roman traffic, only to encounter at the new place the same people and the same finger food.

At other times, cocktail and dinner parties at FAO were organized for different events: the opening of a meeting, the visit of a head of state, the celebration of a new "Ceres," and so on. The excuses were many, but the eating and drinking were always the same.

Of course, Nicla's parties were different. They were elegant and displayed a class that no one could match. Twenty-three years of diplomatic life left an indelible trace in her.

When we returned to Davis, Nicla decided to put her unique expertise to work. It was in this way that Nicky's Fine Italian Cuisine was born. From its inception, this business was intended to remain small in a country where everything must always be "big." Small is beautiful: and Nicla can also make sure that small is delicious.

Catering is a labor-intensive affair. But Nicla has the energy and skills to operate her business all by herself. She wants to follow every single step in a sequence that goes from planning to cooking, displaying, and serving. For each event she uses a new strategy according to season and occasion, a Christmas party being different from a graduation dinner, or a wedding reception. The number of people in attendance also determines what kind of food and service she can offer.

There is a close correlation between old civilizations and good quality food. This is due to a combination of factors that affect eating habits. These include the blessing of a mild climate suitable for growing many different crops; the existence of old traditions that favour enhancement of gastronomic experiences over many generations; and the sophistication of the people, who always demand improvements.

Italy, being a country that enjoys all these factors, is also a place where there is great richness of good quality food. This can be found all over the countryside in the many varied regional cuisines. Even by Italian standards, Nicla is an exceptional cook. She combines delicacy and rare taste, and she can nicely balance together a vast assortment of Italian dishes.

The success of a good Italian meal is closely tied with the type of wines that are served. Wine should improve the flavour of food, while food, in turn, must characterize and magnify the taste of a good wine. It is for this reason that I have gladly joined Nicla's business as the person responsible for the selection and serving of wines at catering occasions. Like a general before a battle, I first carefully study the menu, then I try to get some intelligence information on the people attending the party, following which I proceed to select the best bottles for the event.

I have always regarded wines as living biological entities. In many respects, I consider this type of beverage as delicate and necessary to human life as women. Wines are born in a certain year, they go through a youthful period, when they are fruitful in taste and brilliant in color, then they acquire a nice "body." With age and maturity, good wines reach a peak in flavour and aroma, after which they turn old and pass away, leaving behind a sediment. You cannot treat wines roughly. If you are careless and leave them unattended, they can easily turn sour on you. Just like women and life itself, wines must be first discovered, then appreciated. If they are good, they must be loved, all the way. To the very last drop.

After returning to Davis, we wanted to devote more of our attention to the cellaring of noble red wines. Many new wineries had been established throughout California during our stay in Italy and the quality of their product had improved considerably. Many of these wines were worth aging. Unfortunately, we were unable to build a cellar in our new house on Montgomery. This, however, turned out to be to our advantage: if we could store wines far away from our house, they would last longer. So we decided to start our cellar in Cynthia's house in Sacramento. We recognized that by doing so we were also giving her full proof of our trust. In fact, we did not require a double key to access her cellar as in the bank safe deposit box: she was good enough to guard our wines while starting a collection of her own.

Of all collectible items, wines are unique in the way that they improve in flavour as they increase in economic value. This type of capital gain, that no one so far has been able to tax, has an added advantage when one compares collecting wines to stamps. It is unquestionably tastier (and probably healthier) to sip a bottle from one's cellar than to lick the rear of a rare old stamp.

One more thing must be said about the new house on Montgomery: it is structured and equipped to operate as a four-star hotel, all year-round. This allows to host relatives, friends and friends of friends at no cost to them and at very short notice to us.

There is a brass plate in our nook imprinted with the words: "Albergo Fafozzi—Si Parla Italiano" (Fafozzi Hotel - Italian Spoken). This is a gift from our daughter Marina, who was the first to recognize the value and usefulness of such a hotel, one that can function also as safe kindergarten, restful park with swimming pool, quick cafeteria, and high class restaurant. The hotel, and excellent cuisine, seem to attract people like a magnet. It arranges customers just like a magnet arranges the random scatterings of iron filings: in an oval, orderly pattern, the same pattern as our capacious dining room table.

In many ways it is our "fault" to have expanded into this new activity. We have been always very hospitable to

The house at Montgomery right after completion.

people, both in Rome and Terracina. But in Davis the house is larger and more comfortable. It is also strategically located, close to the UCD campus, to Sacramento, San Francisco, and the National Parks. For this and other reasons we are never alone, but always immersed in friendly humanity. And this, in many ways, is as if we were living a beautiful novel, full of fascinating stories just like our own. In this way the hours, days and years go by very rapidly, keeping us constantly fascinated with the beauty of a never-ending human comedy.

13

Considerations and Conclusions

*Whatever you can do, or dream you
can, begin it. Boldness has genius,
power and magic in it.*

—J.W. Von Goethe

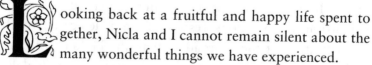ooking back at a fruitful and happy life spent together, Nicla and I cannot remain silent about the many wonderful things we have experienced.

The years have passed so rapidly that it seems impossible that almost half a century has gone by since the day we first met. And all the events that followed seem to have passed at the speed of a jet cruiser. This in itself is a good sign of a happy life. It seems incredible, but it all boils down to speed. If one is sleepless in bed, or sick in a hospital, or waiting for a delayed flight at an airport, time never goes by. Minutes and hours move slowly around the clock and life itself appears to be dull, sluggish, almost lethargic. This is in contrast to a wonderful life like ours, which is instead fast, full, and always vibrating with joy.

Before this speed contest comes to an end, both of us wish to spend a little time to recapitulate our major life events, in the hope of reaching some useful conclusions.

We were born and raised in the right place, at the right time and in the right families. Nothing compares to the city of Rome. One of the most beautiful, fascinating and historical cities in the world, it is simply the "Grand Canyon" of Western Civilization. Its architecture, as well as its history, is multilayered. At the very bottom are the Etruscan constructions, then the early Roman, followed by the Imperial city, the decaying medieval period, the city of the Popes and Michelangelo, the Renaissance, the Baroque, the Neoclassic and, finally, the Modern city with its incomparable richness of churches, palaces, squares, fountains, and parks. Everywhere in this city's historical Center there is an overflow of art and beauty. It was our unique gift to be able to grow and develop in such surroundings.

The time was also right. Many important events took place during our youth from 1925 to 1940. For nearly fifteen years Italy enjoyed growth and apparent economic expansion. Tremendous resources were dedicated to the electrification of the railroad system, the building of roads and some of the first highways, and the construction of dams, aqueducts, schools, and hospitals. The Pontine marshes were reclaimed south of Rome and three modern cities sprang up like mushrooms in the previously unhabitable territory. In this effort by Mussolini "to do something" for the country, there was demagoguery accompanied by waste, errors, abuse, and shortsightedness. However, it is unquestionable that for the first time in many centuries the country was experiencing much-needed improvements.

Then came the period of Mussolini's political and military expansion which gradually led to the disaster of World War II. The "Duce," having become a caricature of himself, used his political power to draft many young Italians to fight senseless wars and revolutions in Spain, Ethiopia, Albania, Yugoslavia, Russia, and North Africa. Nicla and I were fortunate to be young enough to remain outside this absurd sequence of events.

We were also fortunate to be born into our respective families. On the Ronchi-Franz side, a family with long traditions in Veneto and Friuli, there was a solid background in Agriculture and Art. On the Chiarappa-Rass side, there was a good German-Italian cultural mixture with roots in Business and Music. With this background, we were able to grow up in two large and interesting families, continually exposed to the beauty of our city, and to the arts and other resources flourishing in our unique, secure environment.

Schooling was a serious and rigorous business. This was in line with the old European tradition that schools are for learning and not for playing. Most of the time neither Nicla nor myself liked to attend classes, especially when a test was scheduled to take place. Many long hours of study were spent at home each day preparing for these tests. And no one was there to help during study hours. Nor were our respective parents concerned about our recreation time. This was left aside, entirely up to our individual initiative (and of course, only after completion of all the assigned home work). Our parents were not concerned with our "activities," either in sports or social events, as it is so common in modern days.

There is no question that times were very austere when we grew up. It is also true that those were easier times to raise a family, with no TV, no drugs, no gangs, no crimes, no pornography or obscenities, and no constant drive to give children the best of the very best.

One good feature of a war was in its educational effect on growing people. When food was scarce and clothing unavailable, when people were suffering and many were dying, when several human values were under discussion, when life itself could be terminated at any time, all that was superfluous was easily discarded and the basic human values were the only ones that really counted.

Surviving through a harsh war is an education in itself. This enables people to develop and retain a great respect for food, shelter, and friendship. We both received this type of "war education." This proved useful later on in our married life and in our life as immigrants in America. Looking back on this experience, we gained further exposure to a number of situations which also enriched our life. The first was our introduction to such a new and beautiful country as America. From the very beginning, America seemed to be made to measure for us. Here was the country of many opportunities, and these opportunities existed for real. All that was needed was to work hard, keeping a low profile but always ready to step forward at the proper occasion. In America, Nicla and I engaged in types of work we had never done before. First the chicken farm, then the department store, the typewriter factory, and the dairy plant in Connecticut. Following this, were the packing of grapes and my endless walks in the Delano vineyards. Then cleaning houses, doing alterations or studying long hours in Davis. Eight long years of hard work in a foreign country and in a different world. Within this world we were always able to create our own microcosm: with our own records of classical music, our tasty Italian meals, and our selected friends. In the end, this small world we created in the heart of California became home for us. The only home.

Exposure to science and scientific challenge came later in life. The experience of getting a Ph.D. in Plant Pathology at Davis was the first reassuring sign that things were changing for the better. Our many sacrifices started paying off. For me, the scientific training was also a source of novel intellectual values, a new and more orderly way of thinking and of approaching problems. It was also a first encounter with "friendly science." What had seemed cold, ivory-tower academics later became a lively, rational experience, and a great expansion of my mind and my vision of the entire world. Most of my professional career was devoted to science and technology. In both I found great intellectual challenges and many rewarding opportunities. I have loved being a plant pathologist capable of practicing all over the world, without national borders or constraints.

International life and work for a humanitarian organization were also important sources of additional values. The twenty-three years of work for FAO were rich in many ways. First was the opportunity to reunite with our respective families in Rome, and to be able to enjoy and assist our elderly parents in the last years of their lives. Second was the educational opportunity given to Victoria, Marina and Cynthia. They were able to attend first-class schools and to grow up in a beautiful city like Rome. Third was my work in FAO which gave me the opportunity to practice front-line plant pathology, and to test and apply new theoretical approaches to reduce food waste. This work also offered me the opportunity to practice the best type of science: that of feeding people. In doing so I deeply enjoyed meeting some of the best scientists in the world, and visiting some of the most remote countries on earth.

Exposure to the Catholic faith was another important gift. Whereas Christianity was born in Palestine, Catholicism was unquestionably born in Rome and from Rome it reached the entire world. Being raised in Rome meant for both of us continued exposure to this faith as the only faith. However, later in life neither of us observed the strict rules of the Catholic Church. Our religion was never practiced in bigotry, but only in the true spirit of Christianity. It was always directed at assisting others, especially the poor, the needy, the sick. Our religion was also in our morality. We have given to our three daughters the unique opportunity to be educated in Catholic schools and to practice this faith for themselves and their children.

Approaching the end of our lives, we are happy for all we have done. We now have a large and healthy family with three daughters in top career positions, and eight lovely grandchildren. We also have a most beautiful home which attracts many visitors and friends. We greatly enjoy an exquisite cuisine and, occasionally, savor "noble" red wines with good friends and acquaintances. We have discovered that real happiness is to be found in the small things of everyday life: the smile of a child, the color of a flower, the reading of a well-written book, the listening of good music, or the satisfaction of creating something new and beautiful through embroidering, carpet making, or other jobs in the garden or around the house. We appreciate our evening conversation, and, above all, the harmony we try to maintain with everyone. What more is a good life expected to offer?

But life can be so different for different people. In our experience, life is much like an artichoke: tough and spiny on the outside, it can be tender and tasty on the inside. There are many people who never see an artichoke in their entire life: they never eat it, they never miss it. Others only eat the bottom end of a few boiled leaves and throw away the rest. Their enjoyment is limited, their wastage is great. There are only a few who know the many good ways to cook and appreciate an artichoke: they eat it all, and they value it in full measure. Both knowledge and experience are necessary to recognize the simple taste of an artichoke, just as they are essential to prize the many different rewards our wonderful life may bring.

There comes a time when it lies within a person's grasp to shape the clay of their life into the sort of thing they wish to be.

Only the weak blame the parents, the times, the lack of good fortune, or the quirks of fate.

—Louis L'Amour
The Walking Drum

Selected Bibliography

Barzini, Luigi. 1964. The Italians. Hamish Hamilton.

Barzini, Luigi. 1983. The Europeans. Penguin Books.

Bocca, Giorgio.1992. L'Inferno. A. Mondadori.

Chiarappa, Luigi. 1985. Plant Protection at FAO—40 years of service in international pest management. FAO Plant Protection Bulletin 33(4): 131-137.

Di Giorgio, Robert and J.A. Di Giorgio. 1986. The Di Giorgio's: from fruit merchants to corporate innovators. Bancroft Library. Regional Oral History Office, University of California, Berkeley.

Guicciardini, Francesco. 1984. The history of Italy. Translated and edited by Sidney Alexander. Princeton University Press, Princeton, N.J.

Hancock, Graham. 1989. Lords of Poverty.Macmillan Ltd, London

Hofmann, Paul. 1990. That Fine Italian Hand. Henry Holt and Co., New York

Mc Cullough, David. 1992. Truman. Simon & Schuster. New York, London, Toronto, Sydney, Tokyo, Singapore.

Montanelli, Indro and Mario Cervi. 1983. L'Italia della disfatta. Rizzoli

Montanelli, Indro and Mario Cervi. 1991. L'Italia degli Anni di Piombo. Rizzoli

Perelli-Minetti, Antonio. 1975. A life in wine making. Bancroft Library. Regional Oral History Office, University of California, Berkeley.

Robinson, Raoul A.. 1976. Plant Pathosystems. Springer-Verlag. Berlin Heidelberg.

Ronchi, Vittorio. 1977. Guerra e crisi alimentari in Italia. V. Ronchi. Roma

Sheehan, Fred. 1964. ANZIO Epic of Bravery. Univ. of Oklahoma Press. Norman and London

Sulzberger, C.L. 1987. World War II. Houghton Mifflin . Boston

Index

C

E

N